6

# TOWARDS A THEORY OF UNITED NATIONS PEACEKEEPING

# Towards a Theory of United Nations Peacekeeping

A. B. Fetherston
*Post-Doctoral Fellow*
*Peace Research Centre*
*The Australian National University*

St. Martin's Press

© A. B. Fetherston 1994

First published in Great Britain 1994 by
MACMILLAN PRESS LTD
Houndmills, Basingstoke, Hampshire RG21 2XS
and London
Companies and representatives
throughout the world

A catalogue record for this book is available
from the British Library.

ISBN 0–333–61462–3

| 10 | 9 | 8 | 7 | 6 | 5 | 4 | 3 | 2 | 1 |
|----|----|----|----|----|----|----|----|----|----|
| 03 | 02 | 01 | 00 | 99 | 98 | 97 | 96 | 95 | 94 |

Printed in Great Britain by
Ipswich Book Co Ltd
Ipswich, Suffolk

---

First published in the United States of America 1994 by
Scholarly and Reference Division,
ST. MARTIN'S PRESS, INC.,
175 Fifth Avenue,
New York, N.Y. 10010

ISBN 0–312–12275–6                    1000334 213

Library of Congress Cataloging-in-Publication Data
Fetherston, A. B.
Towards a theory of United Nations peacekeeping / A. B. Fetherston.
p.  cm.
Includes bibliographical references and index.
ISBN 0–312–12275–6
1. United Nations—Armed Forces.   2. Pacific settlement of
international disputes.   I. Title.
JX1981.P7F48   1994
341.5'84—dc20
                                             94–19512
                                             CIP

For Laura E. French and Kevin Warnes

# Contents

*Acknowledgements*                                                    xiii

*List of Abbreviations*                                                xiv

*Introduction*                                                          xvi

**1   A Brief History of United Nations Peacekeeping,
      1945—87**                                                          1

   1.  The Founding of the United Nations                 1
     1.1  The Charter                           2
   2.  Main Structures of the United Nations              4
     2.1  The Security Council                  4
     2.2  The General Assembly                  6
     2.3  The Secretary-General and the Secretariat   7
   3.  The Birth of Peacekeeping                          8
     3.1  Post-War Development                  8
     3.2  The Suez and the Congo: A Study of
        Opposites                12
        3.2.1  Suez: The Birth of Peacekeeping   12
        3.2.2  The Congo and Crisis at the UN   13
        3.2.3  Diffusing the Crisis   15
   4.  An Overview of Peacekeeping Operations,
     1948–87                                   16
     4.1  The Nascent Period, 1946–56           16
     4.2  The Assertive Period, 1956–67         17
     4.3  The Dormant Period, 1967–73           18
     4.4  The Resurgent Period, 1973–78         18
     4.5  The Maintenance Period, 1978–88       18
   5.  Conclusion                                        19

**2   UN Peacekeeping in the Post-Cold War World**                     20

   1.  The International Context                          20
   2.  The Rise of Multidimensional Peacekeeping          23
     2.1  The Expansion Period, 1988–93          25
     2.2  Are These Missions Peacekeeping?       30
     2.3  Multiplicity of Functions             31

  2.4  Role Innovations                                        33
3.  Complicating Factors                                       34
  3.1  Management                                              34
  3.2  Financial Problems                                      36
  3.3  Mandate                                                 37
  3.4  Resorting to the United Nations                         38
  3.5  Troop Contributing Countries                            39
4.  Factors Considered Necessary for Success                  40
5.  Conclusion: Consequences of
    Multidimensionalism                                        42

**3  Case Studies: United Nations Peacekeeping in
   Cyprus, Namibia and Former Yugoslavia**                     45

1.  United Nations Peacekeeping Force in Cyprus               46
  1.1  The Creation of UNFICYP                                 47
  1.2  The 1974 Crisis                                         56
2.  United Nations Transition Assistance Group               59
  2.1  Structure of UNTAG                                      62
  2.2  Implementation                                          64
  2.3  Conclusion                                              70
3.  UN Peacekeeping in Croatia and
    Bosnia-Herzegovina, 1992–93                                71
  3.1 UN Peacekeeping in Croatia                               74
  3.2 UN Peacekeeping in Bosnia-Herzegovina                    79
  3.3 Conclusion                                               86
4.  Conclusion                                                 87

**4  Outlining a Theoretical Approach**                        88

1.  Fields of Study                                            88
  1.1  International Relations                                 88
  1.2  Peace Research                                          91
    1.2.1  Positive and Negative Peace                         93
  1.3  Conclusion                                              95
2.  Conflict Theory                                            96
  2.1  Structure and Process of Conflict                       98
  2.2  Causes of Conflict                                      99
    2.2.1  Inherency and Contingency                           99
    2.2.2  Objective and Subjective Conflict                  101
  2.3  Conclusion                                             103
3.  Conflict Management                                       104

3.1 Third Party Intervention 106
3.2 Roles of Intervenors 107
    3.2.1 Roles for Conflict Settlement: Mediation 107
    3.2.2 Roles for Conflict Resolution: Consultation and Facilitation 109
    3.2.3 Roles for Both Settlement and Resolution: Negotiation and Conciliation 110
3.3 Skills of Intervenors 111
3.4 Evaluating Intervention 112
    3.4.1 Ethical Issues in Intervention 114
3.5 Conclusion 115
4. A Contingency Approach 115
4.1 Contingency and a Normative Framework 115
4.2 Escalation and Typology 118
4.3 Why a Contingency Approach? 119
4.4 Critique of the Contingency Approach 121
5. Conclusion 123

**5 Peacekeeping, Peacemaking and Peacebuilding: Definitions and Linkages** 124

1. Introduction 124
2. Peacekeeping 124
2.1 Narrow Functional Definitions 125
2.2 Broad Functional Definitions 126
2.3 Conclusion 127
3. Peacemaking 129
4. Peacebuilding 131
5. Linking Peacekeeping, Peacemaking and Peacebuilding 133
5.1 Linkage at the Macro-Level 134
5.2 Linkage at the Micro-Level 137
6. Conclusion 139

**6 Developing a Conceptual Framework for Peacekeeping** 141

1. Introduction 141
2. Peacekeeping and a Conceptual Framework 141
2.1 Contributions towards Conceptualization 141

2.2 The Ideographic Perspective     143
2.3 Peacekeeping as a Form of Third Party
Intervention:     145
     2.3.1 The Rationale of Third Party
Intervention: Settlement and
Resolution     145
     2.3.2 Problems Caused by Expansion of
the Third Party Role     146
3. Peacekeeping in a Contingency Model     150
    3.1 Peacekeeping in the Escalation Sequence:
Stage Four     150
    3.2 Roles for Peacekeepers at Stage Four     152
    3.3 Conclusion     153
4. A Contingency Model for Peacekeeping     154
5. The Consequences of Utilizing a Contingency
Approach as a Conceptual Framework for
Peacekeeping     157
6. The Potential of Peacekeeping     159
    6.1 Potential of Complementarity     159
    6.2 Building on Existing Knowledge and
Experience     160


**7 Training as a Critical Link between Theory and
Practice**     162

1. Peacekeeping: The Application of Theory     162
    1.1 The Need for Theory: A Summary of the
Arguments     162
    1.2 The Problem of Bringing Theory into
Practice: Training as a Key Factor     164
2. Cross-Cultural Training: An Example of Linking
Theory with Practice     166
    2.1 The Skills Necessary for Effective
Intercultural Interaction     167
    2.2 Techniques of Cross-Cultural Training     170
    2.3 The Case of Canadian Development
Workers Overseas     173
3. Linking Cross-Cultural Interaction Research
with the Practice of Peacekeeping     175
4. Conclusion     177

**8   Training for United Nations Peacekeepers**                      179

  1.  Current Training Provision                             179
  2.  Military Training                                      182
    2.1  Canadian Forces (CF)                      183
    2.2  Irish Defence Forces (IDF)                188
    2.3  The Nordic System: Regional Cooperation   191
    2.4  Secretariat: Briefings for Senior Military
        Staff                   195
  3.  Civilian Training                                      195
    3.1  In-Country Training                       199
  4.  Training by International Agencies                     200
    4.1  United Nations Institute for Training and
        Research (UNITAR)       201
    4.2  International Peace Academy (IPA)          201
    4.3  The Austrian Study Centre for Peace and
        Conflict Resolution (ASPR)   203
  5.  Critique of Peacekeeping Training                      203
    5.1  Practical Critique                         203
    5.2  Theoretical Critique                       207
  6.  Conclusion                                             208

**9   The Conceptualization of Peacekeeping:**
**Implications for Training and Practice**                            211

  1.  Comparing Training and Practice: Finding the
    Training Gap                                    211
    1.1  Military View                              213
    1.2  Civilian View                              216
    1.3  Conclusion: Translating a Theory of
    Peacekeeping into Practice                      218
        1.3.1  Two Essential Tasks   218
        1.3.2  The Training Gap   219
  2.  Inconsistencies in Training and Practice              220
    2.1  Military Training and Peacekeeping
        Training                221
        2.1.1  Living With a Paradox   223
    2.2  The Profession of Peacekeeping            225
        2.2.1  The Professional Soldier and the
              National Service Volunteer   225
        2.2.2  Independent Initiative   226
        2.2.3  Developing a New Profession   227

2.3 The Experience/Expertise Fallacy 228
2.4 Culture Variables 229
3. Future Directions: Recommendations for Research 230
3.1 Development of Training Programmes and Curricula 230
3.2 Improving the Conceptual Framework 231

*Appendix 1: UN Peacekeeping Operations 1948 to 1993* 233

*Appendix 2: Summary of Contrasting Conflict Management Approaches* 236

*Appendix 3: Effects of Escalation on Conflict* 237

*Appendix 4: Contingency Model of Third Party Intervention* 238

*Notes and References* 239

*Bibliography* 265

*Index* 284

# Acknowledgements

I am grateful to the Barrow and Geraldine S. Cadbury Trust for the financial support which allowed me to carry out this work. For allowing me the time to complete the final editing I am grateful to the Peace Research Centre, at the Australian National University. I owe much to the Department of Peace Studies at the University of Bradford, UK, its students and staff, and particularly to Paul Rogers and Oliver Ramsbotham for their unstinting support and help during various stages of this work. Guiding me throughout the development and completion of this project has been Tom Woodhouse, whose excellent insights and comments spurred on the development of my own thoughts in productive directions. My deepest respect and gratitude to Laura and Bruce French without whom none of this would have been possible. Kevin Warnes provided excellent editorial comments throughout the final stages of editing. Most notably he allowed me to read his excellent and thorough Ph.D. thesis chapters on the crisis in former Yugoslavia as background material for my own case-study. Beyond the unfailing academic support, Kevin gave freely of his time and energy in countless ways. This book is dedicated to Laura E. French and Kevin Warnes.

A.B. FETHERSTON

# List of Abbreviations

| | |
|---|---|
| A-G | Administrator-General (Namibia) |
| ASPR | Austrian Study Centre for Peace and Conflict Resolution |
| C-34 | Special Committee on Peacekeeping Operations (Committee of 34) |
| CF | Canadian Forces |
| CF-DPKO | Canadian Forces Directorate of Peacekeeping Operations |
| CIVPOL | United Nations Civilian Police |
| DHA | United Nations Department of Humanitarian Affairs |
| DPA | United Nations Department of Political Affairs |
| DPI | United Nations Department of Public Information |
| DPKO | United Nations Department of Peacekeeping Operations |
| DTA | Democratic Turhalle Alliance, Namibia |
| EC | European Community |
| ECCY | European Community Conference on Yugoslavia |
| GA | General Assembly |
| ECOSOC | Economic and Social Council |
| FC | Force Commander |
| FOD | Field Operations Division |
| FRY | Federal Republic of Yugoslavia |
| ICJ | International Court of Justice |
| ICFY | International Conference on Former Yugoslavia |
| ICRC | International Committee of the Red Cross |
| IDF | Irish Defence Force |
| IPA | International Peace Academy |
| JNA | Yugoslav People's Army |
| NAM | Non-Aligned Movement |
| NATO | North Atlantic Treaty Organization |
| NCO | Non-Commissioned Officer |
| NGO | Non-Governmental Organization |
| OHRM | United Nations Office of Human Resource Management |

| | |
|---|---|
| P-5 | Permanent Five Members of the Security Council (China, France, Russia, United Kingdom and United States) |
| PSC | Protracted Social Conflict |
| PTSS | Post-Traumatic Stress Syndrome |
| SADF | South African Defence Force |
| SC | Security Council |
| SCR | Security Council Resolution |
| S-G | Secretary-General |
| SIPRI | Stockholm International Peace Research Institute |
| SRO | Special Representative's Office |
| SRSG | Special Representative of the Secretary-General |
| SWAPO | South West Africa People's Organization |
| SWAPOL | South West Africa Police |
| UNCIO | United Nations Conference on International Organization |
| UNDRO | United Nations Disaster Relief Office |
| UNDP | United Nations Development Programme |
| UNHCR | United Nations High Commissioner for Refugees |
| UNIC | United Nations Information Centre |
| UNITAF | Unified Task Force (Somalia) |
| UNITAR | United Nations Institute for Training and Research |
| UNMO | United Nations Military Observer |
| UNPA | United Nations Protected Area (Croatia) |
| UNSO | United Nations Staff Officer |
| UNTC | United Nations Training Centre |
| U-S-G | Under-Secretary-General |
| WEU | Western European Union |
| WFP | World Food Programme |

# Introduction

The post-Cold War world has been marred by a proliferation of disputes. Mounting insecurity in many parts of the world has undermined hopes of an immediate peace dividend. The international arena is increasingly characterized by bitter protracted social conflicts, widespread humanitarian crises and unprecedented global ecological hazards. In many instances, the United Nations has been called upon to take concerted and effective action. In response to growing demands the UN has fielded five more peacekeeping operations in the last five years than in its previous forty-three year history. Huge operations in former Yugoslavia, Cambodia and Somalia have increased eight-fold the number of peacekeepers in the field. Peacekeepers are being asked to take on new roles and work in more demanding environments than ever before. Add to this the financial and management problems at the UN, and suggestions of further role expansion, and it is apparent that peacekeeping is approaching a critical juncture.

The overtaxed, *ad hoc* system of peacekeeping does not meet the demands posed by the post-Cold War world. For the UN and peacekeeping to more effectively manage conflict and other crises it is apparent that a framework of intervention will be needed. Boutros-Ghali's *An Agenda for Peace* provides the first step toward establishing such a framework. This study aims to carry this work further. It proposes a theory of peacekeeping based on concepts of peaceful third party intervention. Contingency models form the foundation of this analysis. While the focus is on peacekeeping, a model of intervention within which peacekeeping fits is also proposed. Beyond the theoretical analysis, this work looks at the consequences of conceptualization on the practice of peacekeeping focusing particularly on training. The general purpose of this project is to help form a foundation for further research on the theory and practice of peacekeeping.

Chapters 1 and 2 follow the development of peacekeeping from its nascent stage through to its current period of expansion. These chapters chart the major precedents and crises of peacekeeping from Suez through to Somalia. Chapter 2 concludes the section by providing an in-depth discussion of the challenges posed to peacekeeping by the evolution of its practice and by the new international context.

Chapter 3 offers three case studies of UN peacekeeping in Cyprus, Namibia and former Yugoslavia. These brief studies illustrate the changes and challenges for peacekeeping outlined in Chapters 1 and 2. Moreover, they establish the basis for the proceeding discussion of theories of conflict and conflict management as they relate to peacekeeping.

Chapter 4 summarizes the academic literature on peaceful third party intervention. Concepts such as conflict management, conflict resolution, facilitation, mediation, etc., are defined and explained. Finally, contingency theory and the work of Fisher and Keashly (1991) are introduced. Contingency theory suggests a pragmatic approach to conflict management which makes use of ideas and techniques of third party intervention regardless of theoretical affiliation. Its basic criterion is success. It is argued that such an adisciplinary approach is crucial at a time when conflicts are not only more violent and protracted, but less amenable to traditional conflict management strategies.

Chapter 5 examines United Nations peacemaking and peacebuilding as they relate to the practice of peacekeeping. This chapter defines two levels of interaction: the macro- and micro-levels. It is argued that at the macro-level, links between these three UN functions are tenuous at best. However, these functions are more successfully linked through peacekeeping at the micro-level. This chapter concludes that better coordination of all three roles at both levels is crucial for more effective conflict management.

Chapter 6 argues first that peacekeeping should be seen as a peaceful third party intervention and looks at the ramifications of such an assumption based on the conclusions of the previous chapters. Peacekeeping is then placed within a contingency framework. The consequences of this conceptualization of peacekeeping are analyzed. Finally, a contingency model for peacekeeping is introduced utilizing the work of Bercovitch *et al.* (1991). This chapter concludes by discussing the potential for both peacekeeping and other UN intervention when implemented through a contingency framework.

Chapter 7 opens with a summary of the arguments engendering a theory of peacekeeping. The problem of translating theory into practice is then considered. The subject of training is introduced as a key factor in bringing a theory of peacekeeping into practice and a brief discussion of training theory and method from the field of cross-cultural relations follows. Finally, Moskos's (1976) sociological study of peacekeeping is compared with a study on cultural adaptation by Grove and Torbiorn (1985) to point out the relevance of cross-cultural research and training for peacekeeping. This discussion then leads into Chapter 8's summary and critique of training for military and civilian peacekeepers.

By way of conclusion, Chapter 9 brings together the different arguments of previous chapters. Inconsistencies in practice revealed by the conceptualization of peacekeeping within a contingency model are briefly examined. Finally, this chapter turns to the future with recommendations both for the development of training and further research.

A. B. FETHERSTON

# 1 A Brief History of United Nations Peacekeeping, 1945–87

## 1. THE FOUNDING OF THE UNITED NATIONS

The United Nations was founded in the period immediately following the Second World War. The swiftness with which the new international organization was established owed much to a considerable amount of planning and lobbying by private groups particularly in the United States prior to the end of the war. In addition, and partly as a result of that pressure, United States President Franklin D. Roosevelt, British Prime Minister Winston Churchill and the leaders of the other Allied powers had signed three documents which proved crucial to a gathering momentum toward the creation of a new international organization. In August 1941, aboard a ship off the coast of Newfoundland, Roosevelt and Churchill signed the *Atlantic Charter*, where they put forward the principle of the establishment of a 'wider and permanent system of general security'.[1] In January 1942, twenty-six countries allied against the Axis powers signed the *Declaration of United Nations*. This was the first time the term 'United Nations' was used, and the document affirmed the principles set out in the *Atlantic Charter*. Finally, on 30 October 1943, leaders of the Soviet Union, China, Britain, and the United States signed the *Moscow Declaration* iterating the principle of establishing an international organization which would focus on the maintenance of international peace and security.

These three documents created enough momentum for a conference of the big powers in 1944 in Washington, D.C. which became known as the *Dumbarton Oaks Conversations*. The main objective of Dumbarton Oaks was to negotiate a draft constitution for a post-war international organization which would 'save succeeding generations from the scourge of war'.[2] Although the main facets of a new international institution

1

were outlined at Dumbarton, it was not until later at meetings in Yalta between the Soviet leader Stalin, Roosevelt and Churchill that the crucial question of power-sharing through the newly conceived Security Council was worked out. At the conclusion of the great power negotiations the *United Nations Conference on International Organization* was held in San Francisco, beginning on 25 April 1945. It was at this conference of fifty participating states[3] that the Charter of the United Nations was formally drafted.

While earlier meetings between the great powers as well as the *Declaration of United Nations* had focused on security arrangements and post-war assurances of a peaceful international community, the San Francisco Conference broadened the emerging institution's roles to include the power to act in social and economic areas. Thus the Economic and Social Council (ECOSOC) was established and the new Charter was imbued with references to and guarantees of the basic principles of human rights and individual freedom. The smaller states which had not been privy to the prior decisions of the great powers argued for stronger roles for the International Court of Justice, the Secretary-General, and the General Assembly to counteract the obvious power of the Security Council. In important ways this was a successful undertaking and expanded powers were won in each area by the smaller nations.[4]

The Charter was signed by all the participating states on 26 June 1945. It was ratified by the five permanent members of the new Security Council (China, France, the Soviet Union, the United Kingdom, and the United States – or P-5) and by a majority of states within the succeeding four months, so that on 24 October the Charter of the United Nations came into force. The first meeting of the General Assembly took place the following January in London. The search for a permanent location finally ended when the new Organization was offered a piece of land in New York City. By the early 1950s the buildings along the East river on the Island of Manhattan were ready to be occupied, and the UN headquarters found its permanent home.

## 1.1 The Charter

The Charter performs three basic functions: it sets out the structures of the UN and their interrelationships; it establishes a set of rules and principles which form the legal framework and justification of the UN's action in the international sphere; and it sets out norms for behaviour between states. The main thrust of the Charter rests on the 'maintenance of international peace and security' between states, and although social, economic, and fundamental rights issues of individuals and groups are mentioned, they are secondary to the twin principles of sovereignty and non-interference in the domestic affairs of states.

The UN system is structured around six principle organs: the Security Council (SC), the General Assembly (GA), the Economic and Social Council (ECOSOC), the Trusteeship Council, the International Court of Justice (ICJ), and the Secretariat. The system includes an array of committees, programmes and organs, and specialized agencies.[5] ECOSOC is attached to the General Assembly and most of the UN's programmes, organs and specialized agencies are attached to ECOSOC. The programmes, organs and specialized agencies each have their own mandated relationship with the UN, although the specialized agencies arc autonomous. The Security Council is the only body whose decisions carry the weight of obligation and which are, therefore, theoretically enforceable.

The creators of the Charter envisioned a United Nations which would act through cooperation amongst sovereign states which had abdicated the use of force as a means of gaining their foreign policy goals or settling disputes. In assuming a 'concert', particularly amongst the veto-wielding P-5, the writers of the Charter made two assumptions about the post-war world which subsequently proved misguided. First, it was believed that most aggressive action would conform to the traditional state-versus-state type of conflict. In these instances it would be relatively easy to point to an aggressor, and action would be relatively straightforward. This reasoning stemmed not only from a per-ceived reality of the relative stability of states, but also from the assumption that states operated through their governments and were, to some extent, bound to follow certain behavioural norms within the international system. As will be discussed later in relation to the development of peacekeeping, this vision of an international community functioning as separate and definable state units was only partially accurate. Second, for most of the life of the UN cooperation between the P-5 did not occur. The result was often deadlock. As Claude points out,

> The Council was conceived as an organ by means of which the great powers could exercise a joint directorate over international political affairs, in so far as they could agree upon joint policy and action. By the same token, it was designed to be inoperative in the absence of such agreement.[6]

Although designed so that each of the great powers' interests could be protected through the use of the veto, complete lack of cooperation in the SC was not envisaged. This non-cooperation carried over from the Security Council throughout the rest of the UN system.

While the Charter is supposed to represent a legally binding document to which all members of the UN are signatories, in reality many states ignore the resolutions and principles set out by the Charter and other documents. In general, non-compliance with obligatory resolutions, covenants and other international agreements has been overlooked in favour of the principle of sovereignty. While the Charter thus appears to be a comparatively weak instrument particularly in relation to domestic legal systems, it has, at least, set standards through which precedents have been set. Over the long term these precedents have changed the way states behave. The development of human rights protections is an example of this process. Recent erosion of the principles of sovereignty and non-interference are another example.[7] Such long-term shifts highlight the value of the Charter and other documents in facilitating change and development in the international community.


## 2. MAIN STRUCTURES OF THE UNITED NATIONS

### 2.1 The Security Council

In its capacity as the main organ of the United Nations responsible for the maintenance of international peace and security, the Security Council plays the decisive role for the UN in relation to the settlement of international disputes. It is composed of fifteen United Nations member states.[8] Five are permanent members: the United States, the Soviet Union, United Kingdom, China, and France. The rest are recommended for selection by the General Assembly to the Security Council for a term of two years. Under an informal agreement there are guidelines given for the selection of the ten non-permanent seats which are intended to give the Council geographical representation.

The Council is presided over by a President whose seat rotates amongst the Council members every month by English alphabetical order.[9] It holds periodic meetings in New York City at the United Nations headquarters (the Council has no set meeting times such as the yearly General Assembly). It has two main chambers, one public chamber, and directly adjacent to the public chamber, a private chamber where 'informal consultations' take place which are not open to the public.

Voting can be divided generally into two categories: votes on procedural issues and votes on substantive issues. A vote on whether or not to accept a report by the Secretary-General, for instance, is considered a procedural vote and a vote on a resolution is considered a substantive vote. For the former, a straight majority of nine votes is necessary, for the latter a majority of nine votes is necessary including the concurring votes of the five permanent members.[10]

The Security Council acts on behalf of the membership of the United Nations on issues which threaten international peace and security, and its decisions are obligatory for all states.[11] The Council's mandate potentially covers a very broad range of issues. However, in practice the Council has generally taken a narrow interpretation of what constitutes a 'threat', basing decisions on the foundation of sovereignty and non-interference. Chapter VI of the Charter sets out the techniques which the Council can use for the peaceful settlement of disputes. This includes negotiation, inquiry, mediation, conciliation, arbitration and judicial settlement. In Chapter VII of the Charter the SC is given the power to enforce its decisions. It may 'take such action by air, sea, or land forces as may be necessary to maintain or restore international peace and security'.[12] Before the recent Gulf War, Chapter VII enforcement action was only invoked once – in 1950 over the Korean crisis. At the time this action was only possible because the Soviet Union, which would have vetoed any resolution which would have led to UN involvement, was boycotting the Security Council (a lengthier discussion of the Korean crisis is offered in a later section).

The activities of the Security Council could be likened to a floating iceberg. Ninety-five per cent of its work takes place in private, either in the 'corridor' or in 'informal consultations'. The formal open meetings are, for the most part, merely formalizations of what has already been agreed to behind closed doors. These closed-door meetings involve lengthy negotiations which not only include informal consultations among the SC members, but can also consist of negotiations outside the Security Council with each States' constituency. The development and institutionalization of informal consultations represents a considerable transformation not only away from the intent of the Charter but in Security Council effectiveness.[13]

## 2.2  The General Assembly

The General Assembly is the main deliberative organ of the United Nations. It meets once a year from mid-September until late December, although it may meet at other times if an emergency session is called. Each Member State is represented in the Assembly and has one vote. The Assembly may consider any matter that is of international concern, including matters relating to international peace and security unless the issue is already being considered by the Security Council.[14] In organizational terms the GA's work revolves around six different committees: the First Committee deals with disarmament and international security issues; the Second Committee deals with world economic and financial issues; the Third Committee deals with social, humanitarian, and cultural matters; the Fourth Committee deals with special political and decolonization issues; the Fifth Committee deals with administrative and budgetary matters, and the Sixth Committee deals with questions of international law. Each member of the United Nations has a seat on each committee. The Committees are then divided into smaller working groups which have fewer members but always attempt to have broad geographical representation.

Two Assembly committees which deal specifically with peacekeeping are the Special Committee on Peacekeeping Operations (Committee of 34 or C-34) and the Fifth Committee. The C-34 was set up to consider general guidelines for peacekeeping operations and has not produced much of note. The Fifth Committee is particularly important because it authorizes the budgets for peacekeeping missions.

## 2.3 The Secretary-General and the Secretariat

The Secretary-General (S-G) is the chief administrator of the United Nations. As such it is her/his job to carry out or act upon the directives, resolutions, or decisions made by the other main organs of the Organization. The S-G and the Secretariat staff are classed as international civil servants and although they are citizens of states they are expected to work on a neutral and impartial basis. Staffing at the Secretariat can be problematic particularly for the higher positions. States lobby intensively to get their own candidates in prestigious positions and certain positions have been passed down or 'inherited' by nationals from one State. Not only has this created problems for getting the right person for the right job, but it has inhibited S-Gs from selecting their own staff. It has also meant that many more positions at the upper levels have been created making the Organization top-heavy and creating disorganization and overlap in its work. The combined efforts of former S-G Javier Perez de Cuellar and current S-G Boutros Boutros-Ghali have brought about a reduction of UN staff by some 13 per cent including 57 senior positions.[15]

The S-G's position as foreseen in the Charter is mainly an administrative one. Therefore, the powers of action available for holders of this top UN post appear quite limited. However, over the years two important precedents have been set based on Article 99 of the UN Charter which allow the S-G to take some initiative. These are: the right to conduct inquiries and fact-finding and the right to carry out 'good offices' missions.[16] The late S-G Dag Hammarskjold, noting the importance of Article 99, said it had 'transformed the Secretary-General from a purely administrative official, to one with an explicit political responsibility'.[17] In addition to the potential powers derived from Article 99, the Security Council delegates to the Secretary-General the responsibility for the day-to-day functioning of peacekeeping operations. The S-G then delegates that responsibility to the Department of Peacekeeping Operations under the direction of an Under-Secretary-General.[18]

## 3. THE BIRTH OF PEACEKEEPING

### 3.1 Post-War Development

As has been noted, the construction of the United Nations Organization took place in the aftermath of the Second World War. It was the allied or 'victorious' nations who prepared the new Charter and the greatest of those which developed the power structures of the UN. These 'great powers' focused on developing a format which assigned themselves the largest roles in determining the peace, realized through their permanent representation on the Security Council and their right of veto.

Unfortunately, these great power framers concentrated on enforcement and dealing with the immediate causes of disputes through the Security Council, to the detriment of underlying causes of conflict. In this sense the Council functions much more in a crisis management role than in a conflict avoidance or peace construction role. As Haas points out, 'the preservation of the *status quo* was clearly favored over the provision for peaceful change'.[19] This is supported by the fact that it was the Security Council, rather than the General Assembly, which was empowered to act and enforce.

In addition to its focus on immediate crisis management and the maintenance of a 'peaceful' *status quo*, the Charter did not foresee nor set up structures to deal with the myriad other global problems which, to varying degrees, affect the maintenance of international peace and security. Trans-global issues such as environmental problems, including global warming, ozone depletion, deforestation, pollution, and desertification did not have the same urgency in 1945 as they have since acquired. Population growth and movement and uneven resource distribution have also become increasingly serious problems, as well as mass starvation and incurable diseases such as AIDS. Acknowledging the Charter's limitations, Brian Urquhart, former Under-Secretary-General for Special Political Affairs, notes, '[t]he Charter was written with the disasters of previous years in mind. Not surprisingly, it did not foresee accurately the shape and balance of the post-war world.'[20]

In response to the limitations of the Charter and in recognition of the need to act, transformations have occurred within the United Nations system. It is important to note a few of these transformations because they show how the UN has attempted to adapt to the changes in the international system without re-working the existing structures through amending the Charter (this is a very difficult task with nearly insurmountable political obstacles). Four changes will be noted here covering, expansion in size, alteration in the Security Council practices and procedures, change in the operations of the Security Council, and transformation of attitudes towards issues on the international agenda.[21]

The quantitative transformation, according to Scheltema, refers to the expansion in membership of the United Nations from 50 (51 if Poland is included) to 184. The Headquarters building in New York was originally built with the expectation that the UN would expand to include ninety members at most. The other quantitative change is visible in the expansion of the UN into a huge system including sixteen main specialized agencies, and many other committees, institutions, and bodies, intersecting the system at different points. Non-Governmental Organizations (NGOs) number well over 4000.

Transformation of the practices and procedures of the SC were mentioned in the previous section. They will be briefly summarized here. The concert expected of the P-5 did not function. The negotiations over the use of the Military Staff Committee, which was intended to direct any UN enforce-ment action, and a Standing UN force stalled and have not since been resolved. The SC quickly became a place for public bickering, recrimination and use of the veto. Out of necessity, in order to achieve some level of effectiveness in carrying out its Charter responsibilities, the SC began to meet in private through the use of 'informal consultations'. This change in procedure has meant that public meetings hold no surprises for the SC members as they have worked out their differences in private and know how the voting will go. Scheltema notes,

> What has really happened is that the Security Council has trans-formed itself from a forum for public debate and veto into a deliberative body seeking consensus behind closed doors.[22]

The Security Council's activities to safeguard international peace and security were also transformed in response to the political unviability of resorting to enforcement measures (the one exception was Korea which is discussed in the next section). To counteract this problem peacekeeping was developed.

The final transformation concerns the issues which are discussed and acted upon by the UN. For example, forty years ago the Security Council would not have considered setting up an operation in El Salvador (ONUSAL) for the purpose, inter alia, of monitoring a human rights agreement between a revolutionary force and the government. But human rights as an international issue is now considered the legitimate business of the United Nations.

These transformations are indicative of a system which has been forced to adapt to changes largely unforeseen by its founders and for which no provision for action was available in the Charter. In many ways the Charter has become obsolete; the erosion of the principle of sovereignty upon which it was founded exemplifies this. However, many of the fundamental principles of the Organization, particularly those regarding the rights of individual people, have remained salient as demonstrated by recent interventions on humanitarian grounds in former Yugoslavia and Somalia.

The limitations built into the Charter were only part of the framers' lack of vision. The Organization was founded on the assumption of concerted action by the victorious Allies, especially the P-5 in the Security Council. But as early as the Yalta Conference there were murmurings of the great bipolar conflict to come.[23] Lack of unanimity on most issues and the polarization of the Security Council and the rest of the Organization meant that the Security Council became almost totally incapable of utilizing its collective security machinery for crisis management.

The one exception to this in the UN's early history was the Korean War in 1950. This came about mainly as a result of a boycott of the Security Council by the Soviet Union when North Korea invaded South Korea.[24] During the Soviet absence a resolution was passed in the Security Council which determined that North Korea's action constituted a breach of peace under Chapter VII of the Charter.[25] A further resolution by the Security Council called for the establishment of a unified command under the United States to 'furnish such assistance to the Republic of Korea as may be necessary to repel the armed attack and to restore international peace and security in the area'.[26] This same resolution also authorized the unified command to operate under the United Nations flag. Following the return of the Permanent Representative of the Soviet Union the Security Council became deadlocked. So that the operation could continue a US-backed resolution was subsequently passed by the General Assembly giving it the authority to act in lieu of the deadlocked Security Council.[27] This became know as the 'Uniting for Peace' resolution and its constitutionality is still a matter of debate. The action is important for peacekeeping only in that it established the precedent under the 'Uniting for Peace' resolution of the General Assembly's right to act in a crisis for a stalemated Security Council. It was this precedent that allowed for the establishment of the first force-level peacekeeping operation during the Suez Crisis in 1956. It should be noted that enforcement action in Korea was authorized under Chapter VII of the Charter and therefore did not constitute peacekeeping.[28] The more recent example of enforcement action was the Gulf War. Again, this action, authorized under Chapter VII of the Charter, did not constitute peacekeeping.

In addition to the onset of the Cold War and the demise of the Second World War alliances, decolonization and the rise in nationalism almost immediately rendered some sections of Charter untenable. According to a study by Haas, the latter two issues alone accounted for 39 per cent of conflicts (19 per cent and 20 per cent respectively) from 1945 to 1986. The remaining 61 per cent of disputes were split evenly between civil and inter-state disputes. Many civil and inter-state disputes, according to Haas's study, could also be characterized as post-colonial disputes, i.e. relating to the lack of existence of effective power structures in the wake of decolonization.[29] Haas's breakdown is substantially corroborated by another study done by Miall.[30] Wiseman summarizes the situation:

> data sets which deal with the characteristics of international conflict show that from 1900 to 1941, 80% of wars were between armed forces of two or more states, whereas from

1945 to 1976, 85% were on the territory of one state only and were internally oriented.[31]

The combined problems of decolonization and nationalism meant that most disputes, because they did not fit into the state-system pattern and, therefore, could not be characterized as one state illegally and aggressively invading another, were not within the prescribed remit of the Security Council. The growth in the number of nation-state actors undoubtedly had an effect on the concurrent growth in the complexities of international political relations and it was increasingly difficult in many situations to pinpoint the 'genuine representatives' of a people. As James points out, '[t]he UN security arrangements were not developed with these subtleties in mind'.[32] The Cold War further compounded these problems by creating a situation whereby if the 'West' backed one side, the 'East' would automatically back the other. The effects of this confrontation on the ability of the Security Council to act were decisive. Urquhart notes that, 'the main current of threats to peace flowing from the East-West competition for power and influence ran through the very heart of the Security Council which was supposed to deal with threats to peace'.[33] Whether or not it would have been possible to foresee such developments in 1945 when the drafters of the UN Charter were working is a moot point. The fact was that collective security, the foundation of the new organization, did not work and the Security Council became ineffectual.

These factors created a situation in the United Nations Security Council whereby it could not take action in times of severe international crisis using the methods provided for by the Charter. It was this need to avert the potential escalation of local conflicts into superpower confrontations, coupled with an inability to act, that led to the development of peacekeeping.

## 3.2 The Suez and the Congo: A Study of Opposites

### 3.2.1 Suez: The Birth of Peacekeeping
It was the 1956 Suez Crisis that led to the deployment of the first force-level peacekeeping operation.[34] In previous years two observer missions[35] had been deployed but until the Suez crisis they had not been characterized as peacekeeping.[36]

Because of a poorly planned operation involving French and British forces invading Egypt, the international community was thrown into a difficult crisis involving two members of the Security Council, both holding veto power.[37] The creation of United Nations Emergency Force I (UNEF I), while an important development for the future of peacekeeping, was valuable at the time in that it allowed Britain and France to withdraw without disgrace.[38] UNEF I established a basic set of principles and standards which have served as the basis for the creation of all other missions which have followed. It was the first major precedent. The credit for masterminding this Force goes largely to the then Secretary-General Hammarskjold and a Canadian Diplomat, Lester Pearson.[39] The document prepared by Hammarskjold and Pearson contained five key principles: (1) the principle of consent of the parties to the dispute for the establishment of the mission, (2) the principle of non-use of force except in self-defence, (3) the principle of voluntary contributions of contingents from small, neutral countries to participate in the force, (4) the principle of impartiality and non-intervention (i.e. the force is not meant to participate in the conflict) and, (5) the principle of day-to-day control of peacekeeping operations by the Secretary-General. Urquhart argues that the document was a 'conceptual masterpiece in a completely new field, the blueprint for a non-violent, international military operation'.[40]

UNEF I was quite successful in fulfilling its mandated function of securing a cease-fire and facilitating the withdrawal of foreign forces from Egypt. Based on this experience, there was considerable optimism for the prospects of peacekeeping.

### 3.2.2 The Congo and Crisis at the UN

In stark contrast to the successes of UNEF I, the 1960–64 peacekeeping mission in the Congo (United Nations Operation in the Congo – ONUC), quickly became a source of bitter disagreement in the UN. There had been some controversy over the funding of UNEF I amongst the P-5. But financial controversy over ONUC generated a crisis so serious that the continued existence of the UN itself was in some doubt.

The date for Congolese independence from Belgium was set in January 1960 and, following a very brief negotiation and election process, the country became formally independent on 30 June 1960. The brevity of the planning and preparation given to the independence process resulted in a miasma of Congolese tribal conflict and political wrangling compounded by poor infrastructure and a weak economy. A week after independence Congolese troops mutinied. A short time later the leaders of the mineral rich province of Katanga attempted secession. The Congo operation came about in response to the newly independent government's request for technical assistance and help to maintain law and order.[41] The threat to international peace and security was not so much the internal dispute, which would have been dangerous enough, but the fact that the Congo, because of its rich resources, looked set to become the next superpower battleground.

It was into this civil disorder that 20,000 UN military and civilian peacekeepers were cast, without adequate international support or planning, and with a mandate which was so ambiguous as to be virtually useless. They encountered conflicting pressures from all sides including the numerous internal factions, regional states, and superpowers.

The Katanga secession was finally ended in early 1963, when some sense of security and calm was restored. In return, however, the international community and the United Nations paid a heavy price. Secretary-General Hammarskjold had died along with over 200 peacekeepers, and many more Congolese. The UN was reeling from the shock waves of internal dissension. The Congo itself was in an abysmal economic state, with little effective social, educational or technical infrastructure. As a result the upsurge in interest and support for peacekeeping which had followed the pioneering successes of UNEF I, now turned into bitter opposition. As Urquhart recalls,

> much of the thrust of Hammarskjold's efforts for the development of the United Nations as an active political instrument in times of crisis was... submerged in the later stages of the Congo crisis.... The Congo experience often either wilfully or unintentionally misinterpreted or wrongly perceived, did much to dampen and set back the hopes for the United Nations as the active instrument of peace and conflict control which Hammarskjold's earlier efforts [in UNEF I] had done so much to encourage.[42]

### 3.2.3 Diffusing the Crisis

The Congo operation raised a number of contentious issues. First, the Security Council had become deadlocked after initially authorizing ONUC. The operation had then been continued through use of the 'Uniting For Peace' resolution. The Soviet Union objected to the use of this technique as unconstitutional. Other members also had grave misgivings. Without the use of this resolution the Security Council would have remained deadlocked and the operation would not have been authorized.[43] Second, there was much disagreement about how the operation had been set up, who was seen to have been running it, and the limits and ambiguities of the mandate (especially the question of whether force had been employed during the operation to end the secession in Katanga).[44]

As a consequence the Soviet Union (and others, including France) refused to pay their regular assessment in a protest largely directed at the policies of Hammarskjold. Under Article 19 of the Charter, any member State whose 'arrears equals or exceeds the amount of the contributions due from it for the preceding two years' would lose their vote in the General Assembly. When the Soviet Union fell two years behind in their assessment the United States tried to put forward a motion in the General Assembly which would have disallowed the Soviet vote. Had there been such a vote, the Soviet Union would probably have left the UN, along with its satellite states and other sympathetic states. This could well have dealt a blow from which the UN would not have been able to recover.

The crisis was eventually averted through highly skilled diplomacy and manoeuvring during two meetings of the General Assembly. At the 1964 General Assembly session a decision to abstain from voting deftly avoided a confrontation over the American resolution. In order to function without the vote, the President of the Assembly was elected by consensus. By the next General Assembly a compromise had been reached whereby the United States withdrew the resolution and the Soviet Union received agreement to set up the Special Committee on Peacekeeping (C-34) which was mandated to develop agreed guidelines for peacekeeping operations. The repercussions of this crisis led to a period of dormancy for peacekeeping (see Appendix 1). It was subsequently resurrected in 1973 by Secretary-General Kurt Waldheim in response to the war between Egypt and Israel.

Despite this crisis and the deep divisions it generated over certain issues associated with peacekeeping, operations subsequently continued to be set up on an *ad hoc* basis. The fact that peacekeeping was not written into the Charter meant that it was not supported constitutionally. But the flexibility of the *ad hoc* approach allowed peacekeeping to survive as a working tool of the Security Council.

## 4.  AN OVERVIEW OF PEACEKEEPING OPERATIONS, 1948–87

In this section a brief overview of peacekeeping operations will be given using a slightly revised categorization method first developed by Wiseman. Wiseman thought that when looking at peacekeeping in a case-by-case study, five separate phases become apparent: (1) the Nascent Period, 1946–56, (2) the Assertive Period, 1956–67, (3) the Dormant Period, 1967–73, (4) the Resurgent Period, 1973–78, and (5) the Maintenance Period, 1978–85.[45] Wiseman's categorizations will be utilized. To these, another category has been added by the author which is called the Expansion Period. This last period covers operations from 1988 through 1993 (see Appendix 1) and will be dealt with in the following chapter.

### 4.1  The Nascent Period, 1946–56

As its title suggests it was during these ten years that the foundations for full-scale peacekeeping operations were laid. During this time several observer missions and commissions were set up. The observer missions were in fact peacekeeping but were not called so at the time. Two missions are still in place today, although they have each had to survive changes in the political landscapes in which they operate. The United Nations Truce Supervision Organization or UNTSO was set up in 1948 in Palestine. Today one of the crucial roles played by UNTSO, apart from its observer role, is providing experienced officers for other missions on short notice. This aids greatly in the difficult task of creating each new peacekeeping mission on an *ad hoc* basis, because some experienced personnel are usually available to act as the first wave in new mission areas. Elsewhere, on the border between India and Pakistan, the United Nations Military Observer

Group in India and Pakistan (UNMOGIP) was established in 1949.

## 4.2 The Assertive Period, 1956–67

UNEF I, as mentioned previously, involved not only an expansion of numbers of personnel, but a new level of complexity which went well beyond that of any previous mission. Seven more peacekeeping missions followed. Of these, four were observer missions and three were larger-scale operations. The observer missions during this period were United Nations Observation Group in Lebanon, UNOGIL, in 1958, United Nations Yemen Observation Mission, UNYOM, in 1963, Representative of the Secretary-General in the Dominican Republic, DOMREP, in 1965, and United Nations India-Pakistan Observer Mission, UNIPOM, in 1965. The full-scale peacekeeping missions were ONUC (mentioned above), United Nations Temporary Executive Authority and United Nations Security Force in West New Guinea (West Irian), UNTEA/UNSF in 1962, and United Nations Force in Cyprus, UNFICYP, in 1964 (see Chapter 3). Until the resurgence of peacekeeping starting in 1988 the assertive period was by far the most active one for UN peacekeepers. Each of these operations had some unique features and served to set precedents and provide experiences which are still relevant today. For example, during UNTEA/UNSF, the UN assumed temporary authority over the territory until completion of its transition to an independent state. This included authority for maintaining law and order. In Cyprus, UN civilian police were used for the first time, setting a precedent which was repeated in later-operations.

Considering the controversy surrounding this period of UN history, the number of missions which were established (as well as the innovative measures mandated for them) is surprising. But this period of activity did not last. In 1967, at the request of the Egyptian government led by Nasser, UNEF I was withdrawn from the Sinai, precipitating the June 1967 war. As Wiseman points out,

The Organization pushed to the limits its own legitimacy and competence at a time when East–West antagonism assaulted its very foundations. But the lack of assertiveness in allowing the withdrawal of UNEF at Egypt's insistence without so much as a General Assembly debate on the matter undermined the credibility of the Organization in the management of peace and security.[46]

### 4.3  The Dormant Period, 1967–73

In stark contrast to the energetic activity of the previous eleven years, no new operations were established during the Dormant Period. According to Wiseman, the lack of UN initiatives was not due to lack of conflicts to act upon. He gives three possible reasons for this period of inactivity: (1) history shows that the UN has not acted until a crisis has reached a critical and internationally threatening stage; (2) the new Organization of African Unity was trying to make use of its own regional security measures; (3) the conflicts between the Soviet Union and the United States prevented UN action in either country's 'sphere of influence'.[47]

### 4.4  The Resurgent Period, 1973–78

Three new force-level peacekeeping operations were established in this period. All were in the Middle East: United Nations Emergency Force II (UNEF II), in 1973, in the Sinai, United Nations Disengagement Observer Force (UNDOF), in 1974, in the Golan Heights, and United Nations Interim Force in Lebanon (UNIFIL), in 1978. The latter two, UNDOF and UNIFIL are still functioning. It is interesting to note that between 1965 and 1988 no peacekeeping missions were established outside of the Middle East.

### 4.5  The Maintenance Period, 1978–88

As in the Dormant Period, no new operations were established during these ten years. It is quite possible that one of the reasons for the UN's low profile can be traced to the election to the Presidency of the United States of Ronald Reagan. Reagan's attitude toward the UN was less than cooperative and, in fact, tended to be dismissive. Above all, his administration's attitude toward the Soviet Union, at least in the first half of his eight-year term, was distinctly negative as illustrated by his use of the epithet 'evil empire'.[48] As was noted earlier the adversarial positions of the US and the USSR toward each other made the UN's peacekeeping work difficult and at times impossible.

## 5. CONCLUSION

This chapter has reviewed the historical development of United Nations peacekeeping from its beginnings in the immediate post-war years, through to the Maintenance Period which ended in 1988 with the establishment of the United Nations Transition Assistance Group (UNTAG) in Namibia. The conflict between the US and the USSR was the primary factor triggering the development of peacekeeping and which dominated its subsequent role. Perhaps ironically it was the decline of that bipolar conflict in the late 1980s which transformed the global context of peacekeeping and significantly broadened its potential as a technique of peaceful settlement.

The next chapter will continue the exploration of UN peacekeeping. It will focus on the radical changes in its context since 1988 and the impact of these changes on its practice. Further chapters look beyond present practice and discuss the future of peacekeeping.

# 2 UN Peacekeeping in the Post-Cold War World

## 1. THE INTERNATIONAL CONTEXT

In Chapter 1 it was noted that since the end of the Second World War international conflict has shifted away from inter-state war so that now most international conflict can be categorized as intra-state. It was pointed out that the UN Charter focused on the prevention of inter-state conflict. The post-war shift was not foreseen by the Charter writers, and the UN was largely unprepared to deal with the complexity and deep-rooted character of the type of conflict that emerged. This type of conflict, particularly when it is confined within the borders of one state, does not fall easily within the compass of the Charter's Articles. In addition, and as was discussed earlier, the Cold War made the Security Council incapable of dealing with most conflicts in any truly effective manner.

While the United Nations struggled to survive the Cold War years, conflicts continued, largely unabated. Some statistics are revealing. Eckhardt argues that 'wars have increased in frequency, duration, and deaths from the 18th to the 20th century. The increase of deaths was four times the increase of the world population.'[1] Even discounting the deaths caused by the World Wars (and noting that the century is not yet over), deaths from wars this century have increased over previous centuries.[2] Since the end of the Cold War the number of major armed conflicts has decreased slightly.[3] However, over the same period all armed conflicts have increased, with the largest increase in the category of minor armed conflicts.[4] Wallensteen and Axell point out that although the slight decrease in wars suggests that the international community has some ability to contain major conflicts, '[t]he number of protracted conflicts testifies... to the inability to find lasting solutions to well-known conflicts'.[5] As well as an increase in all armed conflict, the proportion of civilian war-related deaths, which had averaged around 50 per cent since the eighteenth century, increased to 73 per cent in the 1970s and was close to 90 per cent in 1990.[6] One reason for this increase in civilian deaths is suggested by Nordstrom. She points out a pattern of 'increasing reliance on dirty war tactics', arguing that, '[d]irty wars seek victory, not through military and battlefield strategies, but through horror. Civilians, rather than soldiers, are the tactical targets, and fear, brutality, and murder are the foundation on which control is constructed.'[7] Amnesty International statistics on human rights abuses which point out that two-thirds of the world's countries use human rights abuses to maintain political power add substantial weight to her claim.

The scale of human problems and their complex relationship to armed conflict and structural violence were largely neglected or suppressed during the Cold War years so that now the UN and the world community are facing serious crises on a number of fronts. The number of refugees fleeing conflict areas now stands at a staggering 19 million (compared to 11 million ten years ago), with a further 25 million internally persons.[8] The disparity between rich and poor countries is similarly alarming; 'the richest 20% of the world's population receive 83% of total world income, whereas the poorest 20% have 1.4%'.[9] Sivard notes that four out of five cancers can be linked to environmental causes, over 1000 children die per hour from diarrhoeal diseases, and unsafe water and sanitation lead directly or indirectly to 80 per cent of world sickness and disease.[10] At the same time environmental degradation and destruction has continued so that deforestation, global warming, desertification, and pollution are widespread.[11] Indeed the depth of these global problems has led Eckhardt to argue,

In the course of this century, the behavioral violence of wars and revolutions has caused some 86 million deaths, or approximately one million deaths per year. Structural violence, on the other hand, has caused a total of some 1600 million deaths, or approximately 19 million deaths per year. This means that the structural violence of hunger and preventable disease was some 19 times more deadly than the behavioral violence of war in the 20th century.[12]

He argues further that it may only be possible to reduce behavioural violence by reducing structural violence. Finally, a significant change since the founding of the UN has come in rapidly increasing global economic interdependence and the growth of the telecommunications industry sometimes referred to as the 'CNN-effect'.

While the end of the Cold War has enabled the UN to work more freely, the scale of the problems it faces are immense. Added to this, the 'new cooperation', especially in the SC, raised expectations of quick solutions. In the absence of other options peacekeeping was singled out to play a significant role in bringing about resolution of some of the most acute problems leading to the deployment in situations which were substantially different from pre-1988 circumstances. But the severe limitations placed on peacekeeping activity during the Cold War left it largely unprepared for the new demands.

In some respects, peacekeeping has expanded to meet these challenges, but its full evolution has been hampered by the element that once ensured its survival – its *ad hoc* nature.[13] Until recently this reliance on the flexibility inherent in *ad hoc* arrangements was central to the survival and application of the peacekeeping technique. In the bureaucratic and highly politicized world of the United Nations, most diplomats considered frameworks or definitions to be limiting factors which led inevitably to stagnation. While the Cold War set stark and often unassailable limitations on UN attempts to contribute to the maintenance of international peace and security, peace-keeping was a tool of such flexibility that it did not fall fully into the trap of the Security Council's veto. Because peacekeeping operated and in some respects flourished during the Cold War largely because it was *ad hoc* and not written into the UN's Char-ter, there remains a deep suspicion of suggestions that peace-keeping should be placed onto a more firm and permanent footing. However, in the post-Cold War context, increased reli-ance on peacekeeping and its subsequent *ad hoc* adaptations indicate the need to develop alternate management strategies which more effectively cope with the types of conflict we are faced with today. The publication of Boutros-Ghali's *An Agenda for Peace* has gone some way toward bringing peacekeeping into the post-Cold War world by recognizing the importance of utilizing it as one part of a broader intervention process. But much more needs to be done. Later chapters address themselves to developing a conceptual framework for peacekeeping which overcomes 'adhockery' and takes account of the scale, depth and complexity of situations into which peacekeepers are deployed. This chapter concentrates on some of the problems of peacekeeping which have been magnified by its attempts to cope in the post-Cold War world.

## 2. THE RISE OF MULTIDIMENSIONAL PEACEKEEPING

Until 1988, the UN's responses to both its internal political difficulties and the outward change in international conflict and its context have been innovative and, in view of the political difficulties within the Security Council, a considerable achievement. At the same time, the response has been insufficient to quell the rising tide of protracted social conflict and serious environmental and human issues. The demands of the last five years on the UN, particularly on peacekeeping, have been overwhelming.

From 1948 to 1992 around 650,000 personnel participated in peacekeeping operations at an estimated cost of US$8.3 billion.[14] Since 1988, eighteen new missions have been established, five more than in the previous forty-year history of UN peacekeeping (see Appendix 1). In 1992 alone, the numbers of peacekeepers on the ground increased from approximately 10,000 to 62,000, while the budget rose to US$1.4 billion.[15] There are currently around 80,000 peacekeepers on the ground and estimates suggest that this figure could increase to 100,000 by the end of 1993.[16] Of these 80,000 peacekeepers, 4500 are civilian police (in 1987 only 35 civilian police were deployed) and 10,000 are civilian personnel (in 1987 only 1000 civilian personnel were deployed).[17]

In addition to the increase in the application of peacekeeping, the types of missions which have been mandated have also altered. Before 1988, four of the thirteen missions established could be characterised as multidimensional. Multidimensional missions are force-level operations which usually, although not necessarily, include a large civilian component and are mandated explicitly to deal with socio-political and/or humanitarian aspects of the conflict (UNTAG in Namibia and UNTAC in Cambodia are examples). In the five years since, thirteen of the eighteen missions established have had explicit multidimensional functions. In addition, two new missions, UNOMIG in Georgia and UNOMIL in Liberia, have the potential to become multidimensional.

Beyond this, three recent developments are significant. The application of peacekeeping is becoming less inhibited as the line between intra-state and inter-state intervention loses its traditional distinction. In addition, peacekeeping is being applied more often to conflicts which can be characterized as protracted and deep-rooted and which are resistant to resolution through the application of traditional methods of conflict management. The range of activities routinely performed by peacekeepers has consequently expanded. In particular, the demand for peacekeepers to become more energetically involved in explicit conflict resolution activity has greatly increased. Finally, the use of force by peacekeepers has become a significant issue, particularly since the Gulf War. The debate has intensified as the line between peacekeeping and enforcement has blurred.

In the broader context of UN peaceful intervention there are visible indications that, just as peacekeeping is evolving to meet new challenges, so too are other aspects of UN activity. Reforms begun in March 1992 at the UN are attempting, among other things, to improve its management structure. It is hoped that these reforms will make the UN better equipped to handle a rapidly growing work load. *An Agenda for Peace* argues for coordination of UN intervention and puts forward a framework of conflict management.[18] The recent S-G's annual report is a lengthy description of efforts to revamp the UN since the publication of *An Agenda for Peace*.[19] It particularly emphasizes improving the coordination of UN activities in the field. One example of attempts to improve coordination is the establishment of 'Interim Offices' in some newly created states. These interim offices are regarded as 'an experiment in better organizing the multifarious activities of the UN in a particular country'. Their mandate includes 'normal development and public relations functions', but it is expected that they will perform preventative functions by providing timely information and by acting as a direct link between the UN and the state government.[20] These are all indications of attempts to address the problems posed by conflicts in the post-Cold War world.

## 2.1  The Expansion Period, 1988–93

This section will complete the classification and description of peacekeeping missions begun in Chapter 1. This last period, 'The Expansion Period', is by far the most active in peace-keeping history. Several general characteristics set it apart from previous years.[21] First is the cooperative superpower dimension not only in the Security Council but in peace-making activities outside that UN organ. Second, each conflict has significant internal and regional dimensions well beyond the parameters of inter-state conflict. Third, because of the change in attitude toward the UN and peacekeeping by the Soviet Union (now Russia), the role of the S-G in the day-to-day running of operations is not only accepted as a positive situation but is now receiving much more support from the whole Council.

Finally, the UN has taken on new tasks, setting precedents which challenge the non-interference principle and traditional notions of peacekeeping. Missions in Kuwait/Iraq, Somalia and Bosnia, all authorized under Chapter VII of the UN Charter (i.e. consent is not required for deployment) have had a significant impact on the concept and practice of peacekeeping. These missions are not quite 'collective security' but do not quite conform to the three central principles of peacekeeping: consent, impartiality, and the non-use of force. This issue is a particularly difficult one: how exactly do we define peacekeeping? In Bosnia, for example, although the mission was authorized under Chapter VII, in practice it has not had the operational capability (nor the political will) to enforce and has, therefore, continued to operate under traditional peacekeeping principles.[22] While Bosnia provides a particularly difficult case, UNOSOM II in Somalia is more clear cut. In this instance theory and practice met. Force was used and consent was not universally obtained, so the mission qualifies as enforcement rather than peacekeeping. (The issues underlying the problems of classification will be argued in later chapters, where the case for a conceptual framework is made. Here, the issue is avoided, and the missions over which there is some question are grouped together at the end of the section under the heading, 'Are These Missions Peace-keeping?') The remainder of this section briefly summarizes the peacekeeping missions deployed over the last five years.

Following the negotiation of a ceasefire between Iran and Iraq in 1988, United Nations Iran-Iraq Military Observer Group, UNIIMOG, was established to verify compliance with the cease-fire agreement. It was set up along the border between the two countries. UNIIMOG was terminated on 1 February 1991, partly because Iran and Iraq were complying with the 1975 treaty between them, and partly because of the Iraq–Kuwait crisis.

United Nations Angola Verification Mission, UNAVEM, established in 1989, was designed to observe compliance with an agreement between Angola, Cuba, and South Africa on withdrawal of Cuban troops from Angola. This agreement was formulated in conjunction with an agreement on Namibian independence which lead to the establishment of the United Nations Transition Assistance Group, UNTAG, in 1989. UNTAG had a unique and important part to play in the transition to independence and democratic rule in Namibia, and is outlined in more detail in Chapter 3.

A series of new missions were mandated for the Central American region. For the first time since DOMREP in 1965, the UN had a peacekeeping role in a region considered by the United States as part of its 'sphere of influence'. Following negotiations begun by the Contadora Group, including Colombia, Mexico, Panama, and Venezuela, which led to the signing of the *Esquipulas II* Agreement setting up regional security commitments for Central America, the UN was asked by the signatories of the agreement, the five Central American countries, Costa Rica, El Salvador, Guatemala, Honduras, and Nicaragua, to verify observance of the treaty. Thus, United Nations Observer Group in Central America, ONUCA, was established in 1989 and ran until 1992.

Two other operations were also established in the Central American region in conjunction with ONUCA. In Nicaragua, the United Nations Observation Mission for the Verification of Elections in Nicaragua, ONUVEN, was established in late 1989.

This mission was unique in that it was the first time the UN had been asked and accepted the role of verifying elections in a sovereign, already-existing state. Most recently, United Nations Observer Mission in El Salvador, ONUSAL, was established in mid-1991. ONUSAL was an interesting and unique mission because it was put into place while there was still no ceasefire agreement between the El Salvadorian government and the opposition rebel group FMLN. The operation was established, *inter alia*, to verify a human rights agreement, signed in July 1990, between the government and the FMLN. This marked the first time that the UN had undertaken such verification. While this mission has had some success in moving El Salvador toward peaceful resolution of its conflict, it has faced a number of setbacks at the time of writing make its long-term impact on the conflict uncertain.[23]

United Nations Observer Group for the Verification of the Elections in Haiti, ONUVEH, was established on 10 October 1990, by consensus of the General Assembly, in response to a request by the head of Haiti's provisional government. Although the Security Council voiced its support of this mission, it did not actually authorize it. It had been decided that the situation in Haiti did not constitute a threat to international peace and security and therefore was outside the remit of the SC. Although the mission was carried out (authorized by the GA) and a President elected, a military coup followed which undermined the incipient democratic process. Subsequent UN involvement is related below in connection with the United Nations Mission in Haiti (UNMIH).

UNAVEM II, was an extension and expansion of UNAVEM I. Its mission was to verify compliance with the Angolan Peace Accords signed between the Angolan government and opposition rebel group UNITA. Its most important task was to monitor and verify the election process held at the end of November 1992.[24] Although UNAVEM II managed to monitor the elections, the failure of UNITA to accept the results pushed Angola back into civil war.[25]

The United Nations Mission for the Referendum in Western Sahara, MINURSO, was established in 1991. MINURSO's mandate involved verifying a ceasefire, repatriation of refugees, and monitoring the registration of voters and referendum process in Western Sahara.[26] This mission has since been stalled at the pre-registration phase because of differences between the Moroccan government and opposition rebel group POLISARIO over the identification of qualified voters. At the time of writing prospects for the completion of MINURSO's mandate were not good.[27]

The United Nations Transitional Authority in Cambodia, UNTAC, was established in 1992. This mission was mandated to carry out the cantonment, disarming and repatriation of guerilla groups operating in Cambodia; the repatriation of refugees; and the supervision of elections and transition to democratic rule. Like its predecessor, UNTEA/UNSF, UNTAC had temporary authority to carry out some governmental functions during the transition period. UNTAC was completed with the final withdrawal of personnel in November 1993. The UN claimed UNTAC was a largely unqualified success. More circumspect commentators have noted a number of areas which could pose significant obstacles to long term peace and stability in Cambodia.[28]

The United Nations Protection Forces I and II, UNPROFOR I and II, were established in 1992. UNPROFOR I has operated in Croatia. Broadly speaking, its mandate has been to prevent the resumption of fighting and to facilitate movement toward settlement of the conflict. UNPROFOR II, essentially an extension of UNPROFOR I, was set up in Bosnia-Herzegovina as a humanitarian relief operation. Its task has been to ensure the provision of relief supplies to civilians by protecting aid convoys. This operation was the first of its kind and represented a considerable extension of peacekeeping's previous remit. Peacekeeping in the former-Yugoslavia is discussed more fully in the next chapter.

The United Nations Operation in Somalia, UNOSOM I, was established in 1992. It is a humanitarian relief operation mandated to facilitate the delivery of aid to a starving population. It also monitored a ceasefire in the Somali capital, Mogadishu. Following serious problems in fulfilling this mandate and a general deterioration of the situation in Somalia, especially in Mogadishu and the surrounding area, the SC authorized the formation of the Unified Task Force (UNITAF) under Chapter VII.[29] UNOSOM remained a presence in Somalia and liaised with UNITAF. At the end of March 1993, the SC affected a transition from UNITAF to UNOSOM II expanding

UNOSOM's mandate and authorizing it under Chapter VII.[30] Although a great deal of controversy has been generated by the use of force in Somalia and the battles between UNITAF and UN troops and Somali factions in Mogadishu, the UN has had a some positive impact, at least in the short term, in areas outside of the capital.[31]

The United Nations Operation in Mozambique, ONUMOZ, was set up in 1992. It was initially a small observer operation, established to help verify agreements signed between the Mozambican government and the rebel force, RENAMO, ending a long civil conflict. The mandate was subsequently expanded to a Cambodian-like mission. There have been delays in the implementation process caused by disagreement and non-cooperation between the government of Mozambique and RENAMO and the situation remains uncertain.[32]

Four new missions were established in 1993. The United Nations Assistance Mission in Rwanda (UNAMIR) was established in October 1993.[33] It subsumed an existing mission, the United Nations Observer Mission in Uganda/ Rwanda (UNOMUR) which had been set up earlier in the year. UNAMIR was mandated to oversee a transition process similar to those in Cambodia and Mozambique. The United Nations Observer Mission in Liberia (UNOMIL) was established in September to monitor compliance with a peace accord ending civil war in the African state.[34] UNOMIL was unique in that it was the first time a UN mission had been undertaken in cooperation with an existing regional peacekeeping mission (ECOMOG). Another observer mission, the United Nations Observer Mission in Georgia (UNOMIG) was created in August 1993 to verify a ceasefire agreement between Abkhazian and Georgian forces and to investigate ceasefire violations.[35] Although the ceasefire was subsequently broken the UN mission remained to maintain contacts between both sides and Russian troops also in the area and to continue to monitor and report on the situation.[36] Finally, the Security Council decided to create the United Nations Mission in Haiti (UNMIH) made up largely of police monitors and military trainers. The police monitors were mandated to provide guidance and training for all levels of Haitian police and to monitor their activity particularly with respect to human rights. The military trainers were assigned the task of training Haitian

military forces in non-combat roles such as disaster preparation and relief.[37] At the time of writing UNMIH had not been
deployed because of the refusal of Army Commander, Lt.-Gen.
Raoul Cedras to hand over power to democratically elected
civilian President Jean-Bertrand Aristide as per a previously
signed political accord. Following Cedres's refusal to cooperate the SC reaffirmed its commitment to continue to enforce
an oil embargo and economic sanctions on Haiti. While prospects for settlement of the conflict were bleak, worse still was
the situation for the 6.5 million Haitians.[38]

## 2.2 Are These Missions Peacekeeping?

The United Nations Good Offices Mission in Afghanistan and
Pakistan, UNGOMAP was set up in 1988. This operation was
related to the negotiation of the Geneva Accords which led to the
withdrawal of Soviet troops from Afghanistan. The operation was
initiated by S-G Perez de Cuellar through the use of his good
offices, but was sanctioned, although not formally, by the Security
Council. Out of UNGOMAP, which terminated 15 March 1990,
the S-G announced the establishment of Office of the Secretary-
General in Afghanistan and Pakistan, OSGAP, on 15 March 1990,
which consisted of ten officers who were monitors (advisors) in
the area until 31 December 1990. OSGAP was created because
the S-G had been unable to convince the SC to extend the mandate of UNGOMAP and felt some kind of UN presence in the
area was required. This mission was more akin to peacemaking
than peacekeeping.

Two missions were established in Iraq and Kuwait as a result
of the Gulf War. The first, United Nations Iraq-Kuwait
Observation Mission, UNIKOM, was created on 9 April 1991.[39]
The operation has been monitoring a demilitarized zone
extending five kilometres into both Iraqi and Kuwaiti territory.[40] The question of whether or not UNIKOM constitutes
peacekeeping mainly arises from the fact that the operation
did not rely on the consent of both parties.[41]

Almost immediately following the end of the Gulf War and the
subsequent uprising and then repression of the Kurdish population in the North of Iraq, the office of the United Nations Disaster
Relief Coordinator (UNDRO) began a humanitarian operation.
This unique operation involved setting up United Nations

Humanitarian Centres (UNHUC) to assist in the repatriation of the Kurds. Security for this novel operation was initially provided by coalition forces. After extensive negotiations with the Iraqi government, United Nations Security Guards (UNSG) were put into place. According to Formuth, this operation set two important precedents. It challenged sovereignty by 'refusing to permit the non-intervention doctrine to shield a state's genocidal practices against its own population', and it broadened notions of security by defining a humanitarian crisis as a threat to international peace and security.[42] This mission is difficult to define as peacekeeping because it was run from UNDRO not from DPKO, and was for purely humanitarian purposes, i.e. it had no political function. The use of UNSGs was an innovation which represented a compromise between the use of peacekeepers, which was unacceptable to Iraq and the continued use of coalition soldiers, also unacceptable to Iraq. These unarmed guards were made up of the ranks which usually guard the Palais in Geneva or the Headquarters building in New York.

Finally, as mentioned above, UNOSOM II in Somalia was authorized under Chapter VII of the UN charter. Its presence in Somalia did not have universal consent and it carried out enforcement action as authorized by its mandate. This does not conform to the consent and non-use of force principles of peacekeeping and, arguably, does not fulfill the third principle of impartiality.

The number and range of peacekeeping missions undertaken in the past five years has been phenomenal considering previous activities. But the effectiveness of these missions is by no means clear cut. While in the short and medium terms some successes can be noted (Cambodia and Namibia stand out), enhancing the prospects for durable long term peace appears more elusive. This increased activity has had a profound effect on many areas of UN activity both directly and indirectly related to peacekeeping. It is to a more detailed consideration of these effects that we will now turn.

## 2.3 Multiplicity of Functions

The large number of multidimensional operations set up since 1988 has led to a qualitative and quantitative increase in the types of activities carried out by peacekeepers.[43] The following list of peacekeeping functions is taken from Wiseman, but is slightly altered to exclude mention of non-UN peacekeeping and to include some new functions not on Wiseman's original list. These functions are broken down into three groups; military, governmental/political, and civil.

*Military Functions*: observation and monitoring of cease-fires; supervision of the withdrawal of forces; maintenance of buffer zones (UNEF I, UNEF II, UNOGIL); regulation of the disposition and movement of military forces (UNSF/UNTEA, UNTAG, MINURSO); prevention of infiltration (UNIFIL), and prevention of civil war (ONUC); verification of security agreements (ONUCA); disarming of warring factions (UNTAC, UNOSOM, ONUMOZ); supervision of cantonment and repatriation of warring factions (UNTAC); escort/protection of humanitarian aid (UNOSOM, UNPROFOR); mine clearance and training for mine clearance (UNTAC); assisting in retraining and re-forming of military (UNMIH).

*Governmental/Political Functions*: maintenance of territorial integrity (ONUC); monitoring/supervision/provision of law and order (UNTAG/UNTAC/UNMIH); ensuring political independence (ONUC, UNTAG, UNTAC); assisting in the establishment of a viable government (ONUC, UNTAG, UNTAC, ONUMOZ, UNAMIR); security of the population (MINURSO); coping/negotiating with non-governmental entities (ONUC, UNTAG, UNFICYP, UNIFIL, UNTAG, UNOSOM, UNPROFOR, ONUSAL); assumption of temporary governmental authority and administration (UNTEA, UNTAC); administration of an election of a constituent assembly to write a constitution (UNTAG, UNTAC); conduct of elections and referendum (UNTAG, MINURSO, UNTAC, ONUVEN, ONUVEH, UNAVEM II, ONUMOZ); assisting in the formation of local administration (UNIFIL, UNOSOM); verification of human rights agreements (ONUSAL); provision of security for the re-establishment of economic life of local populations (UNIFIL, UNFICYP).

*Civil Functions*: provision of humanitarian assistance (ONUC, UNFICYP, UNOSOM, UNPROFOR); monitoring and regulation of the flow of refugees (UNTAG, UNTAC, UNFICYP, UNIFIL); assisting in the repatriation of refugees (UNTAG, UNTAC, MINURSO); management of local disputes (UNTAG, UNTAC, UNFICYP, UNIFIL); provision of confidence-building measures (UNFICYP, UNTAG, ONUSAL); training police (UNTAC, UNMIH).

This does not represent an exhaustive list. Further, it is important to note that many functions can and do overlap. Some military functions are considered appropriate tasks only for military personnel, but military personnel perform many of the functions in the other two categories.

## 2.4 Role Innovations

Innovations in the practice of peacekeeping were pointed out in section 2.1 and, therefore, will only be briefly summarized here. Election verification in Nicaragua marked the first time that the UN had verified elections in a sovereign, independent state at the request of that state's government. The operation in El Salvador was established to verify, *inter alia*, a human rights agreement between a government and an insurgency movement. A further precedent was set when ONUSAL was deployed before any ceasefire agreement had been reached. In Namibia, UNTAG set up political offices to facilitate the transition process to independence largely through an information and education campaign. These offices performed conflict resolution functions which involved bringing together political party and community leaders. Although this kind of work had gone on before, it had been on a much smaller scale. Moreover, the interesting and innovative thing about the Namibian operation was that the community meetings were the result of a centrally guided and implemented policy. UNPROFOR in Bosnia was the first time a peacekeeping operation was established for explicitly humanitarian reasons. In Cambodia the UN has greatly expanded roles previously carried out in Namibia. The cantonment aspect of UNTAC was unique. UNOMIL in Liberia was the first mission undertaken in coordination with an already existing regional peacekeeping mission. Peacekeepers were deployed preventively for the first time in Macedonia as part of UNPROFOR.

Changes have come quickly when one compares the last five years to the relatively languid earlier period and are likely to continue. Proposals have been put forward for the expansion of peacekeeping into drug interdiction, naval peacekeeping, disaster relief, environmental reclamation, and arms control verification.[44]

## 3. COMPLICATING FACTORS

The expansion of peacekeeping has complicated its functioning along a number of dimensions. This section provides a brief cross-section of the most serious problems and points out areas of peacekeeping activity which have been affected by new reform measures.

### 3.1 Management

Until recently one of the biggest problems for the day-to-day management of peacekeeping operations had been the two-track decision-making set-up at headquarters in New York. Day-to-day control of political and military aspects of missions came under the remit of the DPKO. Day-to-day control over administrative aspects of missions including budget, logistics and communications, was in the hands of the Field Operations Division (FOD) within the Office of General Services (OGS). In the field this split meant that the Chief Administrative Officer reported to the FOD and the Force Commander (FC) and Special Representative of the Secretary-General (SRSG) reported to the DPKO.[45] In September 1993, in an attempt to rationalize management of peacekeeping operations, the FOD was moved into the DPKO. Although it will take some time for the system to fully adjust to this major reorganization, it is undoubtedly an important step toward improving the management capacity and efficiency of operations. The S-G further delineated the separate responsibilities of the DPKO and the Department of Humanitarian Affairs (DHA) so that the DPKO now has responsibility for the 'technical and administrative support for integrated operations in the field including, as appropriate, peacekeeping, peacemaking, electoral or humanitarian components'.[46]

Understaffing continues to be a problem. In 1990 Norton and Weiss argued that, 'experienced and knowledgeable personnel, both civilian and military, are in short supply within the UN Secretariat to cover even on-going operations'.[47] Staffing has not increased significantly since, although the workload has. Related to staffing problems has been the problem of communication between Headquarters in New York and the field. It had previously been the case that when crises arose in the field it was sometimes difficult to reach those in New York who were authorized to make decisions. To rectify this situation a 'situation room' was established staffed by military officers to 'maintain a continuous link with operations in Somalia and former Yugoslavia'.[48] The S-G is considering expanding this to include all UN operations.

In addition to communications problems with headquarters, a Force Commander faces a number of problems in the field. Although good management from the Force Commander's Office mitigates many problems, considerable time is required on the part of the FC to ensure efficient running of an operation. The divide between the civilian and military sections of a mission can be one area of difficulty. Even in the best circumstances military and civilian staff have trouble coordinating activities.[49] Jonah provides some insight as to why this problem exists:

> the problem arises as a result of inadequate career development programs for the field service officers (civilian) and the short tours of duty (usually six months) for military personnel. Consequently field service officers are often appointed to senior positions without appropriate cross training in supervision techniques, or experience in all civilian disciplines. Concurrently the military personnel arrive with little knowledge of the unique factors affecting operations and logistics support in international peacekeeping.[50]

Management is a complex situation at the UN. The difficulties of mounting a multi-national operation where skill level, experience, motivation, and knowledge can differ greatly can be prohibitive. The reform process begun in March 1992 which is attempting to streamline the labyrinthine Secretariat structure and rationalize interaction between Headquarters and the field, has made some inroads. Nevertheless, as Evans succinctly argues,

> Much more is... required to equip the UN to organize and administer peacekeeping operations effectively to meet present day demands and challenges. This will be necessary whether or not there is more selective resort to peace-keeping. The overall numbers of peacekeepers in the field, and the complexity of mandates, is not likely to fall to pre-1990 levels.[51]

## 3.2 Financial Problems

Like management, financial considerations are a crucial aspect of peacekeeping. The UN has been in the midst of an acute financial crisis for years, with no immediate solution in sight.[52] Perez de Cuellar emphasized the seriousness of the crisis in his 1991 annual report.[53] He followed this action by sending a letter to Foreign Ministers of all Member States describing the situation as the 'worst financial crisis' to arise since the beginning of the Organization. The former Secretary-General noted that the crisis was most severe because the UN's role, especially in the maintenance of peace and security, had expanded dramatically, but with no concomitant growth in financial support. Boutros-Ghali inherited an ever-worsening situation. In his *An Agenda for Peace,* he summarized the problem: 'A chasm has developed between the tasks entrusted to this Organization and the financial means provided to it.'[54]

In early August 1993 Boutros-Ghali was forced to resort to the same tactics used by his predecessor; he sent letters to the foreign ministers of approximately 150 states and asked that they pay their overdue assessed contributions. He pointed out that without substantial payment of arrears the UN would be unable to meet budgetary commitments beyond the end of the month. By the end of September 1993 the situation had eased slightly with a reduction in the total of outstanding contributions from US$2.3 billion to an estimated US$1.7 billion (including the peacekeeping budget). Even so, the Under-Secretary-General for Administration and Management noted that just 62 (out of 184) States had paid their full assessment, while a further 59 had not made any payment.

The peacekeeping budget was facing similar difficulties. All but two missions are financed through separate accounts outside of the regular budget. These accounts are based on a slightly different scale of assessment than the regular budget but are still legally binding assessments (Group A states or the wealthiest states pay a higher rate). The total amount spent on peacekeeping since 1948 is estimated to be over US$8 billion. The budget for 1992–3 was about US$3.6 billion, a substantial increase from the budget of US$400 million in 1991. As of September 1993 unpaid peacekeeping contributions stood at around US$1.5 billion.[55]

The perpetual nature of budgetary crises must be tackled as a matter of urgency since it seriously undermines the ability of the UN to deal effectively with ever-increasing demands. Once it is fully funded, the creation of a $150 million peacekeeping reserve fund should help to speed up the UN's initial response to crises.[56] However, it is not just a case of implementing financial reform proposals such as those contained in *An Agenda for Peace* and those set out elsewhere. The underlying problem remains non-payment of assessed contributions by member states and until this problem is overcome, the UN's financial woes will continue to hamper its global peacekeeping role.

### 3.3 Mandate

Mandates derive from multilateral diplomacy. They are crafted through arduous negotiations and a consensus-building process involving members of the Security Council and the parties to the dispute. This consensus process is by no means perfect. Each side has its own partial perception of 'the problem' and how the Security Council and the peacekeeping mission should be dealing with it. Often, because peacekeeping missions are normally established in the face of an ongoing dispute, the process becomes enmeshed in a complex web of interrelationships and power struggles between states. More often than not, in order for a mandate to get the required vote in the Council, contentious issues are left out and ambiguous wording is used.

Forced ambiguities, which reflect the lowest common denominator of agreement, leave peacekeepers caught in the middle of varying interpretations of equivocal documents.

Such vagueness often generates the need for on-going negotiations between the disputants and the Force. UNFICYP, UNTAG and UNPROFOR all provide numerous examples of how mandate ambiguities can plague a peacekeeping mission (see following chapter).

Although the original Security Council document is important, the real test of a mandate's strength derives from a second document which sets out in more specific and practical detail the S-G's instructions for the mission. According to Mackinlay, this second document is crucial to the success of an operation. In his study of four peacekeeping operations in the Middle East (including two non-UN missions), he found that if the second document is worked out in conjunction with the parties involved in the dispute the force will have a better chance of success. While Mackinlay asserts the importance of a second document, he offers this caveat:

> However sophisticated the mandate and the preceding treaty or agreement may appear to be, it is certain that some measure of interpretation and adaptation will be required by the military commander and his staff in order for its [the mandate's] provisions to operate successfully on the ground.[57]

The political necessity of ambiguous mandates is not an aspect of peacekeeping which is likely to change. It is generally considered more important to get a force on the ground than to delay or not deploy at all and allow a destructive conflict to continue.

### 3.4  Resorting to the United Nations

A number of issues are bound up in the lack of willingness of States to bring their conflicts to the UN. Reasons include unwanted public debates over the issues at the UN and the possibility of coming under the international spotlight; unease concerning national sovereignty issues, particularly if a peacekeeping force is likely to be authorized; the possibility that some measure of recognition will be afforded to non-state entities involved in the conflict; and concern over loss of control over future action in the conflict. These considerations often result in a situation in which a conflict is only brought to the UN as a last resort. In commenting on this problem, Urquhart notes that 'the position of the United Nations... has declined... to a last resort, last-minute, reluctantly accepted safety net'.[58]

This negative cycle works both ways. A conflict which the Security Council can act upon because it threatens international peace and security may only be discussed when the situation has reached an intensity level making it impossible to ignore. It is axiomatic that conflicts of high intensity and long duration are the most difficult to resolve. Moreover, insufficient resources have led to situations where the Council has been unable to take concerted action even though help was requested. In one specific case where the Council did take action, the S-G refused to implement the decision citing, among other things, lack of resources.[59]

### 3.5 Troop Contributing Countries

There are a number of aspects of troop contribution which can be problematic from the perspectives of both the contributing country and the Secretariat. The concerns of troop contributors range from financial considerations to number of fatalities (or projected number of fatalities) and type of mandate. All these concerns are likely to be communicated to the Secretariat if a particular operation is not going the way the contributor would like.

From the point of view of the Secretariat, troop contributors can cause a number of problems. All countries participating would like to have their own nationals in top positions, and there is normally a certain amount of lobbying which takes place concerning the selection of Force Commander and other senior field positions such as Chief of Staff. The need to spread appointments amongst contributors gets further compounded because contributors are sometimes reluctant to let go of their best personnel for postings out of the country. This state of affairs can lead to incompetent senior officers holding high ranking positions. Urquhart describes a situation in which a general had been appointed Force Commander for UNDOF. After several months it became apparent that he was 'a soggy, drunken disaster' leaving the 'staff at each other's throats and the Syrians incredulous'.[60] The General was recalled, but not before he had caused many problems. This admittedly extreme example highlights a problem pointed out by Mackinlay; that of sanctioning – or recalling – individuals who are incompetent or are accused of wrongdoing.[61] Such incidents can create tension between the troop contributor and the Secretariat. In addition there may be political repercussions for relations with the disputing parties. These problems can limit the overall capacity of the Force and the Secretariat to function in an independent, impartial and effective manner.

A final problem here has to do with the chain of command. In a peacekeeping mission contingent officers are required to report directly to the FC and are under the FC's command. In addition, officers are not supposed to report to their home governments. In practice, this is not a restriction which is closely adhered to. In some circumstances this propensity to clear actions with home command can led to situations where instructions from home contradict UN orders. The highly publicized case of the Italian Contingent Commander in Somalia is an example. General Loi was recalled home after the UN requested his transfer for alleged insubordination. There were further problems with the Italian contingent when it was accused of making private deals with Somali factions in Mogadishu.[62]

## 4.  FACTORS CONSIDERED NECESSARY FOR SUCCESS

Urquhart lists a number of factors which are essential for the success of peacekeeping. These are: a viable political context; consistently broad support – political, diplomatic, military and financial – for the operation; representativeness in the force; feasibility of the mandate; cooperation from the parties to the dispute; skill and sensitivity in directing the force; quality of command and the military discipline of the troops; no imposition of an external will or solution.[63] Mackinlay's study, discussed earlier, supports the need for consistent broad support and a strong mandate. Evans argues that there are seven conditions which ensure success. These are: clear and achievable goals; adequate resources; close coordination of peacekeeping and peacemaking; impartiality; local support; external support; and a clearly signposted exit.[64]

Heiberg as well as Galtung and Eide note that their investigations suggest the importance of a positive relationship between a Force and the local population for peacekeeping success.[65] Heiberg's study of UNIFIL found that,

> a relationship to local civilians built on communication and confidence is a necessary factor for success; a relationship characterized by mounting hostility, suspicion and lack of communication is a sufficient cause for failure.[66]

Galtung and Eide found eleven factors which contributed to lack of acceptance including, no contact at all with the local population, or highly unpopular fraternization, conspicuous demonstration of power, and forces that never engaged in good deeds (peacebuilding activity).[67]

A study done by Diehl provides further specification of factors related to success or failure.[68] After analysing a number of factors of a case-study sample (six peacekeeping operations, both UN and non-UN), Diehl concluded that the two most significant reasons for failure of peacekeeping are: (1) the opposition of third party states and (2) the opposition of sub-national groups. These findings coincide with Urquhart's conclusions. Alternately, the least significant factors for success were: (1) a clear mandate, (2) financial aspects, and (3) command structure.[69] These coincide less easily with Urquhart and Evans who suggest that both a clear mandate and financial support are crucial to success. According to Diehl, these least significant factors all come under the heading of internal issues. The two factors most likely to lead to failure are external factors, i.e. external to the UN. This suggests that the potential negative impact of factors over which the UN has more or less direct control can be minimized, while factors over which the UN has little or no control can cause great difficulties. Diehl also argues that geography and neutrality are two factors which can have impact on effectiveness.

Haas provides a case-study analysis of peacekeeping success which is similar to Diehl's, but wider in both scope and sample. His findings support the importance of a consistent financial base suggested by Urquhart and Evans. Haas's study also finds that the roles of the Secretary-General and the Secretariat, particularly in terms of leadership, are crucial for success. In addition, Haas notes, that success is normally also associated with the effective application of 'diplomatic and even military pressure of a superpower'.[70] Contradicting Diehl's findings, Haas points out that neutrality is not a requirement of success when certain conditions are met. These conditions are: (1) agreement amongst the permanent five, (2) superpower leadership in the Council concurrent with a two-thirds majority support in the Assembly, and (3) the ability of the Secretary-General to 'construct temporary and shifting coalitions backing an intervention either in the Council or the Assembly'.[71]

Research on the sociology of a peacekeeping force undertaken by Moskos suggests that the most important element for successful peacekeeping is the development of a constabulary ethic within a force.[72] Moskos defines a constabulary ethic as, 'rigid adherence to impartiality and absolute minimum use of force'.[73] This finding seems to contradict Haas's conclusions.

There are obvious problems with our current level of understanding about which elements of peacekeeping (and other interventions) contribute most to success or failure. Indeed, definitions of success vary widely. And findings are by no means congruous. In the new international climate which is pushing the UN toward larger and more complex involvement in conflicts a much better developed and researched understanding of success is needed.


## 5. CONCLUSION: CONSEQUENCES OF MULTIDIMENSIONALISM

As multidimensional peacekeeping has evolved to contend with the changed international context, it has increased the complexity of every level of activity of UN operations. Yet, peacekeeping still has no conceptual base beyond a certain set of principles developed in reference to managing inter-state conflict. Whereas the Security Council has begun to function more effectively (and therefore opened up the possibility of working out strategies for resolving protracted social conflicts) and consequently has been able to put more peacekeepers into the field, no comprehensive review or long-term consideration of peacekeeping as a third party intervention has taken place. Prior to 1988, it could be argued that a conceptual framework for peacekeeping was not necessary since its expansion beyond existing boundaries appeared politically unviable. This political situation has now changed, while, at the same time, protracted social conflicts are increasingly recognized as a major threat to global security. The good management of these conflicts is crucial. In order to enhance the effectiveness of peacekeeping in this new environment it is imperative to move beyond *ad hoc* practices and approaches lacking conceptual guidance. And while it might be argued that thus far peacekeeping has enjoyed some success, particularly in Namibia and more recently in Central America and Cambodia, these successes should be qualified by their short-term emphasis and by a number of serious problems which have surfaced. The failure of some UN-sponsored democratic reform processes have challenged evaluations based on short-term success.[74] UN peacekeeping personnel on missions in Mozambique, Bosnia, Cambodia and Somalia have been accused of human rights abuses, drug trafficking, prostitution, and black marketeering.[75] The financial situation of the UN is, and has been for some time, of crisis-proportions. The effective management of peacekeeping operations, particularly command and control and logistics, continues to be a cause of serious concern, and the DPKO is woefully understaffed given the colossal task of planning, coordinating, and running all current and proposed peacekeeping missions.[76]

Seventy-four of the UN's 184 member states have contributed to peacekeeping, and this number is increasing. Regular troop contributors are having to stretch their resources to meet demand. Yet only six National Training Centres exist for the express purpose of training soldiers (not civilians) for UN peacekeeping. At best, training for both military and civilian peacekeepers can be characterized as partial and fragmented. As previously noted, peacekeeping operations are increasingly complex processes and preparation and training for them should be no less full and appropriate. Provision, to date, has been inadequate.

A significant problem exists with how 'success' is defined. Is success the ability to maintain a ceasefire which can, as Cyprus, Lebanon, former-Yugoslavia, Angola and Western Sahara attest, evaporate all too easily even after years of truce? In addition, a ceasefire is not a solution, only a certain type of *status quo* which must be seen as unsatisfactory for anything but the short term.

Or is success the facilitation of eventual settlement leading to good prospects for a long-term resolution of the conflict? Some recent research indicates the need to develop more nuanced definitions of success, particularly in dealing with ethnic conflicts.[77] Moreover, how success is defined has direct and serious consequences on the techniques which can be utilized for managing conflict.

These first two chapters have provided a brief history of the development of peacekeeping from its inception in the midst of the Cold War to its present post-Cold War state. Although not a comprehensive historical analysis, these chapters have attempted to convey the growing complexity and demands on peacekeeping. Moreover, they have suggested that the inadequacy of the continued application of *ad hoc* methods has presented the UN and the international community with a serious problem which has yet to be fully addressed. The underlying question remains: what can be done to improve the UN's capacity to cope effectively with the myriad problems of the post-Cold War world?

# 3 Case Studies: United Nations Peacekeeping in Cyprus, Namibia and Former Yugoslavia

The three case studies discussed below were selected because they each illustrate a distinct period in the development of peacekeeping from the Cold War period through to the present. Moreover they show the potential of peacekeeping as a means of resolving international conflict, borne out in Namibia, as well as its limitations, seen most clearly in former Yugoslavia.

Cyprus offers an example of 'traditional peacekeeping'. The United Nations Peacekeeping Force in Cyprus (UNFICYP) was established in 1964 and is the longest running force level peacekeeping mission. UNFICYP's history is agonizingly long, controversial, and, perhaps paradoxically, depicts many of the problems and drawbacks of peacekeeping missions as well as many of their positive aspects. Its day-to-day functioning demonstrates clearly the flexible and responsive potentialities of peacekeeping operations. However, the fact that the operation has been in place for three decades with little movement toward settlement displays some of the most serious dilemmas of peacekeeping as it has been traditionally conceived.

As the first large multidimensional operation in the expansion period, Namibia was an obvious selection. Current enthusiasm for peacekeeping owes much to the accomplishments and innovation of UNTAG. More than any other operation, it represents a watershed in the history of peacekeeping, and one of the UN's clearest successes.

The UN's involvement in former Yugoslavia provides an example of the many problems facing peacekeeping in the post Cold War world. The humanitarian mission in Bosnia, in particular, illustrates the new and more demanding environment within which peacekeeping operates. Moreover, the inability of the peacemakers to secure a lasting settlement, exemplified by more than 70 signed and broken ceasefire agreements, points out the inadequacy of the basic conception of peacekeeping as a means to 'buy time' for diplomacy.

Above all, these three examples clearly demonstrate the wide variety of roles peacekeepers take on and the heavy demands and expectations these place on the individuals taking part in peacekeeping missions.

## 1.  UNITED NATIONS PEACEKEEPING FORCE IN CYPRUS

Cyprus is an island in the eastern Mediterranean, covering some 3500 square miles. At present the population is approximately 80 per cent Greek Cypriot and 18 per cent Turkish Cypriot (the remaining few percent are made up largely of British, Armenians, and Maronites). Although of modest size and boasting no significant natural resource, Cyprus has traditionally been viewed as strategically important. It is situated near three major sea routes and is geographically close to Turkey (about forty miles off its coast) and to the Middle East. Its strategic importance has meant that throughout its long recorded history, the mainly ethnically Greek population of Cyprus has come under the influence of a succession of empires.[1] Its most recent colonizer was Britain who became the legal government in the wake of the First World War through the Treaty of Lausanne. Internal pressure for self-rule became politically and militarily organized after the Second World War within both Cypriot communities and Britain's control over the island became increasingly tenuous. Finally, in February 1959, Britain, with the agreement of Greece and Turkey, found a formula for independence on which the Greek Cypriot and Turkish Cypriot leaders could agree.

The London and Zurich Agreements, as they became known, established the foundation for settlement and were later formalized in three treaties (Alliance, Establishment, and Guarantee) and a complex power-sharing constitution. All of these documents were subsequently embodied in the legal framework of the new Republic of Cyprus upon independence.

These complicated structures, combined with embittered inter-communal relations inflamed by the previous years of

violent struggle, were a veritable powder keg causing many –
Cypriots included – to have second thoughts about the prospects for a peaceful transition. However, despite misgivings,
the process continued apace and on 16 August 1960 Cyprus
became an independent state. It did not take long to confirm
that it would be next to impossible to govern Cyprus within the
settlement framework.

For more than two years the Republic struggled with the
constraints imposed by the constitution. But occasioned by
sporadic outbursts of violence and terrorist acts, and owing
to the deeply held differences of opinion, there was little
hope of seriously discussing proposals to overcome the stalemate. The situation reached breaking point. A state of open
violent conflict between the two communities broke out on
21 December 1963, and any hope of a peaceful solution was
abruptly extinguished. In reaction to this threat to peace
and stability in the region, on 27 December a tripartite force
from Turkey, Greece, and the United Kingdom, citing the
Treaty of Guarantee, and with the consent of the Cypriot
Government, began peacekeeping activities throughout
Cyprus. Both the peacekeeping force and subsequent
attempts to find a negotiated solution through the tripartite
powers were unsuccessful. In February 1964, with few viable
options remaining to it, Britain turned the problem over to
the United Nations. After lengthy deliberations, the Security
Council created the United Nations Peacekeeping Force in
Cyprus (UNFICYP) for an initial term of three months.[2]

Thus, the longest force-level peacekeeping operation in
United Nations history was created. Although the task ahead
was viewed as a difficult one, few could have foreseen that it
was the beginning of a three-decade UN presence in Cyprus,
paralleled by political stalemate.


## 1.1 The Creation of UNFICYP

The UNFICYP was established and mandated through Security
Council Resolution (SCR) 186 (1964). The Force's three basic
tasks were, 'to prevent a recurrence of fighting and, as
necessary, to contribute to the maintenance and restoration of
law and order and a return to normal conditions'.[3]

① maintenance of a ceasefire
② restore law e order
③ return to normal conditions.

There were some initial difficulties in deploying UNFICYP mainly focused on the funding issue, but also caused by disagreement over Secretary-General U Thant's interpretation of the Security Council mandate and the normal delays caused by finding troop contributors. The financing of UNFICYP was perhaps the most controversial aspect of the operation, coming as it did in the wake of a general crisis in the financing of peacekeeping operations. This general crisis had led to great problems in both the Security Council and the General Assembly (see Chapter 1). In order to get the desired vote on SCR 186 (1964) the issue of finance was deliberately avoided. The best the Secretary-General could do in the circumstances was ask for voluntary contributions, which he did, and this remained the basis for financing UNFICYP. These financial arrangements meant that the Force was never on a sound financial footing and that the troop-contributing countries had to pay a disproportionate amount towards its continued operation.[4]

By 27 March 1964, Thant was able to declare UNFICYP operational, although it only consisted of full contingents from Canada and the United Kingdom. By the end of April, Finnish, Irish, and Swedish troops were deployed bringing the total size to 6341.[5] The main contributors (those with battalions in Cyprus) were Britain, Canada, Ireland, Finland, Denmark, and Sweden. Austria, Australia, and New Zealand along with Denmark and Sweden contributed to the UN civilian police force, while Austria also contributed a Field Hospital unit.

Deployment was initially set up to coincide with Cypriot administrative districts so as to facilitate close contact and liaison with the government. It was clear from this deployment that UNFICYP's function was aimed not to provide a 'barrier' (although there were a few exceptions) between two combatants or to mount a border patrol, but to work within each community. Such an integrated approach placed UNFICYP in a much better position to facilitate the 'restoration of law and order' and a 'return to normal conditions'. UNFICYP had five operational zones to which contingents were assigned. These were redrawn and troops consequently redeployed several times in the first years of UNFICYP's existence.[6] The highest concentration of troops was in the area around the Cypriot capital, Nicosia, where the situation was the least stable. This volatility was largely due to the existence of a ceasefire line bisecting the city, effectively splitting it into two halves, with Turkish Cypriots on one side, Greek Cypriots on the other, and UN troops in between.

The Green Line, as the Nicosia ceasefire line was known, was originally meant to be a temporary measure put in place to facilitate the institution of a ceasefire in the city. But as one former UNFICYP Chief of Staff noted,

> what was intended as a temporary expedient became a permanent 'frontier' and in the long run was to prove an 'unremitting obstacle to progress towards normalization between the two communities'.[7]

The significance of the Green Line did not come about so much because of any major physical impediments or fortifications (although these were very much in evidence), but rather because of the strong symbolism of division it represented which has since taken on a high international profile.[8] The lasting and potent symbolism of the Green Line carries an important lesson for peacekeepers: that is, even seemingly temporary and insignificant decisions made by peacekeepers can have long and not necessarily positive consequences for the conflict situation.

UNFICYP's function, as it was set out in SCR 186 (1964), was made brief and vague. This was done for political reasons but the vague mandate left the Secretary-General the unenviable task of defining more precisely what functions UNFICYP would fulfil, and perhaps more importantly, what functions it would not. The functions of UNFICYP were set out in more detail in two further documents.

The first document, an *aide-mémoire*, defined the general guiding principles for the day-to-day activities of UNFICYP including guidelines on its legal status, chain of command, and the limits of the use of force. The second document was more specific, and taken together the two documents were meant to provide a coherent directive for UNFICYP and a strong indication to Greek and Turkish Cypriots of the Secretary-General's interpretation of the mandate.

The second detailed document was crucial in determining the daily work carried out by UNFICYP. It detailed a general list of objectives for the implementation of the mandate including: achievement of freedom of movement on all roads in Cyprus, the progressive disarming of all civilians, the return to the normal functioning of the judiciary. Other interim aims were then detailed such as: formulation of a plan to curb the excesses of Cypriot police, particularly because these excesses were a cause of escalated tensions between the two communities, the elaboration of a plan of reintegration of Turkish Cypriot policemen with the Cyprus police force, and consideration of the possibility of establishing joint patrols (including Greek and Turkish Cypriots and UNFICYP) as a confidence-building measure.[9]

Contained within reports by the S-G which followed were clarifications and refinements of these two defining documents. For example, in one report, Thant reiterated the principle of freedom of movement, and stated that UNFICYP had the right to remove fortifications which were endangering the continuance of peace, and to use force to carry out that function.[10] Thant then made a point of pursuing the definition of what constituted self-defence, stating that, '[w]hen acting in self-defence, the principle of minimum force shall always be applied and armed force will be used when all means of peaceful persuasion have failed'.[11]

Underlying all of these 'defining' and 'refining' documents, were three basic assumptions through which the Force operated: the right to freedom of movement, the right of self-defence, and the right to take down fortifications and create buffer zones.

As previously noted, the mandated functions of UNFICYP fell into three categories: (1) the maintenance of a ceasefire, (2) the restoration and maintenance of law and order, and (3) the return to normal conditions.

The first task, the maintenance of a ceasefire, was the predominant focus of UN peacekeeping efforts in Cyprus. As described above UNFICYP was organized into five operational districts. Within each it was responsible for the maintenance of a ceasefire and to this end the Force carried out certain functions. In areas such as the Green Line in Nicosia UNFICYP interposed itself by setting up OPS (observation posts) as well as by carrying out regular patrols. One of the most important tasks of the troops stationed along confrontation lines was to make every effort to prevent changes in the existing *status quo*. For example, if one side tried to move into previously unoccupied buildings and erect new fortifications, UNFICYP would lodge a formal protest and if necessary begin negotiations to effect a withdrawal.

Preventing infiltration of the buffer zone required vigilance of a high order from the UN troops in the area, since any small, seemingly insignificant change could provoke an incident.[12] One method developed to prevent such changes was to label as UN material items in the buffer zone area such as barbed wire or fencing. Another method used was to paint material UN blue. This was done to prevent either side from claiming ownership. Most incursions of any kind into the buffer zone occurred during the weeks immediately following routine rotation of troops (rotation took place approximately every four to six months depending on the troop-contributing country). The timing of these incursions was a test of the resolve, knowledge and ability of the new troops to manage the buffer zone area.

In addition to patrolling confrontation lines, another vital task was the immediate investigation of any shooting or other type of disturbance which could escalate into something more serious. This was true for the whole island, not just along confrontation lines. These investigations constituted a critical part of the maintenance of the ceasefire. Understandably, there were some areas which were more prone to difficulties than others and at these locations, extra patrols and sometimes permanent observation posts were employed.

Breaches of the ceasefire were dealt with through a liaison system which started with the troops on the ground, then moved to the district or zone Headquarters, and finally led up to UNFICYP Headquarters in Nicosia. Part of the responsibility of the troops and officers in each area was to facilitate communication through this liaison system making sure that information about any planned activities by UNFICYP (troop movements or removal of fortifications for example) was received by both sides well in advance. The liaison system was meant to reduce tensions by providing both sides with reliable information and in this sense facilitate communication between the antagonists (such liaison systems are employed in all UN peacekeeping operations).

The second basic function of UNFICYP was the restoration of law and order. Much of this work was done by the UN Civilian Police (CIVPOL) who were involved in accompanying Cypriot police patrols, establishing systems of communication between the UN and the Cypriot police, providing a CIVPOL police presence in areas of high tension, and investigating incidents which involved both communities.[13] CIVPOL had no authority to intervene while carrying out their duties, but their presence and liaison work helped to reduce the number of kidnappings and killings and generally contributed to the restoration of law and order. The significance of a civilian police 'presence' is noted by Rikhye:

> where a reign of terror is a recent memory, and where inter-communal murders, abductions, and victimization are still common occurrences, the presence of an impartial police unit can reduce the sense of insecurity that obstructs any degree of reconciliation.[14]

The third main function of UNFICYP set out in its establishing mandate was the return to normal conditions. It was in carrying out this third function that UNFICYP engaged directly in peacebuilding activities. While the Force's other two functions were vital in creating the conditions within which peace-building could be carried out, it was this part of the mandated functions which allowed for the broadest interpretation of UNFICYP's role.

The work of one particular section of UNFICYP was aimed at restoring economic activity. These activities were described as 'ad hoc measures designed to save lives, minimize suffering and, to the extent possible, restore essential civilian activities' and were carried out through 'persuasion and negotiation exclusively'.[15] Work was carried out in four areas: (1) escorts for essential civilian movements (particularly for those who feared abduction), (2) harvest arrangements including escort during harvest and for deliveries of produce and arbitration of land and water disputes, (3) normalization of public services including post, water, electricity, social insurance benefits, etc., in areas controlled by Turkish-Cypriots, (4) cooperation with non-governmental agencies in assisting refugees.[16]

According to Harbottle, the existence of this small but important section underlined the interdependent relationship between the return to normal conditions, the maintenance of a ceasefire and the restoration of law and order.

Thant viewed this relationship sequentially, arguing that 'decisive steps', meaning the prevention of fighting and the restoration of law and order, needed to precede a return to normal conditions. However, the lengthy *status quo* on Cyprus demonstrates the limitations of such an approach. First, it was not assumed that 'normal conditions' automatically follow from the achievement of a ceasefire and law and order and apart from a few exceptions the peacekeeping force did not take on roles, nor was it directed to, which might have led to reconciliation. Second, 'normal conditions' were defined and limited to the pre-war *status quo*. Since it was precisely those pre-war circumstances which had led to war in the first instance, reproducing them was not an appropriate goal. While much of the work on Cyprus by peacekeeping forces is typical of what is often termed 'traditional peacekeeping', i.e. maintenance of a ceasefire, there were some exceptions.

One exception to the *status quo* rule is particularly interesting because it highlights the importance of peacebuilding tasks within a peacekeeping framework and how they can be creatively organized.[17] In Cyprus, in 1967, a number of murders and abductions in the Paphos district had created some serious problems, including so much fear amongst villagers in both communities that they refused to move beyond the relative safety of their villages. As a result vital agricultural work ceased. In addition, outsiders were reluctant to travel into the area so much so that doctors had to be escorted by UN soldiers while they went on their rounds.[18] In an effort to bring about a return to normal conditions in the Paphos region, Harbottle organized a series of meetings between Greek and Turkish Cypriot community leaders out of which, he hoped, a process of reconciliation might develop.

One of the explicit goals of these meetings was 'to provide a forum for the discussion of possible solutions to inter-communal problems'.[19] Another purpose was 'to bring the mukhtars [leaders] together to discuss their problems among themselves and to give each other peaceful assurances'.[20] Harbottle organized eighteen meetings in all (between fourteen and sixteen actually happened[21]), all chaired by an UNFICYP officer who was responsible for opening each meeting and explaining its purpose. According to Harbottle, it was difficult to assess what effect these meetings had on relations between the villages, but he recounts a conversation with SRSG Osorio-Tafall in which the SRSG said that Harbottle's efforts in Paphos 'had laid the foundation to the gradual rehabilitation of the personal interrelationship that followed'.[22] In a later work Harbottle is more positive. He says,

> The Paphos story illustrates the effect that a low-level initiative, involving the full range of third party action – peacekeeping, peacemaking and peacebuilding – can have on stabilizing a potentially explosive situation which, had it been ignored, might well have escalated to a level of violence throughout Cyprus comparable to that experienced seven years later in 1974.[23]

While it is impossible to provide a detailed assessment of the effectiveness of these meetings, it can be argued that because of Harbottle's work, a reconciliation process was begun and relations improved.[24]

Overall, it is difficult to prove effectiveness of this kind of intervention because it is resistant to quantification (unlike more easily measurable activities such as the removal of a particular fortification or the unmanning of a particular building or area which do not contribute directly to reconciliation). This is especially so when the wider conflict remains deadlocked. When looking at Harbottle's experience it becomes clear that such work is, in any circumstances, valuable if it contributes to greater understanding between the sides and reduces the chances of violence.

Following on from the example set in the Congo, UNFICYP did take on the task of facilitating the return to normal conditions, and in doing so engaged in peacebuilding activities. This is an important point which should be emphasized since it invites the dismissal of notions that peacekeeping and peacebuilding are necessarily mutually exclusive enterprises. Beyond this it should be clear that much of the work of UNFICYP was carried out through negotiation and mediation. This was as true for high level officers at the negotiation table in Nicosia as it was for soldiers patrolling on foot in small villages. Even the most mundane tasks at the lowest level required negotiating ability as small incidents all carried the potential for escalation into more serious conflagrations.[25]

Up until 1974 UNFICYP continued to function as described above, and with a few notable exceptions it was able to help maintain the *status quo*. Although the peacemaking efforts continued on and off, they were, in the main, unsuccessful in resolving even peripheral issues. Still the situation was calm enough by 1968 so that, according to Harbottle, UNFICYP itself recommended that it become less militarily oriented, since there was less need, and more oriented toward a civilian operation which would focus on the facilitation of reconciliation processes.[26] The opportunity to promote such a process was passed up by the Security Council which did not respond to the changing circumstances in Cyprus.

The relative stability attained after 1968, according to James, 'could not be chiefly attributed to UNFICYP, for its nature and purpose did not allow it even to attempt to impose peace on the islanders; it was the restraint of all the parties which, at bottom, accounted for the situation which ensued.'[27] James goes on to say that UNFICYP did play a valuable role in Cyprus and in facilitating a wider regional stability.[28] It seems likely that UNFICYP did play a part in preventing the recurrence of widespread fighting, especially considering the number of weapons and troops packed into such a small area and the potential they created by the sheer force of numbers alone for the escalation of violence. A more detailed assessment of UNFICYP's contribution to the maintenance of the ceasefire has not been carried out. However, the fact that the fighting had been serious enough to warrant the deployment of a force, and that after UNFICYP's arrival was eventually reduced to localized problems lends some weight to the argument that UNFICYP contributed directly to the maintenance of the ceasefire. From this perspective, James's analysis of UNFICYP's role may be too cautious. Considering the existing animosities combined with the escalating pressure that arms imports and troop influxes put on each side to fight, UNFICYP provided an excellent face-saving excuse to stand down.

What is clear is that after 1968 the situation was stable and the emphasis had turned toward negotiations. The recommendation from UNFICYP itself that its role shift to emphasize reconciliation exemplifies the stability of the situation. In this more receptive atmosphere the opportunity for building inter-communal bridges existed (even in the minds of the primarily military staff of UNFICYP). It may be that had the Security Council been able to recognize and take quick and decisive advantage of this genuine lull, the crisis that was about to descend upon Cyprus would never have occurred. In looking back and considering the political and functional obstacles preventing such a move both in New York and in Cyprus, this may be a harsh judgement. But it is important to learn from mistakes and at the very least the Security Council needs to re-evaluate the role it sets for peacekeepers based on such hind-sight. This is a crucial point and will be discussed at some length in later chapters.

## 1.2 The 1974 Crisis

Following a period of political upheaval in Greece tension increased between the two communities in Cyprus. The situation escalated further when Greek national officers serving in the Cypriot national guard staged a coup against the legitimate Cypriot government. This action prompted Turkey to invade Cyprus.

After the Turkish invasion, which left the Turkish military in control of over a third of the Island, UNFICYP's role changed dramatically. Although the tasks mandated by SCR 186 (1964) had some relevance in the new circumstances, the document did not foresee (as it could not have been expected to) the changes which did occur in Cyprus. Despite this, the Security Council did not provide a new mandate for the Force. The relative silence of the Security Council after the invasion, can be largely attributed to the political issues raised by Turkey's action. Arguments within the SC meant that, in all probability, agreement on a new mandate could not have been attained and Secretary-General Kurt Waldheim did not risk setting aside the old mandate in favor of forcing the Security Council to produce a new one. Amid this high-level political wrangling, the Secretary-General had to carefully manoeuvre around opposing views to avoid a showdown in New York, while at the same time provide some direction for his Force in Cyprus.

From Waldheim's point of view one document in particular proved to be useful. The 'Geneva Declaration' was the result of meetings between Britain, Greece and Turkey who had been charged by the Security Council in resolution 353 (1974) with reaching an agreement for Cyprus which would restore its constitutional government.[29] On 30 July 1974 the tripartite conference issued a statement regarding the situation in Cyprus and what should be done about it. This declaration substantially concerned the role of UNFICYP, and although it was never officially authorized by the SC, it served, more than any other document, to provide the direction and authority UNFICYP needed to take up new positions and responsibilities. According to the Geneva Declaration, UNFICYP was responsible for a security zone (called the buffer zone) which was to be established along the Turkish bridgehead and came under the exclusive control of UN Forces. All other forces were prohibited from entry into the zone. In addition, UNFICYP was given the task of providing security for mixed villages.[30]

The day-to-day routine of the peacekeeping force altered and was much more closely associated with the buffer zone area. The Force engaged in confidence-building where possible and tried to encourage farming both in the buffer zone and near it by specifying certain farms which could be cultivated. They also supervised any crossovers that were necessary, for health purposes, etc. UNFICYP continued to carry out humanitarian tasks such as the transportation of supplies and pension and welfare payments to Greek enclaves in the North and the provision of security to those enclaves. UNFICYP also made occasional visits to Turkish Cypriots living in the south and facilitated their continued contact with relatives in the North. Good offices were still made available for negotiations, particularly over public services such as electricity or water when these crossed over the buffer zone.

Along the ceasefire line in Nicosia, UNFICYP sought to create unmanned areas. One successfully negotiated withdrawal was from the Paphos Gate area in Nicosia which had been the source of a number of incidents over the years due to the close proximity of the sides.

After the 1974 crisis, the civilian police were primarily responsible for policing the buffer zone since this area no longer fell under the jurisdiction of either side.

There have been several substantial changes in UNFICYP's composition over the years. In 1973, the Irish Battalion withdrew leaving only a handful of Irish officers stationed at UNFICYP headquarters. The Irish withdrawal was followed in 1977 by the departure of the Finnish Battalion and in 1988 by the Swedish Battalion. In all these cases financial considerations weighed heavily, although the Irish decision was also related to the situation on the Northern Ireland border.[31] Austria provided a contingent to replace the withdrawn Irish battalion. Each of the four contingents (Austria, Canada, Denmark, and the United Kingdom), were assigned to cover a section of the buffer zone.

During 1993 the Force was reduced significantly and, while complete withdrawal was avoided, the future character of the UN's presence on the island is still in doubt and subject to on-going review in the Security Council and the General Assembly. With the increase in peacekeeping commitments elsewhere, major contributors to UNFICYP began to question the continuation of a mission which seemed no closer to resolution than in 1964. Both Denmark and Canada announced that they would no longer contribute battalions to the mission and the Secretary-General was not able to attract new contributors largely due to the disproportionate financial burden of participation. In light of these withdrawals the Security Council voted to recommend a new system of financing whereby costs of the operation not met by voluntary contributions are met through regular peacekeeping assessments.[32] The General Assembly later approved this new method of financing.[33] In addition the Government of Cyprus agreed to pay a third of the cost of the peacekeeping mission. Once this new financing system had been arranged Argentina offered to contribute a battalion.

After a thorough review of the mission, particularly the ramifications of declining interest in Cyprus amongst potential contributors, it was decided that UNFICYP would retain its force-level status. With the arrival of the Argentinian battalion, deployment along the buffer zone has shifted from a four sector arrangement to a three sector arrangement. While there was some concern that the reduction in troops did not provide adequate coverage of the buffer zone, the Secretary-General pointed out that it was the best arrangement that could be hoped for given the huge demands on the Organization coupled with financial constraints.[34]

Given the lack of willingness on the part of Member States to continue contributing to the maintenance of UNFICYP, the future of the force is uncertain. The effect the reduction is likely to have on the three decade old conflict is also uncertain. Moreover, the changes in deployment came on the heels of a new 'confidence-building' initiative by the S-G combined with renewed pressure on all the parties concerned to put old antagonisms behind them and sign a peace agreement.[35] But by the close of 1993 these initiatives had not produced significant movement toward settlement by either side.

## 2. UNITED NATIONS TRANSITION ASSISTANCE GROUP

After years of diplomatic effort, an agreement between the various parties involved in the Namibia conflict was reached at the end of 1988, and the United Nations Transition Assistance Group (UNTAG) was established to assist in the implementation of the settlement package. When independence was finally achieved in March 1990, it was the culmination of decades of struggle by the Namibian people, forty years of effort and pressure by the United Nations and other international organizations, and the end of more than one hundred years of official and *de facto* colonial rule.

Namibia, previously known as South West Africa, covers an area of some 825,000 square kilometres and is bordered by Angola to the north, South Africa to the south, and Botswana to the east. It is mainly arid country with two large deserts, the Namib to the west (running north to south along the Atlantic coast) and the Kalahari to the east. Its capital city Windhoek is situated near the middle of the country. Walvis Bay, a large city on the Atlantic coast, is an economically vital part of Namibia since it is the country's only deep water port (three years after independence South Africa still claims sovereignty over Walvis Bay). The population is relatively small, around 1.4 million, and widely dispersed. The largest population concentration is in the north along the Angolan border in an area known as Ovamboland. There are eleven to fifteen ethnic groups in Namibia (depending on how they are divided), but the

Ovambos make up approximately 50 per cent of the population and are by far the largest ethnic group (others are the Hereros, Namas, Damaras, Kavangos).[36]

For the Namibian people the struggle against colonial rule began in 1884 when the territory formally became a German colony and was renamed German South West Africa.[37] The first rebellion happened shortly thereafter, and indicates the approximate beginning of the struggle for Namibian independence.[38] At the end of the First World War the new League of Nations became responsible for Namibia and in 1920 mandated control of it to South Africa (the mandate gave South Africa administrative powers but did not allow for incorporation and was valid only as long as South Africa carried out its duties in a just and equitable manner).[39] At the end of the Second World War the new United Nations, as the successor to the League, became the body responsible for the administration of the territory.

Increasing international pressure over two decades after the Second World War led by the newly independent African states resulted in the 1966 revocation by the UN General Assembly of the South African mandate. The Assembly stated that 'South Africa had failed "to ensure the material and moral well-being... of the indigenous inhabitants" as the mandate required'.[40]

It was during the years following the 1966 ruling and South Africa's refusal to pass control of the territory over to the UN that an independence movement got under way in Namibia. Several years previously, a labour group known as the Ovambo People's Organization had become the South West Africa People's Organization (SWAPO) in an attempt to broaden its appeal outside of its traditional Ovambo base. SWAPO now took the lead in the push for national liberation and began an armed struggle against South African rule.[41] By this time many other groups had sprung up, and Namibia's struggle began in earnest.

The General Assembly took the decisive step of declaring South Africa to be illegally occupying South West Africa and of renaming it Namibia. At the same time the UN set up the 'Council for Namibia' to govern *in absentia* and provided funds for, among other things, resettling and educating refugees. In ensuing years the International Court of Justice (ICJ) ruled several times to uphold the General Assembly's resolution. And in 1970, in concurrence with the GA, the Security Council passed its own resolution declaring South Africa's occupation illegal, reasoning that the practice of apartheid in the territory went against the terms of the original mandate. Although South Africa remained entrenched in its position, these acts by the UN and the ICJ helped to consolidate and eventually legitimize the independance struggle inside Namibia. They culminated in 1973 when the General Assembly formally recognized SWAPO as the sole and authentic representative of the Namibian people. This was a controversial decision, and some people strongly criticized it suggesting that it would undermine the UN's neutrality. During the next two decades as other African countries gained independence, Namibia came increasingly under the international spotlight as one of the last bastions of colonial rule.

The passage of SCR 385 (1976) and the formation of a 'Contact Group' (negotiating group) the following year signalled the beginning of ten years of intensive negotiation and pressure by a number of parties including the United States, the Soviet Union, Cuba, Angola, the Organization of African Unity, the Front-line States, and the United Nations. This incredible effort bore the desired results in 1988 when agreements were finally signed, and ultimately in March 1990 when Namibia gained independence. The period in between witnessed a long, complex series of meetings and negotiation sessions, periods of conciliation, as well as periods of heightened aggression and violence. This study will not provide a detailed history of the decade. The reader can refer to other sources for more information.[42]

The mandate of UNTAG was derived from SCR 435 (1978) which approved an implementation plan put forward by S-G Waldheim.[43]

The task of UNTAG in its essence was 'to ensure conditions in Namibia' which would allow 'the Namibian people to participate freely and without intimidation in the electoral process... leading to early independence of the territory'.[44] Originally, the mandate was to be carried out and controlled by the UN.[45] This would have meant that the Special Representative of the Secretary-General Marti Ahtisaari would have had direct responsibility for administering the territory during the transition period. As it turned out, the prospect of UN controlled administration, even briefly, was out of the question to South Africa and a more watered down version of the original resolution had to be negotiated. The result was SCR 435 (1978) which gave the Administrator-General (A-G) of the territory, who answered directly to Pretoria, control over the process, and relegated the UN to a monitoring role with no right of enforcement.

Although UNTAG operated within the constraints dictated by the mandate, it managed a high level of effectiveness not only in ensuring that the process was indeed free and fair, but probably more importantly, in reducing violence, and promoting reconciliation.

## 2.1 Structure of UNTAG

Headquartered in Windhoek, UNTAG operated from 1 April 1989 to 21 March 1990 and when fully deployed around the elections in November 1989 comprised almost 8000 personnel. The operation was organized into two large components, one military and the other civilian.

The military component was responsible for three main tasks: (1) monitoring the ceasefire, which included the confinement to base of South African and SWAPO armed forces, and monitoring the phased withdrawal of South African armed forces, (2) monitoring the dismantling of commando units and ethnic forces, and (3) surveillance of borders (to prevent infiltration).

The military contingent was made up of three parts; military observers and monitors (approximately 300), three large battalions (approximately 850 each from Kenya, Malaysia, and Finland), and logistics units (approximately 1700). At maximum strength in early November, the military component reached 4493. The military observers and monitors were deployed by 1 April, but many were without transport or communications (reasons for this are discussed below).[46] They were deployed mainly in northern Namibia and Angola where they monitored the ceasefire, confinement of parties forces to base, and the dismantling of the SA military presence.[47] The battalions were all fully deployed by 1 May. They were concentrated in the north of the territory where most of the fighting occurred and where the most trouble was anticipated.

The civilian component of UNTAG was made up of six sections including the Special Representative's Office, the Independent Jurist, UNHCR, the electoral division, the administrative division, and the civilian police or CIVPOL. The Special Representative's Office (SRO) had overall coordination responsibilities at three levels: (1) with other UNTAG elements, i.e., military and CIVPOL, (2) with the Administrator-General's office, and (3) with the political parties, local community groups, and governmental and non-governmental observer agencies and missions. In addition, the SRO was responsible for negotiating with the A-G and the political parties about the details of transition and for initiating a wide-reaching information dissemination programme.[48]

Deployment was organized through ten regions, each with a regional political office and director. Within those regions were a further thirty-two district offices, each run by a District Head. Along with coordination and liaison work, these offices carried out the information campaign which publicized UNTAG and its various elements as well as the registration and election processes. Many of these offices closed soon after the elections in November but the basic regional and district structure remained the same until March 1990.

The electoral division was made up of a small staff in Windhoek which was responsible for advising the SRSG on the technical aspects of the election and the supervision of both the registration and election processes. They also assisted the SRSG in his on-going negotiations with the A-G over the form and substance of the elections. For the registration and election phases, twenty-three electoral areas were created. For most of these offices a staff-member from the regional or district political office was made district supervisor. During the registration period an extra 180 personnel were brought in, and for the elections numbers of personnel were boosted by 885 people from twenty-seven countries.[49]

The civilian police played a crucial part in the independence process in Namibia since it was their job to monitor the South West African Police or SWAPOL as they carried out their law and order duties. Initially the country was divided in two sectors, north and south, each headed by a regional coordinator. This was later changed when it became apparent that it was unmanageable, and the country was divided into six police districts, each with a commander. Initially, 500 police were deployed but this was increased by 500 and then again by another 500 as the extent of the job of monitoring SWAPOL became evident. By the end of October, approximately 1,500 police were deployed concentrated mainly in the north. The task of CIVPOL was complicated by the continued existence of *Koevoet* (a counter-insurgency unit attached to SWAPOL) and a complete lack of cooperation from SWAPOL. Almost all of CIVPOL's compliment remained in Namibia until the end of March 1990.

## 2.2 Implementation

Once the accords were signed in December 1988, and 1 April 1989 was set as the start date for implementation, preparations for UNTAG began in earnest. The delay caused by disagreements in New York resulted in serious timetable disruptions in the mobilization of UNTAG.[50] By the start date less than 1000 of the 4650 troops had arrived in Namibia, and these were the advance parties which would prepare the way for the later arrival of the three battalions. Moreover, when troops actually began to arrive in some force in the second week of April,

> their preparedness to carry out their mandate came into serious question. Ovamboland residents, who had eagerly awaited the arrival of UN troops, found that almost none of them were familiar with the local language or even accompanied by interpreters.[51]

Civilian police units of UNTAG were not to get to Namibia until 15 April when Irish, Dutch, and Swedish contingents arrived. They were not deployed for a further week. In retrospect, this late arrival and lack of preparedness on the part of UNTAG would not have made much difference if the independence process had begun peacefully. This was not the case, however, and in the early hours of 1 April SWAPO crossed the Angolan border into northern Namibia in force, and a bloody conflict ensued which nearly derailed the peace process.

Early on 1 April SWAPO units crossed over the border from Angola into northern Namibia and engaged in fighting with

SWAPOL. The motivations for SWAPO's incursion remain obscure. From the outside the action seemed reckless in the extreme since it jeopardized the independence process which SWAPO had fought hard to achieve. Moreover, SWAPO could have been reasonably sure that they would do well in the elections. Jaster argues that 'the SWAPO leadership placed high priority on achieving visibility for its guerillas among the people of Ovamboland'.[52] Previous negotiating positions support this point. It may be surmised, then, that the incursion was an attempt to follow through on achieving this visibility. According to the final agreement, SWAPO guerrillas were to withdraw well back into Angolan territory (to the 16th parallel) by the beginning of the transition period. This distance from Namibia and the bulk of SWAPO's Ovambo support in the north may provide some explanation of the 1 April action. It is most likely, though, that only SWAPO's leadership will ever know the full story.

At the time SWAPO crossed the border on 1 April, there were only about 100 UN staff and approximately 900 troops in Namibia.[53] Under the settlement plan withdrawal of SWAPO guerrillas behind the 16th parallel and the confinement of SADF to bases was to have been effected by 1 April when the ceasefire officially came into force. During the last weeks of March South Africa had expressed its concern on several occasions about what appeared to them to be a build-up of SWAPO units close to the border.[54] These warnings were largely ignored possibly because South Africa had suggested similar irregularities in the past which had proved to be less than accurate.

Following some delicate diplomacy an agreement was reached on 9 April whereby SWAPO troops would withdraw behind pre-agreed lines (deep into Angolan territory) escorted by UNTAG troops followed by confinement of SADF to base. Under the agreement SWAPO troops were expected to be out of Namibia by 15 April. However, because information was very slow to disseminate on all sides, and South African troops could not be persuaded to stay away from the UNTAG assembly points, it took much longer than originally anticipated to return the situation to something approaching normalcy. Most SWAPO troops decided to make their own way back without the safe passage offered by UNTAG, and as a result border clashes continued. Toward the end of April it became apparent that some SWAPO troops still remained inside Namibia and the deadline was extended for their withdrawal. By this time though, all three UNTAG battalions were nearing full deployment and were capable of monitoring the situation with greatly increased efficiency. By 13 May SADF troops returned to base and the situation had been restored.

UNTAG was criticized heavily for its lack of preparedness and lack of action. But based on the delays at the UN in New York, this criticism seemed unreasonably severe. Although UNTAG would not have fought SWAPO (this is not the role of a peacekeeping force) their presence on the border before the 1 April deadline might have had two effects: (1) by providing early credible warning of SWAPO's movements UNTAG might have deterred SWAPO's action, and (2) they could have provided reliable two-way information and verification of agreements to SWAPO and SA fighters, to the general public, and to the leadership of the various governments involved. This last point highlights one of the key functions of any peacekeeping force: the provision of reliable information.

By mid-May UNTAG's military component and CIVPOL were fully deployed and the independence process resumed. Most of the forty-two political offices had been opened, and they were beginning the difficult task of informing the Namibian population of each step in the independence process. The period preceding registration was critical in several respects for UNTAG. First, they needed to re-establish credibility with the Namibian people and with the international community in order to allay fears that they would not be able to fulfill their mandate. This was particularly the case in the north, the traditional stronghold of SWAPO support, where sporadic violence continued. Second, the transition process was behind schedule, partly because there remained a number of outstanding and highly contentious issues such as the format of the registration proclamation and the repeal of discriminatory laws which the A-G's office and the SRSG had been hitherto unable to settle.

A recurring and particularly difficult problem in the north was the existence of a police unit know as *Koevoet*. This unit, a black counter-insurgency force which had come under the control of the regular police in 1988, was well-known for its brutality and violent activity against the people of Ovamboland. Although it should have been disbanded under the terms of the settlement plan, it had been operating with a free hand and was continuing to cause havoc in the north. Indeed, by the beginning of June CIVPOL had received over 200 complaints about *Koevoet* and SWAPOL activities.[55] Jaster describes the problem:

> UNTAG's demand that, as a paramilitary group, it [*Koevoet*] be disbanded under the terms of Resolution 435, was initially ignored. *Koevoet* continued to treat SWAPO as the enemy, breaking up its political rallies, assaulting its supporters, and terrorizing villages suspected of pro-SWAPO sympathies.[56]

The presence of this group was jeopardizing the transition process. By the middle of May it became obvious that more police were needed and over the ensuing months the S-G twice requested and received approval for additional monitors. CIVPOL was supposed to be monitoring all police activities, including those of *Koevoet*, but their task was made nearly impossible because of SWAPOL's refusal to cooperate with the UN effort. In addition, some attempts at intimidation were directed at CIVPOL. Eventually UNTAG succeeded in getting *Koevoet* disbanded, but it was only after enormous pressure from Windhoek and New York and continuing complaints and reports of *Koevoet*'s activities that the A-G relented. It was not until 31 October (eight days before the elections) that UNTAG confirmed the demobilization of *Koevoet*.[57] One CIVPOL Commander described it as a process of 'wearing them down' and 'keeping at them' until they complied.[58]

Meanwhile UNTAG's information campaign, run through its political offices, got under way. The initial problem the political offices faced in carrying out their tasks stemmed from the fact that the newspapers, radio, and television were 'deeply partisan' and 'prone to misinformation'.[59] Cedric Thornberry, Director of the SRO, said of the problem: 'ignorance has been generated by deliberate misinformation, and by rather unprofessional print media sapping the capacity for independent judgement'.[60] To counteract this, UNTAG's job was to provide objective information about every stage of the independence process. The political offices focused on out-reach and spent their time visiting churches, unions, political parties, hospitals, and schools attempting to saturate their areas with reliable information. In addition to this, the political offices were engaged in what was described by Thornberry as 'the essential process of reconciliation'.[61] The District Heads were responsible for holding regular meetings with different groups including the political parties to discuss issues and work out problems. In this way the political offices greatly contributed to reducing the likelihood of violence and strengthening the reconciliation process. They also made many useful contacts and were able to keep well informed about potential problems in their areas. This information, in turn, made its way back to Windhoek to Ahtisaari's office.

Registration began on 3 July and continued until 23 September. By the end of that period over 700,000 people had been registered to vote. This considerable task was conducted through thirty-six permanent and thirty-three temporary registration centers as well as approximately 2200 rural registration points covered by 110 mobile registration units. UNTAG had monitors for each registration point to which groups of three monitors were assigned. These groups consisted of a police monitor, an international civil servant, and an interpreter.[62] The registration process had to overcome such obstacles as the high illiteracy rate (60 per cent for the whole population, but up to 80 per cent in some rural areas) and a dispersed population (75 per cent of Namibia's population lives in rural areas).[63]

UNTAG's role in the registration process was negotiated by Ahtisaari to include three important points: that no registration could take place without the presence of a UNTAG monitor, that both the A-G's office and UNTAG would investigate any irregularities or complaints, and that the A-G's office and the SRO would each have a separate lock on the vault where the registration forms would be stored.[64] These concessions were important given the behavior of some of the A-G's staff:

> UNTAG monitors... reported that registrars frequently arrived late and left early, even when long queues were waiting to register, and that registrars moved from place to place arbitrarily and without notice. There was also evidence of intentional errors on the part of local registrars, who in one

instance had spoiled a quarter of completed registration forms.[65]

In response to violence between supporters of the various political parties (most notably SWAPO and its main rival the Democratic Turnhalle Alliance (DTA)) during the registration period, Ahtisaari negotiated a 'Code of Conduct' with the leaders of the nine political parties who were running in the upcoming elections. The first paragraph of the document states, 'everyone has the right to put forward their political principles and ideas, without threat or fear, to every other person, without exception'.[66] It went on to lay down a set of rules for behaviour and a means for on-going communication between political parties through the regional offices of UNTAG. Negotiation of the 'Code of Conduct' was followed up by regular meetings with UN personnel and party leaders at national, regional, and district levels. These meetings were run to facilitate communication and problem-solving between the various parties, with the overall goal of reducing levels of violence and intimidation.

On 21 July the A-G's office published its draft of the election proclamation for public comment. It was, as Jaster points out, 'an inordinately complex system for submitting, verifying and counting ballots' which left 'considerable scope for fraud and manipulation'.[67] Lengthy negotiations ensued which included frequent interventions from New York. Finally, on 6 October, agreement was reached. These negotiations conducted by Ahtisaari and supported by the S-G, were crucial for ensuring that free and fair elections would take place. They represented a significant achievement considering that Ahtisaari had no powers of enforcement relying instead on his powers of persuasion.

By the time of the elections in early November violence had been greatly reduced. Although there were several incidents which might have prevented the smooth running of the election process, all parties seemed determined that the settlement process would continue free from violence, intimidation, fraud or other potential disruptions.

Polling took place over a five-day period from 7 to 11 November. An incredible 97 per cent voter turn-out was recorded, with only 1.4 per cent of the ballots rejected. A seventy-two-seat Constituent Assembly was elected, of which forty-one were won by SWAPO, and twenty-one were taken by the DTA. A two-thirds majority of forty-eight was needed to adopt the constitution and when neither of the two main parties managed this it became obvious that a coalition of some kind would be necessary.

On 14 November Ahtisaari certified that the elections had been 'at each stage free and fair', stating that Namibia had given 'the whole world a shining lesson in democracy' in an election where there had 'been no losers'.[68]

## 2.3 Conclusion

The Constituent Assembly met for the first time on 21 November 1989, and a conciliatory tone was set by SWAPO's representatives who suggested that the Constitutional Principles negotiated in 1982 (but not signed by any of the parties elected to the Constituent Assembly) be adopted as a 'frame of reference'.[69] This motion was carried unanimously. By February in the following year the constitution was adopted by consensus and 21 March 1990 was set as the date for independence.

UNTAG's main task was finished when Ahtisaari declared the elections free and fair. UNTAG civilian personnel who remained until independence began their last task which was to prepare detailed reports for the in-coming UN Development Programme (UNDP) so that their experiences and knowledge would not be lost. The military and police components remained at full or nearly full strength until March 1990. By April, though, the last units of UNTAG had withdrawn and only personnel from the few countries which had negotiated bilateral agreements with Namibia to help restructure and train its military and police, remained.

The UNDP was just one of a number of UN and other international agencies which made arrangements to work in Namibia with the new government, helping to facilitate conditions which would sustain the new multi-party democracy.[70]

UNTAG represents a significant development in peacekeeping away from a purely military focus toward a broadened concept of peacekeeping which included vital aspects of peacebuilding. The tasks that UNTAG personnel were asked to perform were as varied as negotiating the text of a proclamation document, holding meetings to foster reconciliation within local communities, disseminating vital information about the transition process, and monitoring police investigations. While the tasks of UNTAG personnel were varied, one universal requirement was that their interactions with all the parties concerned help to facilitate communication and understanding.

## 3. UN PEACEKEEPING IN CROATIA AND BOSNIA-HERZEGOVINA, 1992–93

Croatia and Bosnia-Herzegovina[71] are located in the Balkans, a region in Europe stretching along the eastern side of the Adriatic Sea. Croatia is bordered in the north by Slovenia and Hungary and to the east by the new Federal Republic of Yugoslavia (or FRY, which includes Serbia and Montenegro). It shares a long, convoluted border with Bosnia to the south and east and to its west is the Adriatic. Ethnically, Croatia is 75 per cent Croat, and 12 per cent Serb (13 per cent other).[72] Apart from a narrow strip of land giving Bosnia access to the Adriatic it is surrounded by Croatia to the north and west and the FRY to the east and south. It is 40 per cent Moslem, 33 per cent Serb, and 18 per cent Croat (9 per cent others).[73]

The inter-ethnic divisions so apparent in the current Balkan crisis developed over a long history in which the region served as a battleground for a succession of competing, and ethnically and culturally diverse empires. Byzantine, Roman, Ottoman and other influences provide the historical background of the current conflict. However, the complex political, social and economic relations in the region over the last five decades were the primary causes of the Yugoslav war. Following the Second World War and Josep Tito's successful civil war a Yugoslav Republic was founded. A federal structure was developed which allowed the six republics constituting the new state to build and largely control their own political, economic and military institutions. Through this structure, Tito sought to balance the competing claims of different ethnic groups, but was unable to reconcile the divergent interests of the Yugoslav republics. After his death in 1980 no new leadership emerged which had the strength to hold the disparate groups and interests together. The lack of political leadership was compounded by general economic difficulties and the decline of communist party rule. By the late 1980s the republics were challenging the federal structure, and although talks were convened, they failed to reach any agreement. During the course of these unsuccessful constitutional discussions all six republics held multi-party elections where the results heavily favoured nationalist parties. A more ominous sign of things to come was a move in some republics to form their own territorial militias independent of the federal Yugoslav People's Army (JNA).[74]

At the same time ethnic tensions in some republics had risen alarmingly. In one highly visible and provocative case the newly elected Croatian leader, Franjo Tudjman deepened suspicions between Croats and Serbs in Croatia when he moved to have bilingual signs changed to display Croat Latin only and hung a new Croatian flag (with the red and white checks of the Croatian heraldic shield) 'from every building'.[75] More substantive moves by Tudjman and his Croatian Democratic Union (HDZ) party came through constitutional changes which disadvantaged the Serb population.[76] In response to increased distrust and tension, leaders of the heavily Serb populated Krajina region of Croatia held a referendum on autonomy in mid-1991 and based on the results formed a 'Serbian Autonomous Region of Krajina'. This autonomous region was later declared the 'Republic of Serbian Krajina' (RSK).

By 1991 the republics were so divided that the possibility of compromise on some form of a unitary Yugoslav state appeared remote. At this juncture the largest gap existed between Croatia and Slovenia's position which favoured some form of sovereignty (possibly within a confederal system), and Serbia's determination, led by Slobodan Milosevic and backed by the JNA, to maintain a Yugoslav state. Milosevic's position was further strengthened by the European Community (supported by the United States) which strongly discouraged the breakup of Yugoslavia. The fragile peace was shattered at the end of June when Slovenia and Croatia declared independence and the JNA sought to restore federal authority. While the Slovene declaration resolved itself relatively peacefully after an initial few weeks of fighting the JNA, Croatia was less fortunate. Not only did the JNA, directed from Belgrade, fight the declaration, but, in the absence of assurances that the minority Serb population would be allowed some degree of autonomy and ensured protection from discrimination within a Croatian state, inter-ethnic war was inevitable. Moreover, the possibility of war spreading throughout the republics and outward into the region loamed over the whole crisis.

Fears of a spreading civil war turned out to be well founded and although Bosnia did not succumb immediately, it began a slow and excruciating slide into violence. The onset of war was dramatically accelerated in early 1992 by the recognition of Croatia and Slovenia and the Bosnian referendum on independence. As Glenny notes,

> The decision by the European Community to recognize Slovenia and Croatia [15 January 1992] pushed Bosnia into the abyss. Once this happened, the Bosnian government had only three roads along which it could travel and each led to war. It could have stayed in the rump Yugoslavia and been ruled over by Milosevic and Serbia. It could have accepted the territorial division of Bosnia between Serbia and Croatia, as suggested by Tudjman and Milosevic. Or it could have applied for recognition as an independent state. The Croats and Moslems considered the first solution unacceptable; the Moslems and Yugoslavs, the second; and the Serbs, the third.[77]

The Bosnian government held a referendum on independence at the end of February 1992, where 64 per cent of the vote was in favour of independence. The Serb communities boycotted the poll and immediately following the vote a number of barricades were raised around Sarajevo by Serb militias and some violence ensued.[78] Although the barricades were quickly brought down, this initial skirmish marked the beginning of the end for any hopes of a peaceful solution to Bosnia's constitutional crisis. By mid-March violence had broken out between Serb and Croat/Moslem militias, particularly in northern Bosnia and Sarajevo such that a series of European Community-sponsored ceasefires had no effect on the ground. The EC and the United States recognized Bosnia as an independent state on 7 April 1992 and on 22 May Bosnia became a member of the United Nations.

## 3.1 UN Peacekeeping in Croatia

From the UN's point of view the conflict in Yugoslavia was an internal affair and therefore did not fall within its remit. Consequently, the Security Council did not take any formal action on the Yugoslav crisis until September 1991. At that time the Council passed a resolution imposing an embargo on the delivery of arms and other military equipment to the area.[79] It was not until several months later, and at the request of the parties involved, that the Security Council considered mounting a peacekeeping operation. On 9 November 1991, the Yugoslav Presidency (made up of a representative from each of the six Yugoslav republics which formed the basis of the federal structure of the state of Yugoslavia) asked the Security Council to consider the situation in Croatia and requested the deployment of UN troops to the area. A meeting of the Security Council was held on 15 November, in which Cyrus Vance, the recently appointed United Nations Special Envoy, put forward five conditions for the establishment of a peacekeeping force in Croatia. These were: the agreement of all parties, a clear mandate, the provision of troops and financial backing by UN members, and the support of the Security Council. Efforts continued toward meeting these guidelines and on 15 December 1991, the Council approved the concept and plan for a UN peacekeeping operation (this was dubbed the 'Vance Plan' after its chief architect).[80] Even so, it was not until two months later, 21 February 1992, that authorization for deployment was given and a further month before peacekeepers began to arrive in Croatia.[81]

The United Nations Protection Force (UNPROFOR) was established for an initial one-year period and was headquartered in Sarajevo, the capital of neighbouring Bosnia. The plan called for the deployment of just over 13,000 troops (twelve battalions), civilian personnel and civilian police.[82] Its main function was to stabilize the situation, creating conditions of peace and security within which negotiations for an overall solution could take place. These overall negotiations were led by Lord Peter Carrington as head of the European

Community's Conference on Yugoslavia (ECCY) until mid-1992.[83] Following moves toward internationalization of the peacemaking effort an International Conference on Former Yugoslavia (ICFY) was created in September 1992, co-chaired by the EC Presidency, represented by Lord David Owen, and the UN Secretary-General, represented by Cyrus Vance (Vance was later replaced by Thorvald Stoltenberg in September 1993).[84]

By 23 March advanced deployments of infantry were under way. UNPROFOR was deployed into four sectors within three UN Protected Areas (UNPAs). Sectors North and South covered the Krajina region of Croatia while Sector West was in Western Slavonia and Sector East in Eastern Slavonia on the border of Serbian region of Vojvodina.[85] These UNPAs were areas in Croatia occupied by armed Serbian militias, where fighting had been most intense and which had a large proportion of Serbs in the civilian populations. Within each UNPA, the UN force was mandated to stabilize the situation (including the maintenance of an 'interim' *status quo* of existing arrangements for local administration and public order), demilitarize or effect the withdrawal of armed forces, protect the local population, monitor traffic in and out of the UNPAs, monitor local police forces and assist in the voluntary return of displaced persons and refugees. The full deployment of UNPROFOR was delayed by several months so that it was not fully operational until late June. The late arrival of some elements of UNPROFOR was caused by some financial wrangling in New York as well as complications created by the outbreak of war in Bosnia.[86] According to a Human Rights Watch report one tragic result of this delay was that 'ethnic cleansing' continued virtually unchecked and by the time UNPROFOR was operational 'most of the area's non-Serbian population had already been expelled' from the UNPAs.[87]

Although UNPROFOR battalions deploying in the UNPAs reported continued violations of the ceasefire and were often restricted in their freedom of movement, they did manage to set up regular patrols, checkpoints and observation posts. They also began the crucial process of establishing liaison neworks.[88]

UN Military Observers (UNMOs) reported that while elements of the JNA were withdrawing from the UNPAs, as called for in the ceasefire agreement, they were leaving behind arms and equipment for local Serb militias. This problem became significantly worse when, on 27 April 1992, Serbia and Montenegro formed the Federal Republic of Yugoslavia. In an attempt to establish its credentials, the FRY immediately announced the withdrawal of all individuals from Serbia and Montenegro serving in the JNA in other republics. The intent was to aid the Bosnian Serbs and to counter mounting international pressure on Serbia and Montenegro. This move effectively stranded large numbers of well-armed troops in both Croatia and Bosnia and led to a huge influx of soldiers into existing militias. In Croatia this meant that the peacekeeping mission was faced with a far more militarized situation than had been anticipated and would now be responsible for demobilizing a much larger number of militia than expected.[89]

During this initial period of UN activity another unexpected problem arose that would do much to undermine the effectiveness of the operation in Croatia. Areas adjacent to the UNPAs (later called the 'pink zones') were held by the JNA but did not come under the UN's mandate (which was restricted to the UNPAs) or the ceasefire agreement. UNPROFOR again found itself in a position of having to mediate in a tense and difficult situation.

Further difficulties continued for headquarters staff in Sarajevo who, according to one report, spent 75 per cent of their time coping with the growing crisis in Bosnia. This had 'an inevitable effect on Headquarters effectiveness'.[90] Overall, the S-G aptly summarized the problems encountered by UNPROFOR noting that '[t]he first few weeks of deployment... have thus made clear the complexity of the challenge which confronts the Force'.[91]

By the end of May UNPROFOR had moved its Headquarters to Belgrade leaving behind a skeletal presence of 120 personnel. Problems persisted in the UNPAs with reports of increasing militarization and economic hardship created, in part, by the flood of refugees from Bosnia. The month ended on a pessimistic note when continued stalemate over the 'pink zone' situation led the S-G to suggest that 'developments since the Security Council approved the Plan for the United Nations peacekeeping operation in Croatia had raised new doubts about the practicability of the operation'.[92]

The increasing complexity of the situation meant that UNPROFOR's mandate was 'constantly expanding as experience on the ground [brought] to light further complexities in implementing the... plan'.[93] UNPROFOR became involved in interviewing individuals who had been forced from their homes, organizing patrols to protect their homes, and compiling data on those groups believed to be responsible for the expulsions.[94] Based on a laboriously negotiated agreement over the 'pink zones', UNPROFOR began monitoring both the withdrawal of the JNA and the activities of local police.[95] UNPROFOR's tasks were enlarged again when it was authorized to carry out immigration and customs functions at the international borders of the UNPAs.[96] Implementation of this extension became difficult because the Serb authorities (based in Knin in the southern part of Krajina, Sector South) placed their own controls and checkpoints at all major crossings.[97]

Closer examination of specific incidents handled by UNPROFOR illustrates some of the serious problems the force faced in carrying out its various tasks. Parts of the Serb-enclaves into which the UN had been deployed were run by Serbian 'gangsters and hoodlums' who were reportedly 'murdering about five non-Serbs a week'.[98] A confidential UN report on the threat posed by these Serbian paramilitary forces stated that there was 'a very real danger of a renewal of widespread conflict in and around the UN protected zones'.[99] UNPROFOR's efforts to monitor and demobilize these militia were largely unsuccessful. In two separate incidents Belgian and Russian peacekeepers 'blockaded' some of these militia. This approach was ineffective as 'in each case, the situation deteriorated rapidly and, to avoid bloodshed, it was decided to suspend the use of force and further negotiations ensued'.[100] After these attempts at 'blockading', however, the militia became 'increasingly hostile to UNPROFOR personnel'.[101]

In another incident on 30 September 1992, tensions rose when a group of Croats attempted to reclaim their homes held by Serb gunman. Russian peacekeepers managed to intercede and prevent what UN officials had warned would be 'a massacre' by convincing the refugees to pull back from direct confrontation.[102] The peacekeepers were successful in preventing further bloodshed by persuading the refugees to go back but the underlying problem remained unresolved.

UNPROFOR also reported that the increasing economic hardship in the UNPAs, especially unemployment and the growing number of refugees, was linked to a rapid rise in crime. The effectiveness of local police deteriorated so that by the end of September, 'no system of law and order [existed] in the UNPAs'.[103]

UNPROFOR had some limited success, most notably in the withdrawal of the JNA from Croatia. Boutros-Ghali reportedly said, 'with the withdrawal of the Yugoslav Army from Croatian soil, a crucial element in the UN peacekeeping plan...had been filled'.[104] It could be argued that withdrawal would have occurred regardless given the FRY's position (this would be less certain in the case of Prevlaka). Coupled with the failure of the international peace process to negotiate an agreement in Bosnia or to broker a permanent settlement for Croatia, the peacekeeping force struggled to maintain the semblance of a ceasefire and made little progress toward fulfilling the rest of the 'Vance Plan'. Apart from preventing all-out war between Croats and Serbs the mission's effectiveness was questionable.

At the beginning of 1993, growing frustration on the part of the Tudjman government particularly over the 'pink zones' issue but also over the return of displaced persons to the UNPAs led to a major offensive by the Croatian Army in the southern part of Krajina (Sector South). A ceasefire agreement based on an earlier Security Council Resolution was signed on 6 April 1993. The agreement called for the end of hostilities and the withdrawal of the Croatian Army (CA) to positions held prior to the 22 January incursion.[105] Over the following nine months two more major offensives by the CA occurred and the situation in the 'pink zones' and the UNPAs continued to deteriorate.[106] UNPROFOR continued its efforts to mediate between the two sides and to carry out its mandate. By September 1993 its role had changed from carrying out the 'Vance Plan' and the various extensions of the mandate to a *de facto* minimalist position: 'The role of UNPROFOR in present circumstances is thus to prevent the resumption or escalation of conflict; to provide a breathing space for the continued efforts of peacemakers; and to support the provision of essential humanitarian assistance.'[107]

## 3.2 UN Peacekeeping in Bosnia-Herzegovina

Over the months following the deployment of peacekeepers in Croatia, the attention of the Security Council and the world press shifted away from Croatia towards the troubles of Sarajevo and Bosnia.[108] In response to international pressure and the obvious threat to regional peace and security posed by the conflict the Security Council progressively stretched UNPROFOR's mandate, which was originally confined to certain areas of Croatia, to include Sarajevo and eventually to include a large-scale humanitarian relief effort throughout Bosnia.[109] Continued fighting as well as reports of 'ethnic cleansing' and other atrocities in Bosnia led the Security Council to pass a resolution on 30 May under the enforcement provisions of Chapter VII of the UN's Charter (the peace-keeping force in Croatia is not authorized under enforcement provisions). The UN imposed sanctions against Serbia and Montenegro, and demanded that a security zone be formed around Sarajevo airport and that the delivery of humanitarian supplies go unimpeded.[110] At the same time the Council began considering a report of the S-G which detailed possible alternatives for the protection of humanitarian aid convoys.[111] Boutros-Ghali argued that such a role for peacekeepers could be problematic and would need to be seriously considered especially if it involved the use of force. The concern was that the use of force could compromise not only the peacekeeping operation and the ICFY negotiations, but also the position of relief agencies operating in the area. Moreover, setting clear and attainable political aims for such enforcement activity was considered virtually impossible. Boutros-Ghali suggested that negotiating agreements for the transport and delivery of aid would be the most preferable option and recommended a more limited operation focused on opening Sarajevo's airport to relief flights.[112]

Foreshadowing what later would evolve into UNPROFOR 2 and full-scale involvement in Bosnia, the Security council extended UNPROFOR's mandate on 8 June 1992.[113] The Council voted to deploy military observers in Sarajevo to supervise the withdrawal of heavy weapons from the city and the surrounding area. This was considered the first necessary step in a process which would eventually see the UN take over control of Sarajevo airport and secure it for the delivery of humanitarian aid.[114] A four-part plan involved the eventual deployment of a battalion which would become 'Sector 5' of UNPROFOR. It further stipulated that fulfillment of the mandate was contingent on the continuation of a ceasefire.[115] Progress toward implementation of the new mandate was slow due, in large part, to the lack of cooperation from the parties and the fragility of the ceasefire.[116] However, after tough negotiations, the UN took control of Sarajevo airport from the Serb militias,[117] whereupon the Council passed a resolution authorizing the deployment of more peacekeepers to the area. Despite the arrival of more troops into Sarajevo the war and the humanitarian crisis continued unabated.[118]

The EC peace efforts under Lord Carrington were characterized by a series of brokered and then broken ceasefire agreements and his tenure as the ECCY's main negotiator finally ended amid some controversy. In the middle of 'on and off' peace talks, Lord Carrington negotiated an agreement with the Bosnian factions which called for supervision of heavy weaponry in and around Sarajevo by UN forces.[119] The Security Council quickly agreed to the plan.[120] However, a nonconsultative approach by Lord Carrington and the rapid response given by the Council led to a serious dispute with Boutros-Ghali and the Secretariat. Boutros-Ghali complained that the new mandate was not only close to impossible to carry out, but had been 'thrust' upon UNPROFOR without adequate consultation and without financial and other material commitments.[121] Boutros-Ghali argued that the UN was already desperately overstretched and that it needed to pay more attention to crises elsewhere in the world. Eventually the dispute was resolved, but it had contributed to a growing feeling in the EC and elsewhere that an internationalization of peacemaking efforts and a new negotiating framework was necessary. Lord Carrington's role was phased out and a new international conference was established and based in Geneva.[122]

The disagreement reflected several serious problems facing the Secretariat. First, the lack of financial support for UNPROFOR and other peacekeeping operations stood in stark contrast to the international community's enthusiasm for providing peacekeepers with new tasks. Second, was the split in the peacemaking process led by the EC under Lord Carrington and the peacekeeping process carried out by the Secretariat. The UN was not represented at the London talks which produced the agreement which tasked UN peace-keepers with the supervision of heavy weaponry. UN officials felt that 'such difficulties could be avoided if the whole peace negotiations were handled by the world organization'.[123] The eventual compromise led to a new peace process co-chaired by the EC and the UN and an undertaking by Boutros-Ghali that future operations in former Yugoslavia would be carried out on a cash-before-delivery basis.[124] This new international focus reflected not only the greater involvement of the UN but also of the United States and Russia and the increasing interest of the Moslem countries in the Bosnian conflict.

Between March and July the humanitarian crisis in Bosnia had worsened considerably. Reports of atrocities in prison camps and widespread ethnic cleansing caused an even greater stream of refugees seeking to escape the war.[125] The work of the international aid agencies became increasingly difficult and dangerous. In one case a UNHCR convoy had 'to negotiate its way through 90 roadblocks between Zagreb and Sarajevo, many of them manned by undisciplined and drunken soldiers of undetermined political affiliation'.[126] Despite these difficulties, in a mid-May Boutros-Ghali argued that Bosnia, 'in its present phase', was not 'susceptible to the United Nations peacekeeping treatment'.[127] An attack on a UN aid convoy heading for the besieged town of Goradze at the end of July shifted international opinion toward taking more concerted action in Bosnia.[128] The stalemated peacemaking process served to fan the flames of increasingly adamant demands for enforcement action.[129]

Under growing international pressure to take action the Security Council adopted two resolutions on 13 August under the enforcement provisions of Chapter VII of the Charter. The first resolution (SCR 770) called upon all states to take 'all measures necessary' to facilitate the delivery of humanitarian aid to Sarajevo and other parts of Bosnia. It further stated that all prison camps in former Yugoslavia must be immediately opened for international inspection.[130] A second resolution (SCR 771) demanded 'unimpeded and continued access to all camps, prisons and detention centres within the territory of former Yugoslavia'.[131] The international response was sluggish, however, even after an Italian transport plane bringing humanitarian supplies into Sarajevo was shot down on 3 September, killing the four crew members. The airport was immediately closed and remained so for a month. A week later, on 8 September, a UN convoy en route from Belgrade to Sarajevo was attacked by Bosnian Government forces and two French soldiers were killed.[132]

It was not until 10 September that the Secretariat presented its report on a 'concept of operations' for Bosnia based on SCR 770.[133] The proposal suggested that UNPROFOR's mandate be extended and the military personnel sent to fulfil SCR 770 placed under the overall direction of the Force Commander. The Bosnia Command, headquartered just outside Sarajevo in Kisljak, was subsequently responsible for Sector Sarajevo and four new zones each with an infantry battalion. Each battalion was responsible for providing 'protective support to UNHCR-organized convoys' inside its own zone.[134] The plan was approved by the Security Council on 14 September 1992.[135]

Although the operation was authorized under Chapter VII of the Charter, it did not (through the end of 1993) use force to carry out its mandate. As Boutros-Ghali argued, this 'new dimension' in peacekeeping did not 'require a revision of the peacekeeping rules of engagement'.[136] In this situation, peacekeepers were expected to negotiate local agreements and talk their way through the roadblocks which dotted the Bosnian countryside. Eight European countries agreed to contribute to and pay for the new force.[137] By early November the UNPROFOR II was comprised of 7000 troops from eight European countries plus an infantry battalion from Canada and a field hospital from the United States.[138] However, the full deployment of peacekeepers was hampered by lack of cooperation from the parties and the need to negotiate the specific terms of their deployment with Bosnian parties on the ground.[139] The most persistent and troubling problem obstructing both deployment and operational effectiveness was the existence of numerous road blocks, controlled by militia groups, which complicated access to many of the areas most in need of humanitarian assistance.

In the face of armed and often aggressive opposition, the French General in charge of the relief operation said, '[t]here is no intention to force our way through any blockade. It is not our mandate.'[140] He went on to say that the UN forces would use persuasion to get the relief convoys through.[141] But the situation was even more complex, involving, as one commentator noted, not just relations with the Bosnian parties but relations with the aid agencies working in the area:

> UNHCR supervises a system of local understandings between Serbs, Croats and Muslims.... UNHCR has to talk convoys through not three sorts of roadblocks but dozens. Imagine the further complications if the European task forces – the British, the French and whoever else comes in – take on ethnic fighters with their heavy weapons. It will take days, not hours, to sort things out. UNHCR believes it is doing a good job already and is exasperated by the thought of new troops interfering.[142]

Conditions in Sarajevo were particularly difficult. One editorial reported that the UN Force had accepted restrictions and harassment that were 'unknown' in other peacekeeping operations.[143] The report concluded by pointing out that morale was low because there was 'no coherent answer' for why the peacekeepers were there.[144] Another report suggested that peacekeepers in Sarajevo had lost confidence in the 'rules of engagement and orders of their Egyptian commander'.[145] In addition, the report noted that the UN headquarters was not guarded at night, the temporary UN civil affairs advisor had disappeared and the three main contingents – French, Egyptian and Ukrainian – could not speak to one another at the lower ranks.

At the beginning of October the Council passed yet another extension of UNPROFOR's mandate. The Council authorized the imposition of a ban on military flights in Bosnian airspace and authorized the UN Force to monitor compliance with this resolution.[146] The ban lacked the power of enforcement and by December 1992 'the US confirmed that Serbian planes had flown more than 200 unauthorized flights; by April 1993 the number of flight violations had risen to 500'.[147] After a particularly flagrant violation of the ban in March 1993, when Serb fighters bombed two Moslem villages, the UN finally authorized the 'shooting down' of unauthorized aircraft in the no-fly-zone.[148] However, this order was interpreted as a measure of 'last resort' and had little impact on the situation. Indeed Human Rights Watch argued that '[b]y April 1993... the destruction of civilian populations and targets was being accomplished by ground artillery, not aerial bombardment'.[149]

While fighting in Bosnia continued, the threat of the spread of violence to other regions in the Balkans, particularly Kosovo and Macedonia, grew daily. To avert the spread of war to Macedonia the UN took the innovative step of deploying a preventive peacekeeping presence into the republic.[150]

From the beginning of the civil war in Bosnia Moslem populations were slowly forced back into enclaves and the UN and aid agencies were regularly prevented access to these areas. In one of the worst cases, in the eastern Bosnian town of Srebrenica, no aid convoys had been allowed through for months. In an attempt to break the siege and get desperately needed aid to the beleaguered enclave, the UN Commander in Bosnia, French General Philippe Morillion announced that he would not leave the town until relief convoys were allowed in. On 19 March a convoy did get through, but subsequent efforts on the part of UNHCR to evacuate the elderly, young, and sick led to 'a stampede of evacuees, some of whom died en route to Tuzla'.[151] UNHCR was criticized for what was perceived as its participation in 'ethnic cleansing' and General Morillion was publicly rebuked by Boutros-Ghali for 'exceeding his mandate'.[152]

Although efforts continued to gain access to Srebrenica and other enclaves, progress was impeded by Serb paramilitary forces. The crisis prompted the Security Council to declare Srebrenica a 'safe area' and demand access to the town.[153] Canadian troops were allowed into the town two days later, but they were then subject to the same siege and Serb forces refused to allow either convoys or troop supplies and reinforcements through.

On 6 May the Security Council voted to add Sarajevo, Tuzla, Zepa, Gorazde and Bihac to the list of 'safe areas'.[154] Continued noncompliance by Serb militias led the Council to pass a resolution under Chapter VII to 'ensure full respect for the safe areas'.[155] The Secretary-General, responding to the request of the SC, presented a report detailing the new requirements for troop reinforcements and redeployments based on the new mandate. The report suggested that a troop level of 34,000 would be needed to ensure 'deterrence through strength' but that the mandate could be implemented, at least initially, with 7600 new peacekeepers.[156] In establishing and securing the 'safe areas', UNPROFOR II was tasked with deterring attacks, monitoring a ceasefire, occupying key points in and around the 'safe areas' and protecting the delivery and distribution of humanitarian relief.[157] In the end the 'safe areas' mandate was not enforced and by December 1993 only several thousand troops had arrived; far short of the minimum level needed to do the job. By the end of July the 'safe areas' were so unsafe that a UN Special Rapporteur on Human Rights reported that Gorazde had been 'bombarded by Bosnian Serb militia artillery for 18 consecutive days in June, which left one half of its houses destroyed'.[158]

More problems for the UN and UNPROFOR surfaced in September when reports emerged from Sarajevo which accused UN personnel of black marketeering and widespread involvement in prostitution.[159]

Peacekeepers were increasingly targeted by Bosnian factions, particularly Serb paramilitary groups, adding to the already great frustration of UN personnel on the ground. This targeting prompted some newly arrived contingents to take a tough line from the outset. Swedish peacekeepers arrived in Bosnia in October 1993. In contrast to other peacekeeping contingents already in the country who can spend days at a time negotiating through road blocks to get aid convoys through, the Swedes were adamant that they would not be pushed around. The Contingent Commander Ulf Hendricsson said, 'I have come to checkpoints where the soldiers refuse to remove the mines blocking our way.... I have told the soldiers if they don't move the mines we'll blow their heads off. We've always gotten through.'[160] He went on to suggest that other countries could 'learn from the Nordic countries how to do UN business'.[161] While respecting this hardline approach, one British peacekeeper commented prophetically, 'I admire the Swedish troops for their attitude, but they've only been in Bosnia for a few weeks. The question is whether their approach will work over the longer run.'[162] Several days later three Swedish soldiers were abducted by Bosnian gunmen (after negotiations they were released unharmed).[163] At the end of

1993, Canada announced that it was reviewing its role in Bosnia. The announcement came on the heels of reports that on 22 December 1993, 11 Canadian peacekeepers were abducted by drunken Serb fighters. The Canadian soldiers were put up against a wall and shots were fired around them. They were released later unhurt but the 'mock execution' renewed doubts about the safety of UN personnel in Bosnia.[164]

By the end of 1993 the international peace conference was no closer to reaching agreement in either Croatia or Bosnia. The situation was no better on the ground, where, according to the UN mediator Thorvald Stoltenberg, 69 separate cease-fires had been negotiated and broken.[165] The Belgian commander in Bosnia, Lieutenant-General Francis Briquemont announced his resignation citing exhaustion. He pointed to a 'widening rift' between the UN in New York and peacekeepers on the ground and when asked what advice he would have for his replacement Briquemont suggested the new Commander 'constantly remind those politically responsible about the difficulties in which they put us [UNPROFOR] because there is no coherence in their strategies'.[166] In a particularly damning statement he said, 'I don't read the Security Council resolutions any more because they don't help me.'[167]

## 3.3 Conclusion

The conflict in former Yugoslavia and the threat of its spread into other areas of the Balkans exemplifies many of the dilemmas facing UN peacekeeping. As one report pointed out, '[t]he proposal to send a larger force to Bosnia highlights the way the Yugoslav issue has been handled – piecemeal, *ad hoc* and usually too late.'[168] The difficult task faced by peacekeeping forces in the region was underlined by British regimental commander, Lt. Col. Bob Stewart who suggested that, '[s]temming from our mission, which is to save as many lives as possible, there are many implied tasks. The first is that it is a peaceful area. In the best case there must be a ceasefire. In the worst case, we ignore what is going on and deliver anyway.'[169] Beyond that, the job peacekeeping forces in former Yugoslavia has much to do with negotiating local ceasefires, maintaining and facilitating a network of contacts, and doing its best in terrible circumstances: tasks that are deeply at odds with the more straightforward military objectives of war-winning for which they have been trained. The difficult back-drop to the peacekeeping force in former Yugoslavia was the unwillingness of the parties to stop fighting, the growing power of local warlords, and a lack of a considered long-term plan for UN intervention made obvious by regular extensions in the UN's mandate and concept of operations in the area.

## 4. CONCLUSION

As the progression of these case-studies indicates, the demands on peacekeeping are compounded by increasingly ambiguous and difficult assignments. The lack of any overall plan or coordinating framework within which peacekeeping might fit has become more conspicuous. UN and EC efforts in former Yugoslavia, especially, appear fragmented, *ad hoc*, and minimally effective. How can peacekeeping evolve into an integrated and effective response to global crises? First, intervention of any form needs to be coherently and consistently conceptualized within a broad framework of peaceful intervention. Second, explicit links between peacekeeping, peacemaking and peace-building need to be better understood and applied by decision-makers and peacekeepers alike. Finally, the peacekeepers themselves need a greater understanding of their role in the overall intervention process, combined with better preparation to carry out that role. These issues are taken up in the following chapters, beginning with a review of theory as it relates to understanding conflict, conflict management and peacekeeping, and culminating with the explication of a theoretical framework for peacekeeping. The final chapters discuss what impact a theory of peacekeeping has on practice, drawing on the example of training.

# 4 Outlining a Theoretical Approach

## 1. FIELDS OF STUDY

The first three chapters provide grounding in the evolution of peacekeeping. The information presented was essentially descriptive. As was noted, peacekeeping is, at present, an *ad hoc* response to international conflict and as such has little or no conceptual basis. The purpose of the next three chapters is to develop a conceptual framework for peacekeeping. In order to begin this process, it is necessary to examine the general theoretical foundations of the fields of international relations and conflict management. It is from this background that third party intervention strategies and contingency approaches have emerged. And it is upon these two theoretical domains that a conceptual framework for peacekeeping will be built. While the present chapter will focus on reviewing broad academic areas, Chapters 5 and 6 will focus on bringing together this conceptual material with the descriptive information provided in the first three chapters. Through analysis of these two areas, a theory of peacekeeping will be developed.

### 1.1 International Relations

International relations is a relatively new social science. It developed as a discipline in the post-First World War era and its purpose was to study and develop ways to prevent international wars. Initially it assumed a basic difference and little connection between international and domestic activities and, therefore, its main concern has been relations between states rather than conditions and activities within states. However, over the last two decades the field of international relations has slowly broadened to include interest in interactions between international non-governmental organizations and also to include analysis of domestic policies as they affect cross-border and global relations. Several different perspectives have influenced this process: idealist, realist, pluralist and Marxist.[1] Only two of these, the realist and pluralist paradigms, will be discussed here.

The post-Second World War era has been dominated by what have become known as the 'realist perspectives'. Realism developed out of the perceived failure of 'idealist' or 'pacifist approaches' which dominated the interwar period. Idealism was seen to be discredited because its reliance on a concert of powers operating through international law did not prevent the outbreak of the Second World War. For realists the outbreak of the Second World War showed that wars could not be prevented through a concert of powers and international law. Instead, they saw an anarchical system where conflict was inevitable and, therefore, argued that preparation for war was the only way to prevent it.

Realism takes the state as its main unit of analysis. It sees this territorial entity as a rational actor interacting with other nation-states in pursuit of its own interests. Competitive and conflictual behaviour is assumed to be inevitable, and war is the ultimate tool for gaining and maintaining power. Realists often reject notions that domestic political, social, and economic conditions have significant impact on developments at the international level. The research focus of this approach is on developing and maintaining a balance of power between the most powerful states. This perspective derives its theoretical base from such historical sources as Thucydides, *The Peloponnesian War*, Machiavelli, *The Prince*, and Hobbes, *The Leviathan*, while in its contemporary form, realism owes much to the contributions of Hans Morganthau.[2] Although realism has not been the only perspective within the field of international relations, it has been the dominant one since the Second World War.[3]

During the 1970s and 1980s, a debate within international relations developed momentum and brought realist, structuralist, and world society perspectives into conflict. Most significantly, this debate has cast doubt on the realist perspective's ability to accurately explain and predict international interactions.[4] Even so, realism has not been removed from its dominant position in international relations.[5]

During this period of debate pluralism or world society perspectives have become more and more prevalent. This perspective, in contrast to that of realism, widens its focus from the nation-state as the basic unit of analysis to include the complex array of interactions at all levels within states and across national boundaries. Pluralists criticize the realist focus on territorial-based power politics as the driving force of relations between states, and suggest that this is simplistic. In particular, pluralists note the global and interdependent nature of economies and environmental problems which are beyond the ability of one state to control. Rejecting the objectivism and positivism of realism, pluralists favour a more normative approach which aims to develop more equitable and just world systems. Further, it is argued that actors, whether multinational corporations, grass-roots peace movements, or individuals, can affect relations at the international level and, therefore, must be taken into account in attempts to explain and understand international interactions, particularly conflictual interactions. Groom argues that, '[c]onfining the analysis to one level, such as the inter-state, is too constraining and so is a limitation to one facet of behaviour, be it economic, legal, sociological, or political'.[6]

Pluralism developed as an interdisciplinary, systems approach to understanding international interactions.[7] While this approach allows for a wider base of analysis than realism, it comes with its own sets of problems. Groom points out that one of the difficulties of the pluralist approach is delimiting the subject area; that is, defining a starting point, deciding what to include, and defining an end point. To overcome this, Groom argues that issues or 'themes' are appropriate starting points and 'the approach is to map transactions in a systematic framework'.[8] Burton, in his studies on conflict, takes the widest view arguing for a generic theory which uses the concept of individual human needs as the starting point suggesting that the denial of these needs explains the phenomenon of violent conflict.[9]

The pluralist perspective is based on a vision of achieving what are assumed to be the common goals of humanity such as human rights, economic well-being, environmental balance, and social justice. Its research focus, then, is in such areas as peace, conflict, security, development, democracy and participation, peace movements, and identity.[10] While realist perspectives look for continuity and balance in the existing order, as they see it, pluralists seek not only to understand the complex mixture of forces which act within that order, but also seek to change it.[11]

Although pluralism as an approach to explaining international relations is not yet fully defined and sometimes seems to lack direction and coherence, it offers a challenging riposte to realist notions of international relations.

## 1.2 Peace Research

While ideas of peace and war date back to the beginnings of recorded history, it was not until The Enlightenment that studies of peace were taken 'as a serious intellectual concern'.[12] One particular focal point for critiques of traditional approaches to conflict and international relations was the refutation of Machiavellian principles articulated in the classic work, *The Prince.* Machiavelli argued that violent behaviour was inherent in human beings and claimed a clear connection between violence and the accumulation of power. As was pointed out earlier, Machiavelli was influential in the later development of realist approaches to international relations. Wallensteen argues that Machiavelli provides a good starting point for the study of peace research because it was attempts to refute Machiavellian assumptions which provided a rallying point for those who disagreed with his views.[13] There are a number of influences throughout the following centuries which contributed to the eventual burgeoning of peace research as a discipline, and utopianism, in particular, gives peace research a distinct influence. However, it was not until the post-Second World War period that it developed into an organized field of study.[14]

Following the end of the Second World War, in response to the development of nuclear capability and the shift to a bipolar stand-off between two superpowers, peace research emerged concentrating on the study of arms control and disarmament and elaboration of theories of conflict. In particular, research focused on understanding conflict process and the range of variables which impact on its escalation and de-escalation. The emphasis of these endeavours was on bringing about conditions of negative peace (the absence of war).

The Vietnam war served to shift the emphasis of the field toward a 'new radicalism' where 'the focus tended to shift from passivity to activism'.[15] During this period ideas of structural violence and positive peace developed and the field underwent a re-evaluation of assumptions which had guided peace research.[16] This served to broaden the range of issues of the field to include such areas as development, economic dependence, ethnicity, and north/south relations.

Today peace research is a multi-disciplinary approach which finds its main inspiration in the social sciences. Some of the distinct areas upon which peace research draws include social psychology, educational psychology, social anthropology, economics, political science, international relations, and sociology. Peace research is distinguished from other fields, in that it goes further than 'conventional conceptions of international relations' and that it is 'conceived as an applied science' encompassing the achievement of negative peace within a wider framework which advocates positive peace.[17] In the sense that peace researchers are advocates, the field has a normative base which distinguishes it from traditional international relations, and utopian and Marxist influences on strands of research within the field provide further demarcation. Galtung provides this description of the task of the peace researcher:

> The values that can be derived and developed from the general concept of peace should be our basic guide to the future, not data from a highly unpeaceful world. Concretely, peace research should not only be concerned with the evaluation of the peace policies of the past, but at least equally much with social critique of the present (criticism) and with the presentation of proposals, even whole blueprints, for the future (constructionism).[18]

Overall, there are two basic strands within the field of peace research; one is centred on studies of the correlates of war, arms and disarmament and conflict theory. This approach focuses more on formulating a critique of Machiavellian thinking which still pervades much of international relations theory and practice today. A second strand is focused on what Galtung terms 'constructionism', that is, emphasizes the articulation of viable alternative social systems which seek to transform present structures. It is here that explicit connection between peace research and peace education and peace movements is most obvious and explicit.[19] Although differences in the methodology and focus of these two approaches sometimes creates tensions and debates, the dual-tracked nature of the field provides a grounding in social reality often missing in other academic disciplines.

### 1.2.1 Positive and Negative Peace

For much of recorded history peace has been defined as the absence of war or the cessation of fighting. This is a negative conception since it defines peace in terms of what it is not and the focus of research, then, is on the prevention of war. Galtung sees negative peace as 'the absence of organized violence between such major human groups as nations', and says that while there is not violence in the relationship there is 'no other form of interaction either'.[20] Based on this characterization, Galtung argues that negative peace can best be described as 'peaceful coexistence' Curle goes further and argues that negative peace is essentially unpeaceful and defines it as,

> a situation in which human beings are impeded from achieving full development either because of their own internal relations or because of the types of relations that exist between themselves (as individuals or group members) and other persons or groups.[21]

Here, Curle disagrees with international relations theorists and some peace researchers who emphasize incremental change within the global system incorporating first the achievement of negative peace and then movement toward positive peace. Curle favours a more transformative approach which recognizes the basic unpeaceful relations which typify even the absence of war and looks to fundamentally change attitudes and structures which limit human development.[22]

It is only recently that efforts have been made to construct a positive image of peace. Galtung, the first to use the term, defined positive peace as 'a pattern of cooperation and integration between major human groups'.[23] For the individual a state of positive peace exists when there is no longer any gap between a person's actual and potential realizations. Direct and structural violence, according to Galtung, are the cause of 'the difference between the actual and the potential'.[24] He later notes that the inspiration for the concept of positive peace 'was taken from medical science where health can be seen as the absence of disease... but also as something more positive: as the building of a healthy body capable of resisting diseases'.[25] Curle sees peaceful relations as 'on the whole doing the participants more good than harm'. In terms of interactions between states, Curle describes a positive peaceful relationship as,

> characterised by close diplomatic ties, frequent exchanges of political, cultural and educational visits, minimal restrictions on commerce and, above all, sufficient mutual trust and understanding to resolve without friction any differences that might arise.[26]

The approaches of both Galtung and Curle differ from Boulding's supposition that distinguishing between positive and negative conceptions detracts from our understanding of peace. Negative peace, to Boulding is an empty concept, devoid of meaning and therefore not useful. He argues for a definition of peace as 'not-war', a term he calls 'inclusive peace'.[27] This concept defines different states of peace from productive activity to peaceful conflict, to unjust peace and places this peaceful activity on the same continuum with war. In other words, to Boulding peace is partly defined by war. Galtung and Curle try to create concepts of peace that are independent of war and violence.

The concept of positive peace is difficult, if not impossible, to define because it represents a state yet to be achieved. In fact, it is probably more likely that positive peace represents not a state or an end-point, but sets of structures which facilitate constructive resolution of conflict and positive human development. In this sense, positive peace is a process or a 'means' rather than an end.

By utilizing the concept of basic human needs, Burton has attempted to provide a more grounded notion of positive peace. He argues that there are three categories of human needs: universal (called 'needs'), cultural (called 'values') and transitory (called 'interests').[28] Universal needs include physical needs (food, clothing, shelter, water, medical care), but also include psycho-social needs such as the need for security, for identity and for distributive justice.[29] It is assumed that the deprivation of these basic human needs causes conflict. The logical corollary then, is that establishing conditions which meet basic human needs is one way to conceptualize positive peace.[30] There are a number of problems inherent in the concept of human needs. Avruch and Black, for example, argue that because the theory is arrived at through deduction, it is impossible to determine operational definitions for the specific human needs posited. Testing the theory then, becomes problematic.[31] Burton, they argue, deduces 'his way to a general theory *from* these postulated needs' and ends up with a kind of tautology.[32] As Avruch and Black's powerful critique indicates, human needs theory has generated a wide discussion and debate which, in itself, has been useful. And the central needs of identity, security and distributive justice seem to have some salience in many destructive conflicts. Further, there is a large body of applied work based, to some extent, on human needs theory, which suggests that, despite its shortcomings, it remains a useful conceptual tool.[33]

Positive and negative conceptions of peace have affected the evolution of different perspectives of international relations. Realist perspectives focus almost exclusively on negative conceptions, while pluralist perspectives and peace research incorporate, to a greater or lesser degree, positive conceptions.

## 1.3 Conclusion

Groom sees realism, pluralism, and peace research (or what he defines as a structuralist approach) as having three distinct research outcomes. Realism leads to the strategist whose goal is 'order and stability based on balance of forces'; pluralism leads to the conflict researcher whose goal is 'legitimized resolution of conflict'; and peace research (structuralism) leads to the peace researcher whose goal is 'post-revolutionary peace'.[34] Although partly accurate, Groom's division still represents a constricted view which fails to take into account, among other things, the transformative nature of pluralism which works outside 'legitimized resolution', and the idea of provention[35] in resolution processes. Moreover, the eclectic nature of peace research is more encompassing than Groom suggests when he limits it to a structuralist approach. Peace research can and does tie into the aims and goals of the pluralist perspectives and the work of the conflict researcher.[36] The example which best expresses the difficulty with such categorizations comes from conflict resolution and Burton's human needs hypothesis. Both of these concepts are difficult to reconcile with a structuralist approach, yet both are concepts within peace research. Although Groom himself admits that the map he provides is primitive, he justifies his approach as providing needed 'navigation points' for the further study of conflict. The importance of Groom's point is in noting that whatever approach researchers take in studying peace, conflict and international interactions, the assumptions inherent in that approach engender a particular range of outcomes or conclusions to their work. This is not to say that the research is therefore invalid; rather, that it is important to be *aware* of the limitations of particular theoretical perspectives.

The rapid growth in interest and research outside of traditional realist perspectives is valuable particularly for the range and complexity of issues brought to bear on the study of peace, conflict, and international interactions. This expansion is also indicative of the value of approaches which tend to be multidisciplinary and which challenge realism's dominance in international relations.

## 2. CONFLICT THEORY

Every human being has long experience with conflict. It is an aspect of our lives which is taken for granted – something that will always be. Conflict occurs at every level of social interaction from the personal to the international. Societies have developed a multitude of ways of dealing with conflict, as diverse as the psychologist's strategy to help a schizophrenic patient whose psyche is in conflict with itself, a judge presiding over a case, or a United Nations official attempting to mediate a conflict between two nations.

Every social science discipline deals with conflict at some level in one form or another and there are a range of theories about its causes.[37] But, according to Deutsch, there can be distinguished several common aspects of conflict that cut across disciplines and levels. First, he suggests that most conflicts are mixed-motive, meaning that the parties involved have both competitive and cooperative interests. Second, while conflict can be destructive, it can also be constructive. Third, cooperative and competitive interests lead to two very different processes of settlement. Fourth, how strong these cooperative and competitive interests are will have a large effect on the outcome of the conflict, i.e. whether it will have a constructive or destructive outcome.[38] Burton differentiates between disputes and conflicts saying that disputes are 'those situations in which the issues are negotiable, in which there can be compromise, and which, therefore, do not involve consideration of altered institutions and structures'.[39] Conflicts, according to Burton, are associated with

> the kind of behavior on the part of persons, groups or nations that goes beyond the normal disagreements and confrontations that characterize much of the usual social, economic and competitive life of societies. Overtly it is behavior that is, or has the potential of being, destructive of persons, properties and systems. The issues that lead to conflicts are not the ordinary ideas, choices, preferences and interests which are argued and negotiated as part of normal social living. They are those whose sources are deeply rooted in human behaviors.[40]

So while disputes are characterized as the ordinary, healthy, and relatively easily soluble problems of living, conflicts are deeper and involve more energy, time, and resources to resolve. For Burton, conflicts are further distinguished in that they are caused by the lack of access to basic human needs. The most extreme form of conflict then, following this description, is protracted social conflict as defined by Azar.[41]

Azar asserts that most contemporary conflicts can be identified as protracted social conflicts or PSC's. He argues that these PSC's are 'identity-related' and occur when,

> communities are deprived of satisfaction of their basic human needs on the basis of their communal identity. However, the deprivation is the result of a complex causal chain involving the role of the state and the pattern of international linkages. Furthermore, initial conditions (colonial legacy, domestic historical setting, and the multi-communal nature of society) play important roles in shaping the genesis of protracted social conflict.[42]

He then goes on to argue that conventional methods of management, derived mainly from realist assumptions of international relations, have been ineffective in finding solutions for these conflicts and will continue to be, since these methods do not resolve underlying causes.[43]

### 2.1  Structure and Process of Conflict

In seeking to understand the basic structure of conflict it is useful to follow Mitchell's triangular model.[44] This model separates conflict into three components: situation, behaviour and attitude. A conflict situation is one in which parties perceive that they have mutually incompatible goals. Conflict behaviour is activity by one party which carries 'the intention of making... [the] opponent abandon or modify its goals'.[45] Conflict attitudes are psychological states or conditions of the people involved in the conflict which interact with the conflict situation and affect (or are affected by) conflict behaviour.

The process of conflict is the interaction between the points of the triad. Changes occur in the situational, behavioural and attitudinal aspects of conflict within the parties, between the parties, and between the parties and the environment. Escalation, de-escalation and conflict widening, according to Mitchell, are the basic dynamic processes of conflict caused by the interactions of the triad.[46] One fundamental driving force behind the dynamic processes of conflict are social relationships. Deutsch's 'crude law of social relations' argues that: 'the characteristic processes and effects elicited by a given type of social relationship (for example, cooperative or competitive) also tend to elicit that type of social relationship'.[47] Psychological parameters play another key role in this dynamic process. Glasl summarizes research findings on the fundamental psychological mechanisms which typify an escalation cycle:

1. Escalation increases projection mechanisms and is increased by them while the parties engage more and more in acts of self-frustration.
2. The conflict moves from the original issues to others, thus increasing the 'issue complexity' of conflicts, while at the same time the parties' cognitive capacity to deal with complexity decreases at the same rate.

3. The social complexity grows because the parties try to make others support their case; systems of coalition and alliances are built up and contribute to a generalization of conflicts – while at the same time parties tend to personalize more and more.

4. As a reaction to the growing complexity of the conflict, the parties adhere to a simplified model of cause-and-effect relationships regarding the conflict, where they see only one problem and only one main source – namely, the other party.

5. The parties expect the worst from the other side and prepare to fight it. This expectation provokes the worst of possibilities, thus causing the exact behavior in the other party that they should try to prevent.[48]

Conflict theorists differ in the emphasis they place on social relationship or psychological aspects of conflict. Those from realist frameworks tend to de-emphasize their importance focusing instead on specific tangible issues which can be apportioned between parties. In addition, they argue, that since much of the research into psychological parameters of conflict dynamics in particular comes from the interpersonal, intra-group and inter-group levels and not at the international level, from a realist perspective its usefulness is questionable. Peace researchers who work on conflict theory, on the other hand, tend to argue that understanding psychological factors involved in conflict processes are central to understanding and effectively managing conflict at any level.

## 2.2 Causes of Conflict

### 2.2.1 *Inherency and Contingency*

As with conceptions of peace, assumptions about the causes of conflict are basic to the tenets of different perspectives in international relations and in peace research. So, whether conflict is, at its root, inherent or contingent is a differentiation which directs areas of study toward different theoretical assumptions and which then produce different methodologies.

According to Eckstein, an event is 'contingent if its occurrence depends upon the presence of unusual (we might say aberrant) conditions that occur accidentally'.[49] In other words, although the conditions which cause violence may exist in society now, it does not necessarily follow that these conditions will always exist. Contingency theory rejects the notion that human beings are innately violent, although it is obvious that they are capable of violence. Manifestations of violence are adaptations to environmental pressure and would disappear if environmental pressures were removed. This is not to say that conflict would disappear, since some forms of conflict are considered essential or functional, but would mean that violent or dysfunctional conflict would disappear.[50] Contingency theory, therefore, assumes that it is possible to manipulate society and other environmental factors to eliminate violent conflict.

Alternately, an event is 'inherent either if it will always happen (e.g. entropy) or if the potentiality for it always exists and actuality can only be obstructed'.[51] The central thesis of inherency theory is that there is something about the interactions of societies and groups that cannot be changed and leads inevitably to violent confrontations. Violence, then, is a norm. Inherency theorists are in disagreement about whether violence is inherent because it is ontologically based or inherent because of unchangeable environmental factors such as limited resources.

Inherency theory postulates the inevitability of violent conflict as well as other types of conflict, while contingency theory postulates the inevitability of some conflict but not violent or dysfunctional conflict. The philosophical position of inherency is a basic premise of the realist perspective, while contingency theory is a basic premise of pluralism and peace research. As Banks points out, this inherent-contingent debate has been the source of division between perspectives for years, but notes that recently the social sciences have moved away from arguing over what may be an ultimately unprovable point.

> The main division between schools of thought reduced itself, in essence, to sterile argument about whether human beings are naturally conflictual or competitive.... All we can observe in practice is that people exhibit both tendencies. The proper focus for debate is, therefore, the conditions under which people are conflictual or competitive. Modern social science has sought this understanding which, I suggest

transcends the traditional discourse, and can give us some assistance in our task of looking at conflict resolution.[52]

Banks goes on to say that the dominance of realism must be challenged since its focus is not on the 'conditions under which people are conflictual or competitive';

> The most basic premise of realism stipulates that violent conflict between states must be assumed to be inevitable. From that premise it is logical enough to deduce that the chances of violence are reduced by preparation for it, and that stability will best be assured in a heavily armed world run by experts in the controlled use of violence.... The basic premise must be challenged if progress toward a stable and peaceful society is to be made. And that is why a pluralist theory of international relations is so important in the construction of a viable approach to peaceful resolution of conflict.[53]

### 2.2.2 *Objective and Subjective Conflict*

Arguments over the objective or subjective nature of conflict form another major line of disagreement among researchers.[54]

The dominant perspective, which is an essential part of a realist view, is that conflict is an objective phenomenon based on interests. These interests, which are assumed to be in short supply, take two general forms: (1) resources such as land, food, water, commodities, weapons, and modern technology, and (2) resources such as societal position and recognition. Based at its most elementary level on the economics of scarcity, conflict exists regardless of the perceptions, values or knowledge of the parties involved. The fact that there are resources which are finite is indisputable, and some researchers focus solely on this particular dynamic as the source of all conflict. Such a limited focus leads to problematic constraints. By assuming that conflict is caused mainly by resource scarcity, objectivists are forced to view the outcomes of conflict as win-lose or zero-sum. The three possibilities for settlement are total victory, total defeat, or compromise; and power is the decisive factor. In addition, Mitchell argues that,

> [a] further difficulty with the objectivist approach can be seen by pushing its major argument to its logical conclusion

and by recognizing that two observers holding different sets of values will interpret the situation in radically different ways.[55]

Most objectivists recognize the intrinsic difficulty pointed out by Mitchell and do take into account some forms of subjectivism in their analysis of conflict. Their main focus in studying conflict, though, remains the objectivity inherent in the assumption of resource scarcity.

Subjectivism takes a much different view of the causes of conflict. The basic assumptions of this approach are: (1) that conflict may have originally been over objective interests but as time goes by these interests are perceived and valued differently by the opposing parties, (2) that the selection of interests itself is a subjective experience based on societal values, (3) that societal values and the cost assessment of those values are constantly changing and therefore are independent of social structures and institutions, and (4) that goal incompatibility must be perceived by the parties involved, otherwise conflict does not exist.

In a subjectivist formulation the definition of 'values' becomes central. Subjectivists suggest that there are certain societal values which are more easily changeable than others. This leads to the conclusion that a pivotal part of the process of ending conflict is understanding the different weight given to a particular value for each party involved in the conflict. In addition, subjectivists argue that it is possible for values to have unlimited supply. In other words, contrary to the objectivist formulation which defines societal values as a limited resource, subjectivists claim that some values can increase in supply as parties in conflict learn to cooperate with each other. An example often used is security, which, according to subjectivists, increases as each side perceives that its level of security has increased.

However, no matter how much certain values are increased, many conflicts are likely to retain some basic goal incompatibility. It is here that it becomes apparent that subjectivist arguments contain elements of objectivism. This is pointed out by Mitchell when he suggests that it is possible to determine as objective fact that at a certain point in time a particular party has certain goals and values.[56] Mitchell then argues that while conflict might be 'objective' at one particular point in time, changes in the parties' aims, calculations, preferences and evaluations that occur over a period of time, render it changeable and hence an intensely subjective phenomenon.[57]

Because values are not seen to be in short supply, and that ultimately it is these values that are the source of conflict, subjectivists argue that they are able to expand the range of the possible outcomes of conflict beyond the win-lose formulation of the objectivists to a win-win or non-zero-sum formulation. Burton suggests that,

> What we should be exploring is whether conflict which is perceived as having a gain or loss outcome can be transformed into conflict that appears to have a positive outcome for all parties by re-examination of perceptions, goals and costs.[58]

It may seem from this discussion that there is a strict dichotomy separating objectivist and subjectivist approaches. This is not necessarily the case, and many researchers have found it most useful to analyze conflict utilizing a combination of the two arguments. Mitchell uses this approach when he adopts a triadic structure for studying conflict.[59] Fisher suggests the utility of such a method of analysis when arguing for a contingency form of third party intervention.[60] Deutsch makes this point when discussing the subjective features of conflict resolution.[61]

## 2.3 Conclusion

In general, these debates over the causes of conflict carry over into realist and pluralist perspectives and peace research. But these associations are becoming less important at the international level at least, as realism begins to lose followers and as more eclectic approaches such as pluralism and peace research are adopted as better or parallel means of analysis. This is not to say that concerns with the root causes of conflict are unimportant. Quite the contrary: they are and will continue to be significant since they help to define methodologies. It is only to say that these basic premises are seen to be less important in the face of the more immediate and overwhelming demands in the present to develop effective methods for resolving conflict and building peaceful societies. In other words, it is less important where a particular method comes from, than that it works. This shift can be seen in the development of contingency models (these will be discussed at greater length in the last section here, and in the following chapter).

## 3. CONFLICT MANAGEMENT

Bercovitch outlines three basic methods of conflict management: '(1) violence and coercion (both physical and psychological), (2) various forms of bargaining and negotiation, and (3) the involvement of a third party'.[62] Bercovitch later modifies the third category differentiating between binding and non-binding third party involvement.[63] Mitchell lists four major strategies of conflict management: conflict avoidance, conflict prevention, conflict settlement and conflict resolution.[64] Of this list the latter two techniques will be discussed in more detail. What differentiates these four strategies and conflict settlement and conflict resolution in particular goes beyond the outcomes that they try to achieve. The strategies, mechanisms and skills of different types of conflict management are inextricably tied to theories about the causes of conflict (see Appendix 2).[65] As Burton notes,

Explanation and procedure are logically related. If, for example, international and communal conflict are considered to be the result of the inherent 'aggression' or lawlessness of states in an anarchical world system, then the appropriate means of management would be multilateral constraints, i.e., international institutions having coercive power and/or great powers employing power-balancing and deterrent strategies.... On the other hand, if it is held that conflicts have their roots in complex behavioral relationships, not fully understood, within and between nations, then analytical processes and explorations of options would seem desirable before resorting to conflict management by power or by modifications in authoritative control.[66]

Conflict settlement strategies aim to establish negative peace, that is, stop fighting or violence, and promote compromise, focusing more often on the objective aspects of conflict. Techniques such as intervention, imposition, conciliation, good offices, mediation, negotiation and peacekeeping are normally categorized as settlement techniques. Settlement procedures are all coercive in the sense that one or all of the parties in the conflict are forced to give up something they otherwise want for the sake of the cessation of fighting. This is not necessarily bad, particularly if a conflict is for the most part about material resources. However, in violent protracted conflicts such coercion may only prolong and deepen the situation.[67] It is possible that settlement can be a first step toward a deeper resolution process, although such a holistic approach happens rarely, if at all. Mitchell defines settlement as a situation 'whereby some compromise solution is achieved "splitting the difference," and allowing both parties to achieve some of their objectives, even if on an unequal basis '.[68]

Conflict resolution is a non-coercive third party intervention strategy that aims to facilitate a self-supporting, long-term end to violence within a framework that is beneficial to all parties. Burton defines resolution as 'the transformation of relationships in a particular case by the solution of the problems which led to the conflictual behavior in the first place. (Such transformation does not necessarily eliminate future problems in relationships, or remove residual antagonisms...).'[69] Laue suggests that there are at least three elements implied in the term resolution: 'the outcome addresses the underlying problems or issues rather than just symptoms or surface manifestations, it is jointly determined, and the process achieves at least some degree of satisfaction for the parties concerned'.[70] Laue suggests that the Camp David Accords were the framework of a resolution process.[71] Burton goes further than Laue and argues that conflict resolution processes are distinct from what he terms problem-solving conflict resolution. Problem-solving conflict resolution does not just involve joint determination or some satisfaction with outcomes, it involves understanding conflict processes analytically followed by the application of that understanding by the parties to the particular conflict situation. In other words, problem-solving involves a *particular kind* of transformative process.[72]

## 3.1 Third Party Intervention

There are many techniques of conflict management, but the focus here will be on third party intervention.[73] A 'third party' has no stake or immediate interest in the conflict into which it intervenes. Although third party intervention can be coercive or binding, such as with legal arbitration, it can also be a non-coercive or non-binding activity. Mitchell makes this distinction when he describes third parties as either 'intervenors' or 'intermediaries', where an intervenor has some power to coerce and where an intermediary has no power to coerce.[74]

Laue defines intervention as occurring

> when an outside or semi-outside party self-consciously enters
> into a conflict situation with the objective of influencing the
> conflict in a direction the intervenor defines as desirable. All
> intervention alters the power configuration among the
> parties, thus all conflict intervention is advocacy. There are
> no neutrals.[75]

Laue goes on to point out that there are three distinct types of advocacy. One is party advocacy, the best example of which is a lawyer arguing a case for a client. A second is outcome advocacy or policy advocacy, where the focus is on a particular outcome. For example, an outcome advocate who wishes to bring about the end of violence, pursues this particular outcome. And finally, there is process advocacy, where intervenors focus attention on facilitation of a positive process which they believe will ultimately help the parties develop their own long-term mutually beneficial resolution.[76] Party advocacy is settlement oriented, process advocacy is resolution oriented, while outcome advocacy can be oriented toward either. In the terms described earlier by Mitchell, an 'intervenor' would be a party advocate, while an 'inter-mediary' would be an outcome or process advocate.

There are several essential features of non-coercive third party intervention: (1) it is non-coercive and voluntary, (2) it involves either outcome or process advocacy through an intermediary, (3) it attempts resolution (this does not preclude attempts at settlement), (4) it is impartial (in the sense that it sees the conflicting demands of the parties from an impartial position, not impartial in the sense that a third party does have particular values and goals which are the basis for its work), (5) it changes the dynamics of the conflict situation.

## 3.2 Roles of Intervenors

It is a significant problem for the study of third party intervention that there is often little distinction made between different types of third party activities. Mediation, conciliation, and negotiation are often used interchangeably or are given quite different meanings. Providing a typology of intervention roles therefore is limited by a lack of agreement on basic definitions. It is important to recognize that how roles are defined (i.e what are the goals of that activity, what are permissible behaviours when engaged in that activity, what are the criteria used to judge when such an activity should be engaged in, etc.) can be traced back to basic premises about peace, conflict, and conflict management.[77]

A list of possible roles for intervenors includes: mediation, negotiation, conciliation, facilitation, arbitration, adjudication, consultation, peacekeeping, good offices, and enquiry/fact-finding. In this section terms will be defined which can relate to the activities of peacekeepers: mediation, conciliation, consultation, facilitation, and negotiation. Here, roles will be categorized loosely in relation to the sought after outcome of the intervention, i.e., roles for conflict settlement (mediation), roles for conflict resolution (consultation and facilitation), and a role that functions within both settlement and resolution frameworks (negotiation and conciliation).

### 3.2.1 Roles for Conflict Settlement: Mediation
According to Bercovitch, mediation is the most common form of third party intervention.[78] He defines international mediation as

> a process of conflict management where disputants seek the assistance of, or accept an offer of help from, an individual, group, state or organization to settle their conflict or resolve their differences without resorting to physical force or invoking the authority of law.[79]

Fisher and Keashly define international mediation as involving

> interventions by credible and competent intermediaries
> who assist the parties in working toward a negotiated settle-
> ment on substantive issues through persuasion, the control
> of information, the suggestion of alternatives, and, in some
> cases, the application of leverage.[80]

It is important to note the difference between these two
definitions of mediation as it explains why mediation has been
categorized here as a conflict settlement strategy. Bercovitch
uses a very broad definition of mediation which covers a
spectrum from facilitation (the least coercive strategy) to supervision (the most coercive or binding). In this sense, Bercovitch's
definition allows for the 'umbrella' term of mediation to
embrace conflict settlement and resolution outcomes depending on the strategy the mediator employs. Fisher and Keashly
conversely make a clear distinction between the two ends of Bercovitch's continuum. Non-coercive strategies produce resolutions while coercive strategies produce settlements. They clearly
separate mediation as focusing on substantive (normally objective or resource based issues) and aiming to achieve a compromise. Mediator strategies can be more or less coercive (thus the
distinction they make between pure mediation and mediation
with muscle) but must be distinguished from strategies which
aim establish a good process, i.e. improve communication,
understanding of the conflict etc., and do not aim to attempt a
settlement (compromise) but seek resolution. Here, Fisher and
Keashly's definition is preferred although this should not be
taken to mean that by default Bercovitch is wrong. Rather, this
analysis looks to make a clear distinction between settlement
and resolution and therefore between process and outcome. It
is quite possible, for example, for a mediator to adopt a non-
coercive strategy which focuses on improving process rather
than the outcome. In this case, though, he/she is no longer a
mediator. The question of how this operates in the real world is
not the crucial point for this discussion. Regardless of the 'label'
applied to a third party it is crucial that *they* understand the link
between the assumptions they make about conflict, and then the
processes they employ to achieve particular outcomes. With this
caveat in mind, for the sake of clarity here, some definitions will
be supplied.[81]

*3.2.2 Roles for Conflict Resolution: Consultation and Facilitation*[82]
Fisher and Keashly define consultation as a technique involving

> interventions, often in the form of problem-solving work-
> shops, in which a team of consultants works with the parties
> to improve communication, diagnose underlying relation-
> ship issues, and facilitate the search toward creative
> resolution of the conflict.[83]

This technique is far more process oriented than mediation.
This is not to say that practitioners are disinterested in achieving
positive outcomes, but it assumes that if parties can establish
positive processes including improved communication, trust-
building, etc., they themselves will find solutions to their problems. At the same time they will have established a framework
which will enable them to deal with problems in the future in a
positive non-destructive way. This is why the outcome of consultancy is resolution.

Facilitation is the strategy employed in problem-solving
workshops. A facilitator aims to achieve better and more
accurate communication.[84] This characterization is confirmed
by van der Merwe *et al.*, who say that 'the facilitator does not
suggest solutions and is primarily concerned with technical
rather than moral issues – i.e. the improvement of communication rather than the promotion of solutions'.[85] Burton gives
the facilitator a more involved and central role as part of a
problem-solving process. He says,

> A facilitator seeks to help the parties arrive at a common
> definition of their relationships, define their separate goals
> clearly, and through facilitated analysis, discover options
> which meet the needs of all. The facilitator is, in fact, a panel
> of four or five persons who work with the parties only in a
> face-to-face situation.[86]

The nearest collation of these definitions is one that views
facilitation as primarily a process of improving communication
but in such a way that the parties develop a greater understanding of themselves, of the 'other' and of conflict more
generally.

### 3.2.3 Roles for Both Settlement and Resolution: Negotiation and Conciliation

Negotiation generally means face-to-face interaction between the parties involved in the conflict without the intervention of a third party.[87] Negotiation can function within either a settlement or resolution framework. The goal of mediation is often to get to a stage of agreement between the parties whereby negotiations can commence. The relationship of negotiation with resolution approaches is less straightforward. Tillett notes, '[i]n most conflicts, the resolution is a necessary prerequisite to effective negotiation; participants who are in conflict, who oppose and distrust each other do not have a good basis for negotiation.... Negotiation apart from conflict resolution essentially represents dispute settlement.'[88] He also notes that it may be necessary in intense conflicts to attain a short-term settlement using negotiation or mediation before resolution can be attempted.

A third party may enter into negotiations with one or all of the parties to a conflict. Peacekeepers are often involved in this activity at a micro-level, for example, when negotiating with a particular party over an issue such as freedom of movement. Van der Merwe *et al.*, note that the 'essential component of successful negotiations is a balance of power.', suggesting that equivalent power reduces the level of coercion in a negotiation process.[89] Fisher and Ury suggest the use of what they describe as a principled negotiation strategy. This strategy is designed to mitigate against the problems of entrenched, extreme positions and a head-to-head adversarial approach to negotiating which, they maintain, is not productive.[90]

Conciliation is defined by van der Merwe *et al.*, as useful in a situation where 'the parties are unable, unwilling, or unprepared to come to the negotiating table to negotiate their differences.... the conciliator thus (a) facilitates exchange, (b) suggests possible solutions and (c) assists the parties in reaching a voluntary agreement'.[91] Fisher and Keashly offer a slightly different version when they suggest that conciliation 'involves a trusted third party providing an informal communication link between the antagonists for the purposes of identifying the major issues, lowering tension and encouraging them to move toward direct interaction such as negotiation to deal with their differences.... the third party does not propose alternatives for settling the dispute'.[92] Part of the aim of conciliation may be to encourage parties to make conciliatory gestures which will lead to further conflict management.[93] According to both sources, conciliation involves a pacification process and gentle persuasion which aims to restore severed communication such that mediation, negotiation or consultation can commence. Whether conciliation aims to engender a mediated settlement or a consultative resolution decides which framework it operates within.

### 3.3 Skills of Intervenors

According to Deutsch, intervenors working at any level need four basic sets of skills in order to be effective. First are the set of skills which relate to building an effective working relationship between the third party and each of the parties involved in the conflict. Here the emphasis is on developing trust and free communication. The second set of skills needed are those which will facilitate the development of a cooperative problem-solving attitude amongst antagonists. Third are those skills which contribute to a creative group process and to group decision-making. Deutsch points out that

> Such a process clarifies the nature of the problems that the conflicting parties are confronting, helps expand the range of alternatives that are perceived to be available, facilitates realistic assessment of their feasibility as well as desirability, and facilitates the implementation of agreed-upon solutions.[94]

Fourth, an intervenor should have substantive knowledge of the conflict including history and current issues. This helps the intervenor suggest alternatives that the parties may not have considered.[95]

Wehr suggests ten essential peacemaking skills which he considers important for effective intervention. These are: (1) conflict situation analysis/fact-finding, (2) empathy, (3) listening/active listening, (4) sense of timing and appropriateness, (5) trust and credibility development, (6) mediation, (7) communication, (8) imagination, (9) joint-costing, (10) crisis management. In addition, Wehr says that all intervenors must have credibility and neutrality.[96]

Honeyman suggests dividing mediation into 'five skill based elements' including, investigation, empathy, persuasion,

invention, and distraction. He adds as an additional requirement that mediators need substantial knowledge of the field in
which the conflict takes place.[97]

Katz and Lawyer employ a training approach which they
developed at the group/organizational level. Their communication and conflict resolution skills training manual divides
skills areas into six parts: information sharing, reflective listening, assertion, conflict management, problem solving and skill
selection.[98] During training each of these six areas is broken
down into its essential elements to be discussed and practised.
The overall aim of this training is to improve communication
by bringing about mutual understanding and respect. The
focus is not on content, since it is assumed that the important
aspect of conflict is communication and once that is improved,
content issues are much easier to cope with.[99]

### 3.4 Evaluating Intervention

Assessing the relative success or failure of an intervention
brings us back to the theoretical considerations which began
this chapter; for how we go about assessment relates directly to
the outcomes that we expect from the intervention. An intervenor who sees conflict as inherent and objective, would define
a positive assessment as one in which the parties reached a
compromise settlement. Whereas, an intervenor who views
conflict as contingent and largely subjective, would be unlikely
to consider such an outcome a success. Rather, such an intervenor would look for a process which indicated that communication, understanding and trust between the antagonists had
improved, and that there was some consideration of the basic
needs of each of the parties involved in the conflict. This kind
of success ultimately rests in reaching the goal of establishing
conditions of positive peace where conflicts are constructively
handled, and violence or coercion are not considered possible
alternatives. The importance of the relationship between
theory and assessment is suggested by Burton. He writes,
'finally we are led back to a theory of human behavior that can
put forward specific goals in relation to which assessment can
be made'.[100] Defining the terms of success and failure, then, is
crucial to the assessment process and can lead to very different
evaluations.

The exact configuration of a 'successful' outcome is impossible to determine. Agreement on the specific elements of a society which is peaceful is unlikely to occur.[101] The international community has agreed on some general parameters through such documents as the UN Charter and the Universal Declaration of Human Rights. Beyond these the definition of 'success' is difficult to enumerate. In any case, success should be seen more as a process than an end, since it is not possible, or desirable, to develop societies that are free of all conflict. Much more important is establishing institutions and cultures of conflict resolution that deal constructively rather than destructively with conflict. These processes are likely to be quite different from society to society.[102] Given this, what can we say about 'success' which is relevant to notions of positive peace?

Success should be based on the overarching value of positive peace tied to an idea of human needs (security, identity, distributive justice) and affected through a consciously bottom-up process. This benchmark of positive peace should act as an ideal or general vision, as a long-term goal, and as a guide for third party intermediary activity. More specifically, the evaluation of success rests, as Ross suggests, on three criteria: '(1) acceptance: the degree to which a solution is accepted by the parties to a dispute... (2) duration: the degree to which a solution is enduring... (3) changed relations: the degree to which interaction between the disputants differs (in a positive way) before and after the settlement'.[103] The advantage of this approach is that it can flexibly include both positive and negative aspects of peace. One problem of such an approach is that it largely ignores structural violence. This general notion of success must be developed further to provide more concrete benchmarks. The two crucial aspects here are: (1) that success be determined in relation to notions of positive peace as well as negative peace where negative peace is seen as only a preliminary requirement for success (this applies particularly to the notion of 'acceptance'), (2) that success be evaluated through objective but also subjective changes in the conflict situation (i.e. a more 'nuanced' notion of success). Developing measures which go beyond purely empirical objective fact-based analysis is the eventual goal since a more 'nuanced' approach to success has to tackle, *inter alia*, the problems of subjective aspects of conflict as well as structural violence.

### 3.4.1 Ethical Issues in Intervention

Assessment is a value-judgement and since this is the case it would seem important to focus on the ethics of intervention and develop ways to evaluate an intervention not only for its value-orientation but also for its impact on the conflict.

Laue and Cormick have developed an ethical framework for intervention.[104] Laue lists some key questions which he says intervenors must ask themselves 'at every point of their activity' covering questions about, whether to intervene, choice of goals, definition of target, choice of means, and assessment of consequences.[105] Wehr offers a five-point list which he calls a conflict intervention guide arguing that the decision to intervene must be based on some criteria.[106] Burton also stresses the importance of establishing a criteria for intervention, suggesting that intervention can be looked at as two separate issues, 'whether or when intervention is required, and the quality of intervention (including consideration of the relevant intervenor)'.[107] Burton then proposes the use of the terms 'restrictive' and 'constructive' to help assess quality of and need for intervention. Restrictive intervention refers to 'policies that intervene in systems transactions for some immediate reasons, in ways that threaten the system, and the changes and adjustments that would be made if the system were to operate freely'.[108] Constructive interventions, according to Burton, are those 'policies that seek to assist in processes of adjustment to change'.[109] By seeking to understand more fully these types of issues it may then be possible to develop appropriate strategies for intervening in conflicts and at the same time develop better assessment tools.

Lewer and Ramsbotham have developed a framework or set of standards for ethical humanitarian intervention based on ten principles.[110] They argue that each principle should be met before intervention is contemplated. They add that if the use of force is contemplated then additional, more stringent standards must be met. These principles could usefully be applied to peacekeeping both in terms of the decision to intervene, planning (including a coherent long-term intervention process and long-term goals), implementation, and, importantly, evaluation.

## 3.5 Conclusion

This discussion of third party intervention is not meant to be an exhaustive search of the field and its literature. The purpose has been to provide a broad indication of the general area and some of the main perspectives and arguments. Interest in third party intervention is growing, particularly from within perspectives which are attempting to build theoretical and practical alternatives to realist approaches. While the study of third party intervention has advanced significantly, it is clearly evident that there are no easy, straightforward answers to bringing an end to the serious international and domestic conflicts with which the world is faced today. In this context the problems of protracted, deep-rooted conflict often seem insoluble and the need to find coherent and effective responses has become overwhelming. Settlement approaches to conflict management which currently dominate are not capable of providing the needed response. The lack of success of these traditional management approaches suggests the need to try alternatives. One particularly hopeful alternative is an approach which brings together a variety of efficacious strategies under one coherent applied framework. It is toward the development of such a framework for conflict intervention that we will now turn.

## 4. A CONTINGENCY APPROACH

### 4.1 Contingency and a Normative Framework

A contingency approach to conflict intervention is based on the premise that all conflicts have both subjective and objective elements. In addition all conflicts go through an escalation (and de-escalation) process which is recognizable, and which, depending on the level of escalation, exhibits either objective or subjective elements more strongly. Evidence suggests that mediation is most effective in early stages of an escalation process when objective or substantive issues are prevalent, and alternately that it is less effective in later stages of conflict when subjective elements have come more to the fore.[111] It is surmised then that intervention types such as mediation, which focus on objective elements of conflict, will be more effective at certain points in the conflict; and intervention types such as consultation, which focus more on subjective elements of a conflict, will be more effective at other points. Furthermore, the utilization of different methods at different points in the conflict can be interrelated. Fisher and Keashly call this 'complementarity'. Working within a contingency approach, then, means utilizing an appropriate intervention strategy which has been shown to be most effective at particular points in a conflict process. This type of accurate knowledge is gained by in-depth analysis of past interventions. It is designed to yield empirical data regarding the success or failure of a particular intervention at a particular time.[112] The more that such information is available, contingency theory suggests, the more likely it is that optimally timed and effective interventions can be utilized.[113] The overarching goal of this process is more effective conflict management.

It is also claimed by supporters of contingency theory that it produces empirical evidence in a way that ideographic and prescriptive approaches do not. An ideographic approach sees all conflicts as unique, so much so that evidence of what worked in one conflict will not have any useful application in other conflicts. In other words, generalization or theory-building is unlikely to produce useful results.

The prescriptive or normative approach, on the other hand, begins with a general theory which prescribes a particular approach. Evidence is then sought to support the approach. Conflict theory which is prescriptive tends to focus on the need to overcome communicative and perceptual difficulties in conflict. It operates through the premise that once such barriers have been removed resolution will be possible. The problem is that little in the way of evaluative or empirical evidence is or can be produced to support these claims. In addition, because this method begins with a general theory which has an overt value-orientation, any evidence which is put forward is open to the criticism of subjectivism or the self-fulfilling prophesy. A further problem exists if the theory is based on ideas which are inherently untestable through empirical methods.

Contingency approaches offer a middle ground. Intervention success or failure can be seen as contingent on particular factors which can be analyzed. As Bercovitch *et al.*, put it, '[t]he contingency approach encourages systematic empirical research because it stipulates variables and attributes with explicit operational criteria'.[114] Contingency theory is an attempt to reconcile settlement and resolution strategies but maintain a distinct value-orientation. It then becomes possible to develop new methodologies which combine empirical and normative strategies as well as a range of other tools. In a paper discussing the implications of the end of the Cold War on international relations theory, Gaddis argues,

> My point... is not to suggest that we jettison the scientific approach to the study of international relations; only that we bring it up to date by recognizing that good scientists, like good novelists and good historians, make use of all the tools at their disposal in trying to anticipate the future. That includes not just theory, observation, and rigorous calculation, but also narrative, analogy, paradox, irony, intuition, imagination, and – not least important – style.[115]

There is an important caveat to this process. It could be argued that a contingency theory itself is a normative approach, and therefore any conclusions that are reached are value-driven and, in some sense, prescriptive. No empirical evidence, particularly of the type suggested here, i.e. analysis of past interventions, can be free of value-judgements which yield particular results for one set of researchers but which might yield quite different results if analyzed by another group of researchers.[116] For this reason it makes sense to be cautious when looking at the empirical evidence which provides the basis for building a contingency model. This is not to say that the process is not important. Indeed to decide against a contingency theory leads back to an ideographic approach. The need to find some way to manage conflict which is more coherently based on past experience, which is not just prescriptive and which avoids the dead end of ideography leads, with all due caution, to contingency theory. Prein echoes the need for care when he warns,

> Such models are based on the assumption that a certain strategy is to be chosen, given a certain problem or conflict.

But conflicts are not given: Conflicts are complex and dynamic processes, of which it is difficult to say what exactly the conflict is. The characterization of a conflict is a matter of definition; several different perspectives are usually possible and those perspectives are – especially in conflict situations – often incompatible. Moreover, the normative prescriptions, which link a certain conflict with a preferred intervention strategy, arc often quite simplistic.[117]

There are certain considerations which may lead to the choice of contingency theory above overtly value-oriented prescriptive approaches or covertly value-oriented descriptive approaches. It may be that more emphasis must be placed on ethical issues in intervention and methods of assessment than have been evident previously either in theory or practice. Overall it may be that a contingency process must be judged by what Laue terms a 'concept akin to "fairness as the basis of justice"'.[118] So, while within a contingency model approaches with distinct value-orientations may be used, the long-term super-ordinate goals are specific. This may point to a multi-tiered assessment approach, which can judge a particular method in and of itself, but also judge that method as part of an overall process.[119] This argument suggests that contingency theory does and should provide a normative framework, and ultimately that framework is driven by the values inherent in the concepts of positive peace and conflict resolution. To further clarify the point, a major value of contingency theory, apart from providing empirical evidence which may help increase the efficiency and appropriateness of third party interventions, is that it can take what is best from disparate approaches, for example conflict settlement strategies which may have an important short-term impact on a conflict process, and link them up with a broad, long-term conflict resolution goal.

### 4.2 Escalation and Typology

In order to develop a contingency approach, a typology of intervention strategies needs to be developed (see above), and stages and processes of escalation and de-escalation need to be identified.

In an early, now classic, work by Wright, four stages of escalation are identified.[120] More recently, Glasl identifies nine stages of conflict escalation, and he groups these stages into three phases. He then matches these stages to strategies of intervention.[121] Fisher and Keashly further refine this approach and establish four stages of escalation: (1) discussion, (2) polarization, (3) segregation, and (4) destruction. At each stage the relationship between antagonists changes significantly. Communication, issues, perceived possible outcomes, and strategies employed change over time (see Appendix 3). For each stage, Fisher and Keashly identify strategies of intervention (see Appendix 4).[122] While Fisher and Keashly's model suggests a linear definition of escalation, it is also possible to view their four stages as both time specific, so that parties in a conflict go back and forth through these stages, and non-linear, so that different levels in a conflict and among parties may be at different stages of escalation or de-escalation. The Northern Ireland conflict is a good example of this non-linearity. Obviously, a more refined escalation/de-escalation process needs to be identified. Fisher and Keashly are themselves aware of this, and put forward their ideas as starting points for more research, not as final categorizations.[123] It may also be pointed out that this escalation scale could be more useful for international conflicts, i.e. conflicts between two states, rather than intercommunal conflicts which are often much more complex, involve more actors, and exhibit elements which can be associated with protracted social conflict. Developing the model to incorporate more complexity perhaps making it less linear might make it more applicable to PSCs. Nevertheless, the stages that Fisher and Keashly adopt are based most strongly on Glasl's research and there is a growing body of evidence supporting the validity of his work.[124]

### 4.3 Why a Contingency Approach?

Four important reasons for making use of a contingency approach were mentioned above. It will yield empirical evidence where other approaches have failed to do so, it offers the potential for developing more sophisticated methodologies, it can usefully and coherently link what have been considered disparate approaches, and it has an overarching value-orientation which can incorporate a more nuanced notion of success.

Fisher and Keashly point out that with the increasing reliance on third party intervention as a means of managing

conflict, our understanding of those situations and our skills
for dealing with them must be improved. This is particularly
true with those conflicts which have become protracted and
deep-rooted. They sum up their argument by saying,

> The over reliance on one or another method to the detri-
> ment of others needs to be re-examined. In both theoretical
> work and practical application, a healthy eclecticism should
> be encouraged, with of course due caution exercised in
> regard to ethical and professional concerns. Within this
> context, the appeal of a coordinated and sequenced
> approach is increasingly apparent. The contingency model
> provides an initial picture of such an approach based on a
> rationale that accepts the objective and subjective mix that
> underlies most conflicts. The model also provides for the
> complementarity of a variety of third party methods, as
> opposed to seeing these as competing or contradictory. It
> therefore provides a useful point of departure for further
> understanding of pacific third party intervention and for
> ultimately increasing its efficacy in dealing with protracted
> social conflict.[125]

Other academic studies which call for multi-role strategies and
further research and refinement of the existing body of work on
third party intervention seem to support this claim. Rothman
argues for supplementing traditional intervention roles with
problem-solving approaches and offers a typology which develops his theory.[126] Ury points out that 'a significant opportunity
lies in coordinating, for any given conflict, the various existing
third party efforts – governmental, intergovernmental and non-
governmental – so that they build on each other's strengths and
compensate for each other's weaknesses'.[127] Van der Merwe *et al.*
suggest that third party intervention is part of a broader
approach to conflict 'where intervenors may have to move
between a variety of behaviors'.[128] Mitchell notes that 'in coping
with many conflicts, a wide variety of management techniques
may be simultaneously employed'.[129]

Finally, Azar concludes his discussion of protracted social
conflict by suggesting what is closely related to a contingency
approach. He says that conflict management (translated here
as conflict settlement) 'may be regarded as a necessary
preliminary step in the process of conflict resolution'.[130] Alter-

nately, conflict resolution 'may be undertaken through problem-solving forums in order to bring the parties to the point where official negotiations can be effective'.[131]

There may be other benefits. As an approach to third party intervention, a contingency model can then be applied to each type of intervention. For example, if it is decided that mediation is needed, then it should be possible to look at a detailed contingency model that could be used for mediation, peace-keeping or other types of third party intervention. Bercovitch *et al.* have begun to formulate such a model of mediation based on studies which indicate when and what types of mediation are most effective using specifically defined process and context variables.[132] This type of contingency model could be adapted for all intervention strategies so that a model of intervention would be two-tiered (perhaps more), i.e., a contingency model within a contingency model.

### 4.4 Critique of the Contingency Approach

In a preceding section the problems associated with a value-oriented approach were outlined and discussed. These problems, as Prein pointed out, can be troublesome. In defining a typology and an escalation/de-escalation process, these problems resurface. There can be very large discrepancies, for example, in how mediation is defined. As was previously noted, this can be seen when comparing the work of Bercovitch *et al.*, and Fisher and Keashly. These definitional differences not only reflect underlying theoretical differences in the specific instances which were just mentioned, but reflect a wider problem, which is the difficulty in creating a typology that is specific enough to be useful and which can be agreed upon. This problem is not likely to disappear in the near future. Some crucial definitional problems concern how one defines active and passive mediation in terms of coerciveness. A definition closer to community mediation would suggest that mediation is a non-coercive activity, while definitions such as the one put forward by Bercovitch *et al.* include coercive mediation. A further problem in creating a typology which accurately delineates intervention activities, arises because a mediator could act, in certain instances, more like a consultant (as these terms are defined by Fisher and Keashly). Although there are problems with the process of developing a typology, if this process is seen as a starting point, as Fisher and Keashly suggest, then there is room to utilize research to refine such concepts as mediation, consultation, and negotiation. Indeed, such a process of refinement is part of the work of Wehr and Lederach. They define a new type of mediator they describe as 'insider-partial' as differentiated from the more traditional conception of a mediator as 'outsider-neutral'.[133]

There is the further difficulty of how well a typology and an escalation/de-escalation process relate to complex protracted social conflicts. When attempting to apply intervention strategies, it may be more useful to look at conflict in a less linear manner. Such an approach could allow for differences over time and within and between parties in the conflict, as was mentioned above, and would provide a flexibility to work intervention strategies at multiple levels simultaneously. A similar type of conflict management process was relatively successful in Nicaragua, and may provide some interesting directions for further research.[134]

Finally, there is little evidence to support the use of consultancy approaches at the international and intercommunal levels. One of the main reasons for this may be that consultancy approaches are based on a high degree of confidentiality, and so it is difficult, if not impossible, to get enough information about them to judge their effectiveness as conflict management tools. As much as prescriptive theory leads us to the conclusion that consultancy approaches should be effective, if they are to be used within a contingency model, it is crucial to pinpoint exactly where and when they can be expected to have the most positive results. Some research at the organizational, community, and individual levels exists to support the claims of the consultancy approach, but how well it translates into the international scene is still largely unknown. This leads to the difficult problem of recognizing the need to find a middle ground between strict empiricism and prescription. While it is important to recognize the need for evidence which begins to tell us where and when different intervention strategies may work best, it is also important to recognize that some of the most promising work in third party intervention, i.e. consultancy, is not necessarily testable through strictly empirical processes. But this does not automatically lead to the conclusion that it should be discarded. Different methods of assessment need to be found.

Although contingency theory has a number of problems, it still seems to offer the best possibility for more effective management of conflict. In addition, there is a healthy inter- action between theory and practice built into this method which should not be underestimated.

## 5. CONCLUSION

In the complex world of international and intercommunal conflict, it is not surprising that a variety of management methods have been developed. But approaches have been disparate and there has been little or no coordination among them. Considering the number of serious protracted conflicts occurring around the world, an approach which tries to coordinate and target intervention strategies is important not only for how it might affect current practice, but also for how it might add significantly to what we know about conflict and conflict management.

With the increasing demands on the already overloaded *ad hoc* function of peacekeeping, the development of a frame- work of intervention based on a contingency approach is significant. The next two chapters will take up this point in detail arguing that the effectiveness of peacekeeping and other UN interventions could be greatly enhanced if conceptualized and practised through such a framework.

# 5 Peacekeeping, Peacemaking and Peacebuilding: Definitions and Linkages

## 1. INTRODUCTION

Peacekeeping, peacemaking and peacebuilding represent three distinct categories of UN intervention. Examining the links between these three areas of activity (with particular emphasis on peacekeeping and how peacebuilding and peacemaking link with it) provides some indication of: (1) the scope of linkage, (2) significant gaps, and (3) the extent to which conceptualization of the UN's third party role is needed to provide a framework which could direct and coordinate these UN activities. The following chapter then looks specifically at initiating the development of a conceptual framework for peacekeeping.

## 2. PEACEKEEPING

Because of its historical roots, peacekeeping has avoided institutionalization (see Chapter 1). Definitions which have been applied to peacekeeping have therefore been functional and descriptive. In this sense they focus on the general functions and specific mechanics of peacekeeping, from describing which jobs peacekeeping forces perform, to who is involved, to how operations are set up. These are labelled functional definitions here because they describe peacekeeping with only minimal relation or reference to its third party role, to an explicit theoretical framework or to a model of peaceful settlement of disputes.

124

## 2.1 Narrow Functional Definitions

Peacekeeping has generally been defined as a function in itself, with peacemaking added as a separate but related activity. Examples are numerous. Sherry coined the term 'controlled impasse' to describe peacekeeping, arguing that there are a large number of conflicts which are 'objectively insoluble' and are perpetually in a state of 'controlled impasse'. He goes on to argue that many conflict situations can only be settled 'from a change in historical circumstances, which in the long run tend to make irrelevant even the most intractable conflict situations'.[1] This definition implies that the main role of peacekeeping is one of waiting for history to make a conflict and the peacekeeper's role redundant. In a later publication Sherry says, 'peacekeeping is the reverse of military action: it is the peaceful application of a military presence in the interest of a political process'.[2] This definition suggests greater emphasis on the possibilities of peacekeeping, and such new emphasis makes sense considering political developments at the UN and the renewed interest in peacekeeping as a tool of peacemaking. The main function of the peacekeeper, though, is to ensure the maintenance of a *status quo*, or a controlled impasse.

Similar in tone to Sherry, James describes peacekeeping as providing 'a barrier against... unwanted war'. Norton and Weiss describe peacekeeping as 'an interim step – a stop gap – to buy time for active diplomacy'.[3] According to Holst, peacekeeping amounts to a confidence-building measure assisting parties in holding a ceasefire.[4] Russett and Sutterlin suggest that peacekeeping is a deterrent.[5] Coate and Puchala say that 'peacekeeping policies prescribe courses of collective international action aimed at preventing or halting armed conflicts'.[6] Finally, peacekeeping has been defined as an expression of the will and intention of the international community to prevent or forestall a conflict.[7]

These definitions, while describing some functions of peacekeeping, do not provide a functional definition that gives an adequate picture of peacekeeping as it is practised today. Namibia and Cambodia stand as eloquent examples. More problematically, these definitions fail by the lack of any attempt to explain the relationship of peacekeeping as a form of third party intervention to a concept of positive peace, as described in the previous chapter and as set out in the UN's Charter. Peacekeeping is a form of third party intervention aimed at facilitating the peaceful settlement of disputes; therefore, the question of how it relates to those principles is crucial. Even if the most narrow definition of 'facilitation' is emphasized, i.e. facilitation as controlled impasse, the centrality and importance of the relationship remains. And it is this relationship that is largely unexplored.

Peacekeeping in the sense of Sherry's definition as well as the other definitions mentioned, is a tool for the maintenance of the *status quo* largely indifferent to the deep-rooted economic and social issues which accompany protracted conflict. This point is argued by Simonia.[8] In some cases Sherry's determination may provide an accurate description of an on-going situation. Both UNFICYP and UNIFIL are examples of controlled impasse. But his definition ignores two things: (1) a conceptualization of peacekeeping as an integral part of a larger process of peaceful settlement of disputes and, (2) the activities carried out by peacekeepers.

## 2.2  Broad Functional Definitions

These definitions are distinct from narrow functional definitions in that they prescribe an active part for a peacekeeping force in facilitating settlement. Haas argues that 'one purpose of peacekeeping is the creation of conditions of stability and trust facilitating eventual settlement'.[9] This sentiment is echoed by Skjelsbaek who says, '[t]he essence of the peacekeeping function is to dispel distrust and incite a minimum of confidence'.[10] Rikhye, Harbottle and Egge go further and describe peacekeeping as a 'peaceful intervention, where a third party acts in the capacity of an impartial referee to assist in the settlement of a dispute between two or more other parties'.[11] While they use the terminology of peaceful intervention, mediation, negotiation, conciliation, etc. and exhort the prospective peacekeeper to gain 'understanding of the problem at the root of the conflict and of the human relationship involved', they do not provide these terms with a theoretical framework which would, in turn, provide direction for practice.[12]

The International Peace Academy uses the following definition of peacekeeping:

> the prevention, containment, moderation and termination of hostilities between or within states, through the medium of a peaceful third party intervention organized and directed internationally, using multinational forces of soldiers, police and civilians to restore and maintain peace.[13]

In 1991, the then Under-Secretary-General for the Office of Special Political Affairs,[14] Marrack Goulding, provided the following definition of peacekeeping:

> United Nations field operations in which international personnel, civilian and/or military, are deployed with the consent of the parties and under UN command to help control and resolve conflicts which have a clear international dimension.[15]

More recently Goulding has employed a somewhat different definition of peacekeeping:

> Field operations established by the United Nations, with the consent of the parties concerned, to help control and resolve conflicts between them, under United Nations command and control, at the expense collectively of the member states, and with military and other personnel and equipment provided voluntarily by them, acting impartially between the parties and using force to the minimum extent necessary.[16]

All of these definitions fall short of both the conceptual and practical realities of present day peacekeeping. The details of how such roles as facilitation, assistance, control, and resolution are to be carried out are neglected. Crucially, they fail to provide peacekeeping with a concrete link to broader processes of conflict and its management.

## 2.3 Conclusion

While broad functional definitions provide clearer explanations of peacekeeping, as with the narrow definitions their lack is not in what they say, all of which can be attributed in some sense to the technique of peacekeeping, but in what they leave out. The real difficulty in providing a comprehensive functional definition of peacekeeping is that as peacekeeping takes on more and more functions the definitions get longer, more general and less useful.

Although many of these examples point out the need for a coordinated and coherent approach for UN activities, including a deeper understanding of the impact on conflicts of these activities, they do so without specific reference to such an approach. As a result these accounts pose more questions than they answer, and continue, perhaps even deepen, the confusion about what it is that we expect peacekeepers to do. Do peacekeepers control conflict, deter conflict, maintain a *status quo*, act as a barrier to unwanted war, buy time for diplomacy, represent the will and intention of the international community, act as a confidence-building measure, act as a peaceful intervention, act as an impartial third party referee, assist in settlement, implement settlement, facilitate settlement, dispel distrust and hatred, help to resolve conflict, create conditions of stability and trust, additional activities, or all or none of the above?

The argument is not that peacekeepers do not do these things or at least have not done these things at one time or another. The point here is that not only is it not clear what peacekeepers should do and how they should go about doing it; but neither is it clear precisely what they actually do. This situation makes it difficult if not impossible to evaluate, improve, change, direct or otherwise influence their actions. For example, how should a soldier in UNIFIL or UNFICYP help to dispel distrust and hatred and create conditions for stability and trust? The mere presence of peacekeepers is no guarantee that such roles will be fulfilled, and again there is no coherent direction provided for carrying out those roles.

Analysis of peacekeeping by some authors has led to attempts to formulate a definition of peacekeeping placed within a system based on the concept of positive peace. Along with trends in peacekeeping toward multidimensionalism and interventions into protracted intra-state conflict situations has come a re-evaluation of the United Nations as the main international focal point for building a global society that reflects the principles embodied in the Charter. The realization that peacekeeping on its own will not be effective in helping to facilitate the resolution of conflict is growing. Simonia, for example, points out that definitions of peacekeeping describe how to maintain or return to the *status quo* and do not attempt to discuss or analyze peacekeeping's relationship to the underlying causes of conflict.[17] Similarly, Malitza argues that peacekeeping 'can win full credentials only in a larger structure including peacemaking and peacebuilding'.[18] Not only does the role of peacekeeping in relation to an overall coherent approach to attaining the ideals set out in the Charter need revision, but the roles that peacekeepers take on at the operational level need to be evaluated and reconsidered in light of such revision. The possible consequences of failing to take on such an approach are put into a more specific context by Formuth, who argues,

> Unless the benefits of the global economic system are more widely distributed, many marginalized segments of the developing country populations will have no incentive to cooperate in its security and stability. Absence of accommodation will cause major increases in migration to developed countries, a resort to radically nationalistic policies, further increase of humanitarian emergencies, civil and regional strife and greater suffering.[19]

## 3. PEACEMAKING

Peacemaking according to Boutros-Ghali is 'action to bring hostile parties to agreement, essentially through such peaceful means as those foreseen in Chapter VI of the Charter of the United Nations'.[20] The specific tools of peacemaking are set out in Article 33 of the Charter. It states that the parties to a dispute should 'seek a solution by negotiation, enquiry, mediation, conciliation, arbitration, judicial settlement, resort to regional agencies or arrangements, or other peaceful means of their own choice'.[21] These techniques are detailed in a publication produced by the Secretariat in 1992 entitled, *Handbook on the Peaceful Settlement of Disputes Between States.*[22]

It is by now historical fact that the UN's peacemaking capability was greatly reduced during the years of the Cold War. Like peacekeeping, the end of the Cold War has enabled the

UN to revive and revamp its peacemaking efforts. Although this is cause for optimism, some serious problems with peacemaking efforts linger. One major problem occurs in the timing of referral of conflicts to the UN for consideration. Almost universally, conflicts are brought to the Organization only after they are so serious that facilitating resolution presents a difficult if not insurmountable challenge. *An Agenda for Peace* tries to address this issue by looking toward developing the UN's preventive diplomacy and post-conflict peacebuilding capacity. The implication is that Chapter VI does not provide scope for effective preventive action.[23] In the on-going reform process at the UN, geographical offices have been created within the Department of Political Affairs (DPA) with the responsibility for information collection and analysis. The aim is to utilize this information to get early and effective action on situations before they escalate into violent conflicts.[24] The S-G has considered a proposal to turn the DPKO into the Department of Peace Operations (DPO). As part of this proposal the section working on preventive diplomacy in the DPA would be brought into the new DPO.

Peacemaking as it relates to peacekeeping has been defined as 'the negotiation for agreements on disputes, whereas peacekeeping is the implementation of those agreements'.[25] In the *Peacekeeper's Handbook* peacemaking is described as 'negotiation and mediation'.[26] Malitza gives this definition:

> In this light, war (open conflict) is synonymous with the cessation of all peaceful interactions and their substitution by a violent confrontation. Peacekeeping is the effort to stop that violence and peacemaking is the attempt to restore the severed interactions.[27]

Perez de Cuellar adds that peacekeeping 'can only be a palliative if it is not made to serve as a prelude to, or accompany, negotiations towards a comprehensive settlement'.[28] Further, noting the importance of peacemaking for peacekeeping, he wrote, 'experience has shown that the mere continuance of a peacekeeping operation does not by itself generate movement towards a settlement'.[29]

It is apparent that peacemaking and peacekeeping are being linked in the way described by Perez de Cuellar. This is confirmed by Boutros-Ghali in *An Agenda For Peace*. The cases of

Namibia and Cambodia are examples of the potential of such an approach. In both cases a detailed settlement plan was agreed upon before peacekeepers were put into the field. This was followed up with further negotiations on the ground by the peacekeepers working out the details of the transition process. However, problems experienced with the missions in Western Sahara, Angola and Mozambique are evidence that even if a settlement has been negotiated before the arrival of peacekeepers, this is no guarantee of success.[30]

Further problems for peacekeeping come with operations like UNPROFOR in Bosnia. For the short term there seems to be an indisputable imperative to get peacekeepers on the ground to distribute humanitarian aid to civilians. But like Cyprus and Lebanon, UNPROFOR was put on the ground prior to the agreement of a settlement plan. It is a disquieting prospect that the UN's mission in Bosnia could become another of peacekeeping's 'silent vigils'.

Based on the descriptions presented above, peacemaking as it relates to peacekeeping can be characterized by the following: (1) it is being used more frequently and, perhaps consequently, is being re-evaluated, (2) it has a constitutional base, (3) it involves negotiation and mediation at the macro-level between parties to the dispute and works either alongside or prior to peacekeeping, and (4) its main goal is to facilitate the settlement of disputes leading to the cessation of hostilities and the rejuvenation of positive interaction.


## 4. PEACEBUILDING

Peacebuilding is the third main area of UN activity associated with the peaceful settlement of disputes. Its relation to peacekeeping has received less attention than the link between peacemaking and peacekeeping. But as a means of preventing the recurrence of hostilities, reconstructing economic and social interactions and facilitating resolution, peacebuilding is crucial.

Boutros-Ghali points to the importance of post-conflict peacebuilding, which he defines as, 'action to identify and support structures which will tend to strengthen and solidify peace in order to avoid a relapse into conflict'.[31] Elsewhere,

Boutros-Ghali notes that peacebuilding amounts to 'rebuilding the institutions and infrastructures of nations torn by civil war and strife; building bonds of peaceful mutual benefit among nations formally at war'.[32] Evans gives a more detailed version of peacebuilding noting that strategies which aim to forestall conflict or ensure that it does not recur fall into two categories: international regimes and in-country measures.[33] International regimes which are 'designed to minimise threats to security, promote confidence and trust, and create frameworks of dialogue and cooperation' apply. In-country strategies include pre-conflict peacebuilding (a kind of preventive action) to compliment Boutros-Ghali's notion of post-conflict peacebuilding. These strategies focus on economic development and institution building.

Offering a definition with a different emphasis, the proceedings of the International Conference on Peacebuilding, held in 1986, said:

> Peacebuilding is a positive, continuous cooperative human endeavour to build bridges between conflicting nations and groups. It aims to enhance understanding and communication and dispel the 'wandering rocks' of distrust, fear and hate.[34]

Malitza describes peacebuilding as 'the deliberate and systemative build-up of interactions, dense and durable, initiating a state in which the resumption of conflict would be improbable'.[35] Finally, Coate and Puchala say, 'peacebuilding policies prescribe action aimed at eliminating the social and economic sources of tension that are among the causes of war'.[36]

The UN's peacebuilding activity is carried out by agencies within the system such as the World Food Programme (WFP), UN Development Programme (UNDP), and the UN Children's Fund (UNICEF) and by specialized agencies like the World Health Organization (WHO) and the UN Educational, Scientific and Cultural Organization (UNESCO). In addition, a large number of non-governmental organizations are engaged in peacebuilding activities, often alongside peacekeeping missions.

The need to coordinate peacebuilding activities with other areas of UN involvement is a growing concern. The intention to better manage peacebuilding activity is reflected in the emphasis of Boutros-Ghali's reform agenda. The creation of the Department of Humanitarian Affairs with its mandate to work toward integrated relief efforts, as well as the proposal to further rationalize UN missions by creating a Department of Peace Operations indicate movement toward prioritizing peacebuilding. In relation to peacekeeping there has been little coordinated activity except in the case of UNHCR and the repatriation of refugees and more recently in the humanitarian relief operations in Bosnia and Somalia.

## 5. LINKING PEACEKEEPING, PEACEMAKING AND PEACEBUILDING

The difference between macro- and micro-levels as they relate to peacekeeping was first noted by Galtung and Hveem in their research on participants in peacekeeping forces. They were interested in how the peacekeepers themselves understood their roles. Galtung and Hveem used a continuum measure of minimum role definition to maximum role conception. They describe this measure as 'located on an axis from *distance* from the social reality in which they [the peacekeepers] were embedded to *closeness* and involvement'.[37] This is a particular way to understand the specific micro-level roles of peacekeepers. Here both macro- and micro-levels will be employed to clarify the specific roles of peacekeepers as they fit into a broad process of conflict management. Rosenau's definitions of macro, macro–micro, and micro levels will be utilized. He argues that global pattern and transformations in interactions can be conceptualized along three dimensions:

the distribution of power in world politics through which states, IOs, and other key actors respond to each other (a macro parameter); the authority relationships through which governments, multinational corporations, ethnic groups, and other large collectivities are linked to individual citizens (a macro–micro parameter); and the analytic and emotional skills of citizens through which they respond to the course of events (a micro parameter).[38]

The following section will employ the macro and micro parameters as useful means of identifying different patterns of relationships between peacekeeping, peacemaking and peacebuilding. The following chapter will discuss in greater detail the macro–micro parameter as a key aspect of the conceptualization of the peacekeeping function.

## 5.1 Linkage at the Macro-Level

Peacemaking, peacekeeping and peacebuilding at the macro-level are described most often as separate but interdependent activities.

Peacemaking is the area of activity in which diplomats or specially appointed high level UN Secretariat officials act as mediators and/or negotiators in conflict situations. In relation to peacekeeping, peacemaking can (1) work in parallel with a peacekeeping mission, (2) provide a settlement package prior to peacekeeping and then continue involvement through the implementation phase (although at this juncture peacemaking is carried out for the most part at a lower level), or (3) work without reference to peacekeeping. The operation in Cyprus is an example of the two processes working in parallel. The peacekeeping mission in Namibia shows how peacemaking can define the shape of the peacekeeping or implementation process. The United Nations Good Offices in Afghanistan and Pakistan (UNGOMAP) is an instance where high-level peacemaking operated without peacekeeping. Boutros-Ghali lists some of the functions carried out by peacekeepers and peacemakers which contribute to peacebuilding:

> Through agreements ending civil strife, these may include disarming the previously warring parties and the restoration of order, the custody and possible destruction of weapons, repatriating refugees, advisory training support for security personnel, monitoring elections, advancing efforts to protect human rights, reforming or strengthening governmental institutions and promoting formal and informal processes of political participation.[39]

Peacebuilding is carried out by a number of different UN agencies, sometimes in coordination with each other, but in many cases not.[40] US Ambassador to the UN, Madaline

Albright, was outspoken in her criticism of lack of cooperation between UN aid agencies. She pointed out that the creation of the DHA, which was supposed to act as the coordinating body of aid efforts, had changed little since the head of the Department, U-S-G Jan Eliasson, had been given the job but not a mandate powerful enough to carry it out.[41]

At the macro-level peacebuilding is normally not linked explicitly to peacekeeping processes, although there are exceptions. For example, in Cyprus and Cambodia, UNHCR worked closely with the peacekeeping force. In Namibia one of the designated tasks of the peacekeepers who remained until independence was to write detailed situation reports for the incoming United Nations Development Programme (UNDP). Peacebuilding is considered a separate activity to peacekeeping, and although they may work in conjunction on occasion, more often they do not. The UNDP role in Cyprus is a good example. Cooperation between UNFICYP and UNDP is minimal.[42]

Experiences in Somalia, Cambodia and Bosnia provide less innocuous examples of how little coordination can occur between peacebuilding agencies and peacekeeping operations. According to one report, a UN technical team sent to Somalia to gather information about areas most in need, 'failed to consult the voluntary aid groups that have been working inside the country for months'.[43] The implication was that lack of consultation meant that the mission took much longer than necessary to compile its report, thereby slowing down the process of getting vital aid to starving Somali people. The resignation of the Secretary-General's Special Representative to Somalia, Mohamed Sahnoun, was reportedly sparked by Sahnoun's outspoken criticism of the UN's slow reaction to the crisis.[44] In Cambodia, the failure again of a UN peacekeeping mission to consult with agencies already working in the country resulted in massive inflation in rates for rented property. The rent-hikes compromised the position and work of those agencies without the resources to pay such high sums. According to some sources, if the UN had taken a different, more consultative approach such inflated rents could have been avoided (thereby also benefiting Cambodians who could not afford the inflated prices either).[45] Recent reports from the NGO Médecins Sans Frontiers have been highly critical of the UN and its attempts to coordinate aid efforts particularly in Bosnia but also in Somalia.[46] Among the most serious failures reported in Bosnia were accusations that the peacekeeping force used humanitarian aid as a bargaining chip and prevented refugees from entering UN-controlled areas because of 'political agreements made with the warring parties'.[47] An especially damning conclusion contended that, '[t]he difficulty of keeping the peace in the midst of war, a contradiction in terms, has meant that the UN's humanitarian operations have progressively breached humanitarian law and that UN troops increasingly violate the rules of war'.[48]

The effect of this peacekeeping activity on UNHCR's work has been particularly problematic, creating concern about the 'militarization' of aid and the loss of neutrality.[49] So troubled by the situation, the High Commissioner for Refugees, Sadako Ogata, was compelled to write,

> [e]xtreme care must be taken... to ensure – and to preserve the image of – impartiality, neutrality, and the humanitarian nature of UNHCR's operations for the benefit of refugees and displaced persons on all sides of a conflict.... Given these concerns, the closest consultation and coordination must be promoted between the peacekeeping forces and the humanitarian operation at every level.[50]

Adding their view to the debate, the International Committee of the Red Cross (ICRC) noted: '[t]he danger in the way the UNHCR are being compelled to work... is that it too often leads to "imposing" humanitarian relief. And once one starts to impose one becomes part of military action. And once that happens one is part of the problem, not the solution.'[51]

These debates clearly show that effective coordination is not yet a reality. Linkage between peacekeeping, peacemaking and peacebuilding at the macro-level has been limited both in theory and in practice. Effective coordination is difficult when there is no overall structure providing direction for activities.

The reality is that not only have the processes not been linked in any consistent or comprehensive way to each other, but that they have not been related in any concrete sense to an examination and analysis of the causes of conflict and of approaches to relieving those causes. If these processes are to have impact on a conflict situation, they must be driven by a direct, concrete, and coherent relationship to an overall conceptual approach to conflict management.

As has been previously noted, prevention of fighting to allow time for peacemaking is not necessarily an adequate justification for peacekeeping. The consequences of such intervention are serious but are not often considered beyond the acute crisis of the moment. The usual reasoning is that peacekeeping saves lives by preventing violence. This is commendable and important. The problem is that after the crisis has passed little effort has been made to test and analyze the results so that future crises can be met in a more effective and organized fashion. The new international context not only provides a political opportunity to do something about this, but is also generating situations which demand the development of such an approach. In the increasingly challenging post-Cold War environment it is vital that conflict and other crises are addressed more substantially than through the reactive, piece-meal approaches which are currently utilized and which are becoming less and less effective as the problems mount.

## 5.2 Linkage at the Micro-Level

Peacekeepers carry out activities at the micro-level which approximate the definitions of peacemaking and peace-building. This is not to say that peacekeepers negotiate comprehensive settlement packages or that they set up and carry out programmes of economic aid. But peacekeepers do negotiate, mediate, and facilitate, and they do carry out many humanitarian and other peacebuilding functions.

The definitions of peacebuilding outlined above suggest that peacebuilding entails several distinct functions. First, peacebuilding is activity targeted specifically at rebuilding economic and/or political infrastructure. So, for example, when peacekeepers sit on village roofs in Lebanon to deter shelling from destroying houses, rebuild bridges in Bosnia, provide security for farmers in Cyprus, construct roads, run a democracy education campaign and re-train police in Cambodia, they are engaging in micro-level peacebuilding. Second, peacebuilding is activity targeted specifically at reconciliation, or restoring severed interactions. When peacekeepers in Cyprus organized village meetings between Greek and Turkish

Cypriots attempting to rebuild trust and create an atmosphere in which the villages felt safe enough to leave their homes, they were engaging in peacebuilding. When political offices in Namibia organized weekly meetings between opposing political parties and community groups to resolve local conflicts, they were engaging in peacebuilding. Indeed, every time a peacekeeper interacts with a civilian or a member of the opposing military forces, for whatever reason, she or he has the opportunity to carry out this type of peacebuilding function. Third, peacebuilding is the provision of humanitarian aid. When peacekeepers deliver relief supplies in Bosnia and Somalia, they are engaging in peacebuilding.

For peacemaking the link is equally apparent. A Canadian officer points out that 'negotiations are required at all levels of the peacekeeping organization, for those both directly and indirectly involved, from the world forum of the UN, to the individual soldier on duty at an isolated OP [observation post]'.[52]

The argument here is not just that peacekeepers engage in micro-level peacemaking and peacebuilding, but that:(1) such activity should provide a basic rationale for peacekeeping, (2) peacekeepers are uniquely placed to begin processes of reconciliation and reconstruction as well as facilitate communication at all levels in the conflict-torn communities in which they operate, (3) a much more considered and controlled approach which would legitimize these activities is needed, and (4) in order to carry out these functions in an effective, coherent and testable manner, peacekeeping needs to be directed from within a conceptual framework of peaceful third party intervention.

Some argue that peacekeepers, particularly military peacekeepers, are not suited to such roles and that they should be carried out by other organizations and at other levels. But this argument misses the point. Peacekeepers already carry out peacemaking and peacebuilding at the micro-level in response to crisis situations and extreme need. Indeed, Norton and Weiss argue that, '[a] major justification for the force in southern Lebanon at present is humanitarian'.[53] The humanitarian relief operations in Bosnia and Somalia are further evidence that peacebuilding activities are an important, if not the major, justification for peacekeeping. UNTAC's mandate included a human rights component which was tasked not only with monitoring human rights abuses but with carrying out an educational campaign.

To say that such roles are inappropriate for peacekeepers is to deny what they already do. It also denies the international community and conflict-torn countries one of a very limited number of conflict management methods available to the UN. Not only does this contradict immediate needs but it denies peacekeeping's part, both real and potential, in a larger process of conflict management. These micro-level activities are the heart of peacekeeping. An approach to peaceful third party intervention which maintains a *status quo* without reference to the suffering of the communities involved and without concrete connection to a coherent and considered approach to the underlying causes of the conflict must be viewed with extreme scepticism.

It is apparent that theoretical work based on data gathered in the field is the kind of evidence that will be needed to provide peacekeeping with well-grounded justifications for intervention. Linking macro- and micro-level activities and recognizing, evaluating, and reorganizing the peacemaking and peacebuilding activities of peacekeepers in the field would go a long way toward ensuring that peacekeepers would have a positive and effective impact on a conflict situation. These necessary changes, though, will be difficult if not impossible to realize unless understood and implemented through a conceptual framework of peaceful third party intervention.

## 6. CONCLUSION

What would peacekeeping look like when placed in a broader framework? What implications would such an analysis have on the practical operation of peacekeeping? Would such an endeavour produce a useful conceptualization of peacekeeping? How might these changes in the conception and operation of peacekeeping contribute to the peaceful settlement of disputes? These questions will be examined more carefully in the following chapters. It can be suggested here that, thus far, definitions of peacekeeping have been inadequate because they have not been placed within a larger framework.

Moreover, it is the contention here that in order for peace-keeping to continue to expand in size, number and complexity of operations, a theoretical framework must be developed which provides a structure from which to analyze the utility of peacekeeping as a third party intervention and as a tool of conflict management. Because of the increased use of peace-keeping in protracted social conflicts, we need a more coherent approach to judging its positive and negative effects and developing its methodology to improve performance.

It is not enough to send a force into the field with a vague notion that they should be impartial and help to facilitate settlement. To act as a third party in a protracted violent, polarized conflict is an extremely difficult and delicate task. Diplomats, academics and others who have acted in the capacity of a third party are generally well trained, highly expe-rienced individuals with a good base of knowledge about the particular conflict. On the whole, peacekeepers have limited preparation and experience.

It is evident that much more work needs to be done to fill the wide gap between the practice of peacekeeping and the concepts embodied in the practice of peaceful third party intervention. As Boutros-Ghali points out, '[t]he authority of the United Nations system to act in this field [peacebuilding] would rest on the consensus that social peace is as important as strategic or political peace'.[54]

# 6 Developing a Conceptual Framework for Peacekeeping

## 1. INTRODUCTION

Conceptual confusion over the UN's role in the post-Cold War world is manifest. Boutros-Ghali has argued that '[p]eace enforcement must be an option, for diplomacy without strength will not be regarded as serious'.[1] His case for enforcement is argued vigorously in *An Agenda for Peace* and elsewhere.[2] Contradicting these arguments for the use of force, he commented during a visit to Mozambique, '[w]e need peace but we cannot impose peace'.[3] Perhaps most accurate was his comment in a speech to the United Nations Association in the United States where he said, '[n]ew and complex questions arise every day. We do not yet have the answers.'[4] These statements are indicative of a general confusion over how to deal effectively with conflicts like those in Somalia and former Yugoslavia. This chapter puts forward one option which might usefully be developed and applied toward the goal of finding better means of managing both potential and on-going conflicts.

## 2. PEACEKEEPING AND A CONCEPTUAL FRAMEWORK

### 2.1 Contributions towards Conceptualization

Along with the expansion of peacekeeping into uncharted areas of activity and the numerous proposals for further expansion, there has come an increased recognition of the need for more formal organization and articulation of specific guidelines and goals for the use of peacekeeping.[5] This goes further than specific reform questions. As Perez de Cuellar noted:

141

For the longer term, we need to speculate on where peace-keeping fits into the underlying effort to build the international rule of law and a reliable system for the maintenance of international peace and security.[6]

The former Secretary-General articulates the problem addressed in this chapter. That is, with the expansion of peace-keeping, it is necessary to begin understanding and operating peacekeeping from within a broader framework of conflict management. Goulding, in an effort to bring together the various strands of peacekeeping, proposed the following formula:

Peacekeeping certainly is evolving.... But I think that what is happening is that the species which has been called peace-keeping is evolving into a genus, also called peacekeeping. The genus will include a number of species; classical peace-keeping is one of these and there will certainly be occasions in the future when it will again be required. Large new composite operations, like the one in Namibia, are another species. There is perhaps a third species, namely field operations which have no military component at all.[7]

Harbottle has developed a broader framework for peace-keeping based on the concept of peacebuilding. He identifies three methods of third party intervention: peacebuilding, peacemaking and peacekeeping. However, he characterizes peacemaking and peacekeeping as forms of peacebuilding. According to Harbottle, when the peacekeeper's role is understood within this framework, as essentially a type of peace-building, then the range of roles that peacekeepers perform are given a basis for legitimization and, coordinated with peace-making and other peacebuilding activities, implementation.[8]

Harbottle is not alone in pointing out the wider implication of peacekeepers' efforts and the need to recognize the potential for effective peacebuilding carried out by peacekeepers at the community level. Nor is he alone in arguing that fulfilling such potential requires the development of an overall framework coordinating all third party efforts within a particular conflict and on a regional basis as well.[9]

Harbottle also addresses the issue of how theory translates into action. He notes that,

The typology of peacekeeping with which this Handbook is concerned is structured on the concepts of mediation, negotiation and conciliation being the precepts on which the soldier peacekeeper bases his initiatives for settling disputes and preventing violence – not relying on his self-loading rifle.... In essence, therefore, the theoretical concept behind third party peacekeeping is that the ending of conflict and control of violence can be achieved by other means than by enforcement and/or counterviolence.[10]

Harbottle shows clearly why peacekeeping is classified as a peaceful third party intervention, and points out that the consequence of that classification is the application of a particular methodology. He also argues that the peacekeeper's role is twofold, the ending of conflict and the control of violence. For Harbottle, it is this view of peacekeeping that should guide activity in the field.

Accordingly, at the macro-level, there is the argument that some kind of link should be established between peacekeeping, peacemaking and peacebuilding which is more substantial than has previously been the case. At the micro-level there is the argument that peacekeeping constitutes a peaceful third party intervention and therefore peacekeepers' roles fall into a typology of activity described in Chapter 4 (i.e., mediation, negotiation, facilitation, etc.).

As was discussed earlier, there are indications of growing support both inside and outside the UN for the construction of a framework for third party interventions (including peacemaking, peacekeeping and peacebuilding). Some shift in this direction can be seen at the macro-level of UN peacebuilding activity. Movement toward greater coordination can be seen in the establishment of the Department of Humanitarian Affairs and the creation of interim offices. Such changes are urgently needed if the international community is to make positive contributions to the long-term resolution of both potential and on-going conflicts.

## 2.2 The Ideographic Perspective

An argument often used against the development of a conceptual framework is the ideographic one. The ideographic position is that each peacekeeping operation is unique and that lessons, on the whole, do not carry over; therefore it is impossible to develop a conceptual model of peacekeeping. An ideographic argument is also used against the development of a theory of mediation.[11]

To argue such a point means that one can never move beyond the confusion and profusion of third party intervention methods which exist now and which, in many cases, are ineffective. It is simply not true that we can learn nothing about how and when peacekeeping is most effective by analyzing past operations and looking at the wider research field of third party intervention. For instance, Cyprus is often cited as an example of why it is important to link effective peacemaking with peacekeeping. Lebanon is cited as an example of a situation where peacekeeping was not the appropriate conflict management strategy. Western Sahara and Angola both provide depressing examples of the difficulties in implementing pre-negotiated settlement packages, whereas UNTAG is an example of the successful implementation of a pre-negotiated settlement package. All these examples should provide lessons for on-going and future operations.

The ideographic approach does not hold up at another level. The principles which form the basis for the use of peacekeeping provide a skeletal conceptual framework which has carried over from mission to mission and which defines the concept of peacekeeping. If each operation were so individual as to hold no useful information for others, then it would also be the case that these basic principles would not have retained their salience seen in the continued application of operations based on consent, impartiality and the non-use of force.

Ultimately, though, it is the need to develop a more effective means for dealing with conflicts which provides the main argument against ideography and for the conceptualization of peacekeeping. A conceptual approach provides the means to test and select strategies and to develop complementarity between and among those strategies. The work of Bercovitch *et al.*, and Fisher and Keashly, provide examples of the utility and importance of the conceptualization process and the information it produces.[12]

## 2.3 Peacekeeping as a Form of Third Party Intervention

### 2.3.1 The Rationale of Third Party Intervention: Settlement and Resolution

In Chapter 4 the concept of third party intervention was discussed at some length. The concepts of positive and negative peace, conflict settlement and conflict resolution were defined and a typology was introduced. The question asked in this section is where does peacekeeping fit into the concept of third party intervention?

Definitions of peacekeeping suggest that it can be seen both as a conflict settlement and as a conflict resolution activity (see Chapter 5). The case-studies illustrate this point. In Cyprus peacekeepers' activities have been, in large part, directed toward the maintenance of a status quo situation; a conflict settlement strategy. Similarly, the humanitarian mission in Bosnia while negotiations on partition take place in Geneva reflects a settlement strategy. In Namibia, the information campaign associated with the elections and the wider settlement process, and particularly the work of the political offices in facilitating talks between rival political parties demonstrates attempts to improve communication and understanding between groups and to promote positive relationships. This kind of activity is more strongly associated with conflict resolution than conflict settlement. As these case studies indicate, peacekeeping is in a unique position since it displays elements which can be associated with both conflict management styles.

Multidimensional peacekeeping, as exemplified by UNTAG, can be seen as a strategy which is more closely related to conflict resolution; while classical peacekeeping, as exemplified by UNFICYP, is more closely related to conflict settlement strategies. As has been argued, the increased use of multidimensional peacekeeping parallels the more active involvement of the UN and peacekeeping forces in protracted social conflicts. In addition it is apparent that multidimensional operations exhibit elements of both types of third party activity. The crucial difference between classical and multidimensional peacekeeping is more a matter of degree and of concerted organization. In multidimensional operations third party roles associated with resolution strategies appear to be taken on more explicitly, often sanctioned or initiated from above, while in classical peace-keeping, such roles appear to occur by individual initiative and haphazardly rather than through any strategic planning and specific implementation. The 'Code of Conduct' initiated in the SRSG's office in Namibia was a national strategy. The community meetings organized by Harbottle in Cyprus, on the other hand, were initiated and implemented locally.

It seems likely that this split in roles coincides with the number of civilians involved in an operation versus the number of military. That is to say, multidimensional operations have a much higher percentage of civilians who appear to take on resolution roles more easily than their military counterparts, who tend to focus exclusively on settlement strategies, in particular on the maintenance of a ceasefire.

When considering the evolution of international conflict, it appears that a combination of conflict resolution and conflict settlement strategies is most effective.[13] Peacekeeping as an intervention strategy is capable of utilizing both resolution and settlement techniques as multidimensional operations have shown. How these strategies can be most efficaciously combined and which roles most effectively achieve the aims of each strategy are matters which warrant further study.

### 2.3.2 Problems Caused by Expansion of the Third Party Role

The development of the third party role of peacekeeping is a response to the need for new management strategies for protracted social conflict. This section will argue that there are serious repercussions for peacekeeping associated with its development. Attempts to address the problem of finding more effective ways of dealing with international conflict can be seen in the application of multidimensional peacekeeping. While these activities are commendable, the sheer size and complexity of the resulting operations produces huge challenges. These challenges ensure that such an approach to peacekeeping, operated in isolation and without reference to theoretical developments and analysis, is unlikely to achieve more than short-term alleviation. This conclusion rests on the assumption that the international community as a whole and the UN in particular, wish to find more effective ways of resolving the numerous on-going conflicts or have the wherewithal to take specific action. The claim here is that peacekeepers have demonstrated that peacemaking and peacebuilding carried out by peacekeepers at the micro-level and in relatively uncomplicated circumstances can work. The problem now is that in order to apply this experience to more serious intercommunal conflict through the use of larger and more complex operations, a conceptual framework must be developed within which activity can be guided and results can be assessed. The consequences of failing to take this necessity seriously are seen in Cyprus, Lebanon, Angola, former-Yugoslavia, Mozambique, and Somalia.

The multiplicity of roles and the expansion of the concept of peacekeeping has created some difficult problems. First, there is the difficulty of the shift in attitude and specific skill requirements inherent in taking up a third party role. Problems in this area are particularly acute for military personnel but affect civilians as well. As Skjelsbaek argues,

> Soldiers in peacekeeping forces face a double challenge. In order to have respect of the armed forces of the adversaries, the parties to the conflict, they must demonstrate military competence... on the other hand, non-military methods like dissuasion, persuasion, and negotiation constitute the essence of peacekeeping. [14]

Moreover, peacekeeping lacks clear and specific meta-goals which would not only link peacekeeping to other interventions, but would provide much needed direction for the peacekeepers on the ground. Such linkage would make it more likely that the peacekeepers themselves would understand their significance and place as part of an intervention. Further, peacekeepers could be trained not just for specific skills related to their technical jobs, but for more general skills related to carrying out their jobs in the peacekeeping environment.

A significant problem exists with the concept of linking peacekeeping and peacemaking to induce conflict management. According to Bercovitch *et al.*, mediation by leaders of international organizations has a 4 per cent rate of success.[15] They suggest this result may be caused by 'the more limited resources of international organizations compared to governments, but may indicate the greater intractability of disputes that are referred to leaders of international organizations'.[16] Haas's results seem to support this claim.[17] In addition, conflicts of long duration and high intensity are less amenable to mediation.[18] These findings do not inspire confidence in the effectiveness of linking peacemaking and peacekeeping. For protracted social conflicts to be resolved, peacebuilding has to become a central element in the management process, a point which is argued by Azar.[19] Roles taken on without reference to the central importance of peacebuilding and conflict resolution may provide short-term halts to fighting, but are very unlikely to affect a long-term peaceful relationship.

Finally, a major problem with the expansion of peacekeeping centres on the decision to intervene. Thus far it has been an implicit assumption of peacekeeping and those who authorize it that such an approach is right. But is it?

Miall's recent study which looked at 81 conflicts between 1945 and 1985 concludes that the UN is more successful in dealing with inter-state than intra-state disputes, and that it is ill-equipped to cope with internal disputes and conflicts where intangibles such as value differences are primary causes of the problems. He goes on to say that diplomats, while good at negotiating territory and resource conflicts, are not as successful at negotiating when basic values are at stake.[20] If this conclusion were applied to peacekeeping, as it is currently practised, the UN might be advised to stay out of conflicts such as Lebanon, Western Sahara, Somalia and former Yugoslavia.[21]

Along the same lines as Miall's results, but in relation to peacekeeping, Diehl argues that the UN has more success in inter-state rather than intra-state conflicts.[22] Moreover, he points out that peacekeeping used in any context requires a value-judgement. He concludes,

> we have seemed to imply that no peacekeeping operation is better than an unsuccessful one. But, is this really correct? If peacekeeping can halt the fighting and stop bloodshed, even for a short time, is this enough to justify a peacekeeping operation? The answer requires a value judgement.[23]

It is quite possible that in the absence of reference to a specific, broad framework of conflict resolution the value judgements implicit in decisions made by the UN to intervene were inappropriate for the particular conflict situation in question. Weber makes this argument when he writes,

Difficulties with the very concept of peacekeeping go beyond even those questions of the politics of international law to politico-philosophical issues that question the validity of the peacekeeping idea itself. The very act of suppressing violence, it has been argued, can have negative consequences. Peacekeeping without peacemaking and peacebuilding 'may generate even more unmanageable conflicts later on'.[24]

Galtung reaches similar conclusions to those of Miall, but his work is specifically related to peacekeeping in its role of the 'fire brigade'. He argues that

A good case can be made for peacekeeping in a horizontal conflict, in a conflict between equals with no element of dominance.... In these few cases peacekeeping cannot, deliberately or not, be a means to maintain a dominance structure; it is truly a third party. But if it intervenes and freezes a *status quo* in a vertical conflict between periphery and center, then, whether wanting to or not, it is simply a party to the conflict siding objectively with the side most interested in preserving the *status quo*.[25]

Applying Galtung's conclusions would result in the very limited use of peacekeeping. However, Galtung argues that if peacekeepers also took on some of the roles of peacemaking and peacebuilding, then the dangers of intervening in vertical conflicts would be mitigated.[26]

The point is not to argue against any use of peacekeeping, but rather to note that the assumptions upon which its use is based may not be sound. Whether or not this is the case is an argument which cannot yet be made. Although some studies have been carried out, evidence is sparse. For example, apart from the studies just mentioned, in Chapter 2 a number of different studies yielding different results on what leads to successful peacekeeping were presented. Such evidence is enough only to point out how much more work needs to be done. The rest of this chapter turns its attention to developing a means to improve decision-making and implementation processes.

## 3. PEACEKEEPING IN A CONTINGENCY MODEL

The purpose of the previous sections was to highlight the need for a conceptual framework for peacekeeping. This section will try to develop such a framework for peacekeeping, relying for the most part on third party intervention literature. To this end, this section will examine the implications of viewing the third party role of peacekeeping from within the framework of a contingency model. The model which will be the basis for this discussion is the one formulated by Fisher and Keashly and examined in Chapter 4. Fisher and Keashly's model can be compared in some ways with the trilateral activities of the UN – peacekeeping, peacemaking and peacebuilding, where peacemaking is roughly equivalent to mediation, and peacebuilding can be seen as a broader version of consultancy, or more accurately, consultancy can be seen as one aspect of peacebuilding. This relationship is pointed out to suggest that the UN has many of the tools required to utilize a contingency model, and also has considerable experience.

### 3.1 Peacekeeping in the Escalation Sequence: Stage Four

According to Fisher and Keashly, peacekeeping is used only after a conflict has escalated to STAGE 4 when a conflict is defined as destructive (see Appendix 4). This is an obvious, but crucial point. Once conflicts reach the destructive stage, they become much more difficult to manage and require not only skilful peacemaking and peacekeeping, but also peacebuilding measures to promote effective management.[27] Peacekeeping without appropriate coordination with other interventions and without the will and direction to contribute to a management process beyond violence control will face insurmountable odds in achieving anything beyond a *status quo.*

Peacekeeping when operating from the rationale of a contingency model can be visualized in a two-tiered approach, with peacekeepers working in the area of operation at the micro-level facilitating settlement or facilitating a more positive atmosphere, coupled with peacekeeping, cooperating and coordinated with peacemaking and peacebuilding efforts at the macro-level. This means that peacekeepers act as an inter-

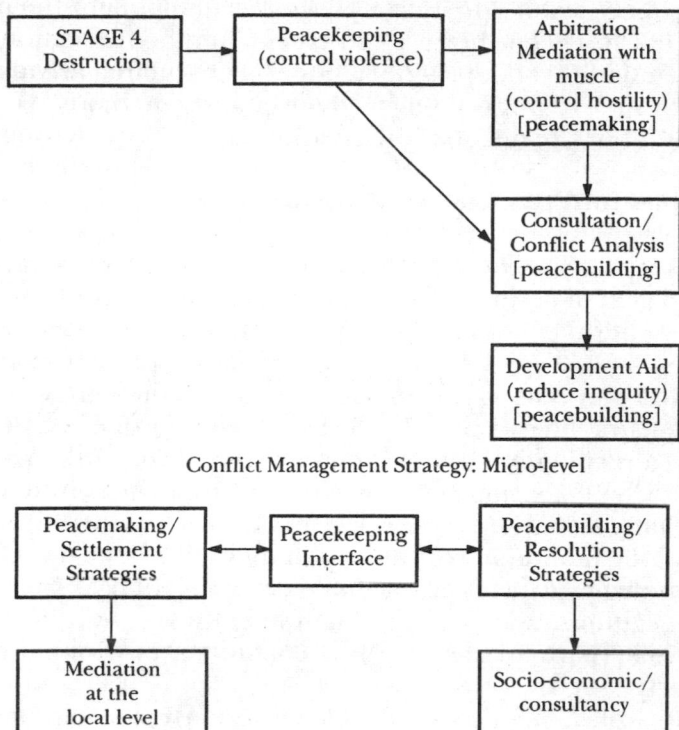

Conflict Management: Macro-level
(Fisher, 1990, p. 237, Escalation Stage 4)

*Figure* 6.1    Peacekeeping and a contingency framework

face between traditional peacemaking, or mediation as defined by Bercovitch *et al.*, and peacebuilding efforts, including both third party consultancy and socio-economic processes (see Figure 6.1). Operationally, it makes good sense for peacekeepers to coordinate activities on the ground since security in a war-zone is inevitably problematic. In addition, peacekeepers could coordinate and facilitate local peacebuilding activities, providing a centre through which micro-level activity is carried out.[28]

Because of peacekeeping's application at an early stage in the de-escalation process, micro-level activity might be usefully understood as pre-peacebuilding, with peacekeeping laying the groundwork for later, more concerted and direct efforts once a more stable situation has been achieved. Such preparatory work has been shown to be crucial in other areas, such as pre-negotiation and pre-mediation.[29] Particularly interesting here is recent work applying consultancy methods to pre-mediation or pre-negotiation situations.[30]

## 3.2 Roles for Peacekeepers at Stage Four

Peacekeeping in this context must take on more than the limited goal of control of violence or establishment of a democratic political process. There are numerous examples of the problem of a 'one role' or 'minimum role' approach. Perhaps the most devastating examples of this are the post-election situations of Angola and Haiti. Peacekeeping does not function in a vacuum but must respond to the needs of the parties in conflict, i.e., become part of a bottom-up process. And while multidimensional operations can be seen as an attempt to go beyond the minimum role approach they fail to take on resolution strategies which can facilitate reconciliation at the local level. Legitimization and coordination of these resolution roles is crucial, particularly in the demanding environment of protracted social conflict.

Three roles, then, each of equal importance, are legitimated within this model. First is the role of conflict control which provides the base level of activity for peacekeeping and precedes the application of *either* of the other two roles. Second is the facilitation of an atmosphere conducive to negotiations and settlement, and in the long-term movement toward resolution. Third is the facilitation of an actual settlement and resolution process. These roles encompass the expansion and multiplicity of roles indicated in Chapter 2.

At the micro-level peacekeeping operates as the medium through which peacemaking and peacebuilding activities are put into action (see Figure 6.1). This model assumes that the conflict control role is being fulfilled effectively, since without some level of conflict control, other activities are either difficult or impossible. The near derailment of the implementation process in Namibia following SWAPO's 1 April incursion provides a case in point. However, this does not mean that conflict control is the most important role or more central than other activities. It is also important to emphasize that the micro-level model does not imply that peacekeepers should be engaged in macro-level activities. Peacekeeping operations are not equipped to mediate settlement packages or to put into place large-scale socio-economic programmes. Peacekeeping should be seen in much the same way that pre-negotiation is, as laying the groundwork for more comprehensive peacebuilding and peacemaking activity, or in providing the first crucial phase of an already negotiated settlement package. This is also in line with the philosophy of many humanitarian aid organizations which see emergency aid as the first step toward re-establishing self-reliance.

## 3.3 Conclusion

Boutros-Ghali has suggested that new demands on peacekeeping require a comprehensive approach which he calls 'peace operations'. He argues that UN involvement in conflict must go beyond traditional peacekeeping, so that its role is

> not merely to send peacekeeping forces to separate combatants, but to intervene in the whole national reconciliation process; in the restructuring of the government; in the rehabilitation of the country; in the return of thousands and thousands of refugees; in the rebuilding of the bridges and the highways; in the restructuring of the political apparatus.[31]

It is important to be fully aware that this complex level of involvement necessitates, first, a more concrete and accurate understanding of the processes of conflict and conflict resolution; second, a more complete understanding of how peacekeeping or 'peace operations' fit into such processes; and third, grounded in this knowledge, a more specific and coherent methodology for the application of peacekeeping or 'peace operations'. Peacekeeping, functioning from within a contingency model provides the outline of a framework for understanding conflict processes which can begin to provide direction for application. Initially the most important aspect of this process is the collection of data which can be analyzed and then used to further inform practice.

## 4.  A CONTINGENCY MODEL FOR PEACEKEEPING

The previous section dealt with peacekeeping within a contingency model. This section concentrates on a contingency model for peacekeeping. The model shown in Figure 6.1, macro-level, indicates how peacekeeping fits into a broader conflict process. Figure 6.2 shows a model, taken from a study on international mediation by Bercovitch *et al.*, which is adapted here specifically for peacekeeping. The model is based on the collection of information from a data-set.[32] It establishes the outcome of intervention as the independent variable and process and context issues as dependent variables.

The specific definition of a successful outcome or successful conflict management is an essential element of the model. This definition could be a range of outcomes from failure (resumption of war, for example), to complete success (the establishment of a stable democratic society, for example), with a range of options in between. The first step, then, in applying this model to peacekeeping is to develop a specific definition of success. It would then be possible to direct a data analysis to begin to answer two general questions: (1) in what conflict context is peacekeeping most likely to have a positive impact; and (2) through the application of which strategy is peacekeeping most likely to contribute to a successful outcome?

In their research on mediation, Bercovitch *et al.* found that the context variable 'intensity' was a strong predictor of mediation success. As the number of fatalities rose in a given conflict (i.e. the level of intensity rose) the chances for successful mediation declined.[33] By analyzing the process variable 'mediator strategies', they also found that mediators who employed strategies which were more directive or substantive had a higher rate of success.[34]

For peacekeeping, it would be possible to analyze the process variable of 'peacekeeper strategies' as predictors of success. For example, such an analysis might find that violence control functions were fully successful 0 per cent of the time, while operations which carried out the violence control function as well as facilitative functions were fully successful 70 per cent of the time.

The use of this model to analyze peacekeeping missions would begin to provide a broader picture of when peace-

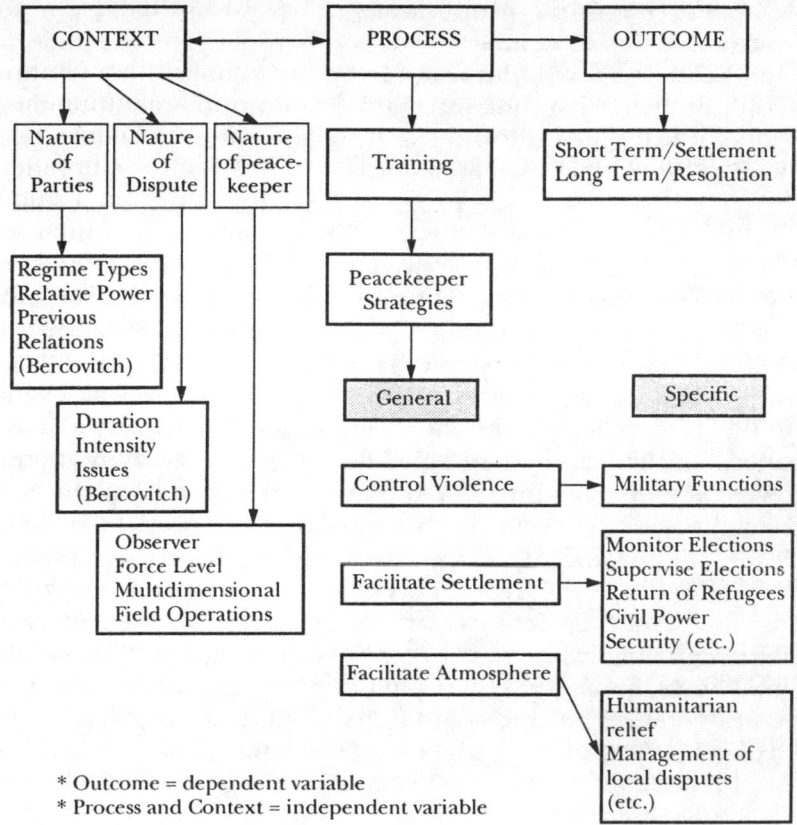

*Figure* 6.2    Contingency model of peacekeeping
*Source:* From Bercovitch *et al.* (1991). p. 11.

keeping is most successful (i.e. what context variables are the
best predictors of success) and how peacekeeping is most
successful (i.e. what process variables contribute most to
success). Through such an analysis a pattern would begin to
emerge which would help to direct later decision-making.
Bercovitch *et al.* summarize the benefits of adopting such a
method of research:

The contingency approach which we advocate avoids mere
description or prescription, allowing us instead to test logi-

cal and empirical propositions. The propositions are so articulated as to confirm or disconfirm patterns of relations and consequences, thus improving our scholarly knowledge of how mediation functions in the real world, and providing practical insights into how best to make it a more effective means of conflict management.[35]

A study by Diehl, partly reviewed in Chapter 2, is similar in aim to the contingency approach of Bercovitch *et al.* but focuses on peacekeeping. Diehl develops a definition of success based on peacekeeping's 'ability to limit armed conflict between the protagonists' and its 'role in the resolution of the underlying dispute between those protagonists'.[36] Diehl's definition of conflict resolution is equivalent to what we have called conflict settlement here. Based on his analysis, Diehl develops four guidelines for the use of peacekeeping. First is the importance of securing the support of the parties involved in the conflict (consent) for the deployment of the mission. Second is the use of peacekeeping primarily for interstate conflict. Third is deployment in locations with geography which enhances the ability of peacekeepers to perform supervisory roles. Finally, peacekeeping missions need to maintain a neutral stance to the conflict situation and the parties involved.[37] According to Diehl, following these guidelines should lead to more successful peacekeeping.

Diehl's observations are based on a data-set list of pre-1988 operations, and therefore his study emphasizes factors which can be considered part of traditional peacekeeping. His conclusions should be re-tested in the light of the developments in peacekeeping since 1988. One consequence of these developments for such an analysis is the need for a more sophisticated model, such as the one utilized by Bercovitch *et al.*, which accounts for the complexity of conflicts and the resultant increased complexity of peacekeeping operations. Moreover, an explicitly empirical approach, like that utilized by Bercovitch *et al.*, which attempts to clarify and separate specific factors, explain definitions of success and failure, and identify independent and dependent variables, is necessary. Even so, Diehl shows the possibilities of applying such an analysis to peacekeeping, provides some initial ideas for constructing a model specific to peacekeeping, and thus offers a beginning point for further research.

## 5. THE CONSEQUENCES OF UTILIZING A CONTINGENCY APPROACH AS A CONCEPTUAL FRAMEWORK FOR PEACEKEEPING

Peacekeeping placed within a contingency model does not necessarily demand a revolutionary change in strategy or methodology. The real consequence of putting peacekeeping in this context is a shift in perception. Many of the activities that a contingency model points to are activities which have been or are being carried out by peacekeepers on the ground either with or without a planned programme. The case-studies bear this out. The shift in perception is crucial because it not only legitimizes these activities but shows that peacekeeping without peacemaking and peacebuilding, especially in protracted social conflict situations, will be ineffective in the long term, and possibly also in the short term.

Once peacemaking and peacebuilding (at the micro-level) have been given as much emphasis in the minds of peacekeepers as conflict control activities, it is possible to carry out such activities in a coordinated manner and it is possible to train peacekeepers to fulfil these roles. Even if it is not politically feasible to coordinate the three areas at the macro-level, coordinating peacekeeping at the micro-level at least begins the groundwork of what might be called a 'pre-resolution' or a 'pre-peacebuilding' phase. This has taken the form of coordination of local level resolution processes, either at the initiative of local people or at the initiative of the peacekeepers. Such local level resolution activities took place in Namibia and Cyprus. These resolution activities went beyond being reactive, and in both cases were to some extent proactive, i.e they tried to go beyond dealing with one specific problem at one point in time and tried to establish a longer-term process which would deal with future problems.

A contingency model provides a testable hypothesis which gives decision-makers information from which to make more informed choices. Bercovitch *et al.*, and Fisher and Keashly, provide examples of the type of evidence that analysis through a contingency approach can reveal.[38]

It might be argued that one negative consequence of this approach is that it places enormous and widely varied demands on peacekeepers. This is a potentially troublesome point which might be mitigated in several ways. Training is one obvious answer, and a good one. But training alone will not be enough. Instead, an approach such as one utilized in Namibia may be more practical. In this case, teams of peacekeepers were used. A team might consist of representatives from the military, police, and civilian sectors where each was assigned specific tasks. For example, the civilian might be the only member of the group with specific training and experience in negotiation. However, in order to negotiate more effectively with the opposing military forces, the knowledge and experience of a UN military officer might be crucial. Such sharing of expertise would avoid the need to expect too much from a particular individual or group, but would ensure that personnel with appropriate training were on hand to deal with specific situations. And while all peacekeeping personnel would undoubtedly benefit from some training in conflict resolution techniques, employing teams would relieve the pressure on peacekeepers. Training and job requirements could be directly targeted to specific tasks, which in turn would create a clear division of labour and more explicit expectations, an important factor considering the increased demands on peacekeeping. The corollary to this is that peacekeepers would be less likely to be faced with situations for which they had no training or experience. In Namibia teams consisting of UN security personnel (usually civilian police) and UN election personnel (either for the purpose of registration or election supervision) worked together to monitor the A-G's staff.[39] However, a basic level of training for all peacekeepers which includes instruction and practice in conflict resolution is necessary since, as Skjelsbaek points out, 'non-military methods like dissuasion, persuasion and negotiation constitute the essence of peacekeeping'.[40]

Finally, a significant consequence for peacekeeping is in the area of training. At the moment, military functions are stressed in training and in practice. There has been a significant rise in the number of civilians participating in peacekeeping. Indeed, a recent UN document highlighted the varied roles that civilians, including police, have carried out in the past and are likely to handle in the future. However, the emphasis on the military side of peacekeeping is still considerable.[41] The following chapters take up the issue of training more specifically and focus on what kinds of training and how much training peace-keepers routinely receive. These chapters will consider the consequences of placing peacekeeping within a contingency model for training by relating the types of training peace-keepers currently receive to functions they carry out in the field.

## 6. THE POTENTIAL OF PEACEKEEPING

### 6.1 Potential of Complementarity

The potential of a contingency approach rests on the complementarity of various strategies. In other words, if mediation stalls at a particular point in the conflict process, consultancy can be employed. There is a growing body of evidence from the organizational level as well as from the international level which provides support for the potential of complementarity.[42] Wehr and Lederach examined the *Esquipulas* process in Central America and concluded:

> The effective combining of such local resources with external third parties in *Esquipulas* can be seen a contribution to the theory and practice of international third party intervention. We suspect that international mediation would be more effective were the various external and internal mediators and the moderator within the context to be systematically identified and enlisted: a deliberate citizen volunteer presence, a mixed team of outsider-neutrals and insider-partials, a resident conflict transformation group working on a deep-seated conflict situation.[43]

The system of Commissions which worked so effectively in Nicaragua was structured into the *Esquipulas* agreement. The experience offers a striking lesson for peacekeeping missions and demonstrates the effectiveness of active facilitation of communication and conflict resolution from the bottom up.

Prior to 1988, coordinating a contingency approach (at least within a peacekeeping operation) was well within the UN's capability. Writing in 1990 Coate and Puchala argued that peacekeeping operations had been reasonably successful in coordinating 'activities of organs, organizations and other actors whose participation and contributions... [had] been essential'.[44] While coordination had not been problem-free, they argued that its overall success could be attributed to two factors: first, peacekeeping operations functioned, for the most part, in a vertical chain of command (in contrast the horizontal coordination between aid agencies); second, peace-keeping tasks had been relatively simple.[45] The increasing complexity of missions places a question mark over the poten-tial for effective coordination and problems in this area have been noted elsewhere. Fulfilling the potential of peace-keeping, then, rests on recognizing the positive foundation which exists in the form of experience as well as the conse-quences of the expansion of peacekeeping. The key is to act on this information appropriately.

## 6.2  Building on Existing Knowledge and Experience

A contingency approach for peacekeeping and for interven-tion in general opens up great potential for improving the effectiveness of conflict management in general and peace-keeping in particular. However, it creates challenges. A com-prehensive examination of past peacekeeping operations, including those which are on-going is necessary. Analysis of the empirical evidence available needs to be translated into viable strategies. Peacekeeping has made initial moves toward meet-ing the challenges of effective conflict management through the refinement of multidimensional operations. The huge variety of roles that peacekeepers have already filled and the experience of forty-plus years of practice, make it apparent that much of the raw material for a coordinated and effective approach to peacekeeping within a system of conflict manage-ment already exists. It is the recognition and legitimization of the peacekeepers' roles through a more precise understanding of how peacekeeping operates within a contingency model of conflict management, coupled with specific procedures to use and target these roles most effectively, which is vital and which must be developed. As Diehl and Kumar reflect,

> We hope that our analysis has demonstrated that UN peace-keeping troops have considerable potential for generating joint positive solutions to international conflicts. Yet this is

possible only if we can recognize the limits if their applicability to some situations on the one hand, and expand the
horizons of their roles on the other.[46]

The proposition to be tested is whether peacekeeping missions
which are operated from the rationale of a contingency model
are more likely to bring about long-term resolution and less
likely to become embroiled in a civil war or support an
unpeaceful *status quo.*

# 7 Training as a Critical Link between Theory and Practice

## 1. PEACEKEEPING: THE APPLICATION OF THEORY

### 1.1 The Need for Theory: A Summary of the Arguments

The three previous chapters expound a particular theoretical approach to peacekeeping. This approach is based on the application of peacekeeping conceptualized through a contingency model of conflict resolution. It has been demonstrated that the basis for this reconsideration of peacekeeping derives from three main sources. The first is the argument that international conflicts have fundamentally changed, and new approaches are needed to facilitate their resolution. The second is the argument that the UN has partially responded to the new challenges posed by the shift in conflict by first creating the *ad hoc* technique of peacekeeping and most recently by moving toward multidimensional peacekeeping. Not only has peacekeeping expanded in numbers of operations and in roles performed during those operations but it has become more complex and more explicitly committed to and involved in conflict resolution processes. The third is the examination of the conceptual basis of the third party role of peacekeeping which poses significant challenges to the current practice of peacekeeping at both micro- and macro-levels.

These three arguments culminate in the postulation that in order for peacekeeping to continue to be practised effectively within the new environment, two basic changes are necessary. First, the rationalization and application of peacekeeping must be derived from a theoretical framework which takes into consideration both the means and end of an over-arching peace process. And second, this theoretical framework then must be

162

used to provide peacekeeping with the rationale for its own specific forms or modes of activity.

It was then argued that a contingency model provides a skeletal conceptual framework of an over-arching peace process, within which peacekeeping can be set. Once peacekeeping is conceptualized through the framework of the contingency model, the rationale for three general roles becomes apparent. The first role is that of conflict control which provides the base level of activity of peacekeeping preceding the application of either of the other two roles: either the facilitation of an atmosphere conducive to negotiations and settlement, and in the long-term movement toward resolution, or the facilitation of a pre-negotiated settlement and resolution process.

This explication of peacekeeping's third party role derived from the conceptual approach of contingency theory can then be translated into specific roles for peacekeepers (see Figure 6.2). The most significant result of this analysis is that the baseline for any peacekeeping mission is conflict control. But it is crucial that conflict control then be paired with one of the other two roles, both of which necessitate the use of conflict resolution processes in peacekeeping. In other words, the micro-level peacemaking and peacebuilding activities of peacekeepers are vital aspects of any operation. The specific skills associated with the third party conflict resolution processes of peacekeeping, peacemaking and peacebuilding are primarily negotiation, mediation, facilitation, consultation, conciliation, reconciliation and communication.

Given these arguments two points become clear. The first is the need to develop and carry out empirical research which will provide concrete evidence regarding a number of different aspects of peacekeeping. The second is the need to bring this theory of peacekeeping into practice.

It is this second task which will be the focus of the following three chapters. Training is the key factor in this process. Coherently developed and coordinated training programmes, which are based on and derived from a contingency theory of peacekeeping, will enable peacekeepers to understand and implement their essential third party role. The problem is that the current state of training does not reflect the reality of the peacekeepers' situation.

## 1.2 The Problem of Bringing Theory into Practice: Training as a Key Factor

It has only been relatively recently, since the late 1980s, that training for peacekeeping has become an acknowledged issue.[1] This interest in training has led to some advances in the provision and overall coordination of peacekeeping training in the UN. However, the training issue, and peacekeeping more generally, continue to suffer from a lack of theoretical and practical coherence and direction. This point was made in a set of recommendations submitted by the Committee of 34 to the Special Political Committee during the 1991 General Assembly session. The report states:

> The expansion and diversification of peacekeeping operations should encourage efforts to set up a set of general guidelines to govern them. Some kind of definition of peacekeeping should be developed, thereby reducing the level of ambiguity with regard to the concept and practices of such operations.[2]

The need to link the development of a theoretical base for peacekeeping and its methodology goes beyond 'reducing the level of ambiguity'. This conceptual point has been argued and was briefly summarized in the opening section of this chapter. The methodological point to be made here is that any development or expansion of peacekeeping practice should include the development and expansion of training. One of the results of such a development in training would certainly be a reduction in the current levels of ambiguity regarding concepts and practices. Another result would be the provision of training in conflict resolution techniques as well as a range of other skills.

The crucial significance of training in the process of developing effective peacekeeping is two-fold: first, training provides the means for dissemination of the meta-goals guiding peaceful intervention and implementation of third party activities designed to accomplish those goals, and second, training provides an important link in the testing of the conceptual base of peacekeeping. These interactions can be visually represented as a cycle of development where conceptual analysis leads to developments in training which lead to changes in practice. These

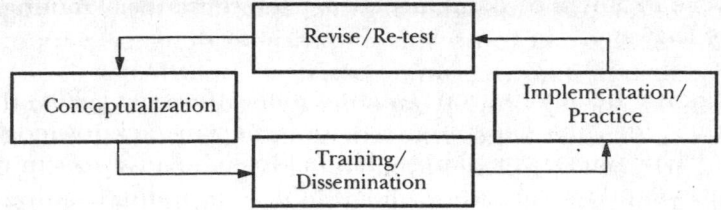

*Figure* 7.1    Cyclical development of the theory and practice of peacekeeping

changes then initiate testing and revising which finally feed back into the conceptualization process (see Figure 7.1).

Before launching into the detailed description of current training provision provided in Chapter 8 and the analysis which follows in Chapter 9, the remainder of this chapter will briefly examine theory and practice of training from the field of cross-cultural interaction. The purpose of this exercise is not to provide a critical analysis of the scope and effectiveness of various training techniques. Such a task, although important, is beyond the scope of this work. The purpose of this examination is to point out the link between theory and methodology in the field of cross-cultural interaction as a critical consideration for the effectiveness of training programmes, and as such, an important consideration for peacekeeping training programmes. Another purpose is to examine the methods and theories utilized in cross-cultural training in order to provide comparative evidence for the proceeding discussions (evidence of this kind is non-existent for peacekeeping training). A final purpose is to provide a common set of terms through which training provision can be considered.

The use of information available in cross-cultural training has another significance. All peacekeeping missions engage in cross-cultural interaction at two levels: (1) between the Force and the parties to the conflict, and (2) between the various national contingents within the Force. For this reason it is likely that cross-cultural training has direct significance for peacekeeping training beyond a comparative analysis. The penultimate section of this chapter examines a sociological study of a peacekeeping force which lends some support to the notion such a direct link.[3]

In general, the remainder of this chapter and those which follow are written not to provide empirical evidence to support a particular training programme based on a particular theory of learning or specific work from other fields of study, nor are they written to develop a specific curriculum for peacekeeping training. This activity too is beyond the scope of this work. The purpose of the following discussion is to point out gaps, inconsistencies, and deficiencies which provide support for the arguments of this book summarized above and which point to areas which require more considered examination in the future.

## 2. CROSS-CULTURAL TRAINING: AN EXAMPLE OF LINKING THEORY WITH PRACTICE

Cross-cultural training refers to a broad area of research and training which is intended to prepare individuals to work and live successfully overseas. Groups which utilize such training are varied and include military and business people, overseas development advisors, aid workers, and travellers. Albert describes the task of cross-cultural training as preparing

> individuals to understand as much as possible the differences in norms, roles, values, behaviors, and so on. More importantly, in as much as possible, we ought to prepare them for the fact that we cannot fully prepare them, that there will be many surprises, and many things that they will have to learn by themselves. We should therefore, help individuals learn how to learn in the new culture.[4]

Working and living in a different culture is something that all peacekeepers must contend with, although some will undoubtedly have more direct contact with the host country and the conflicting parties than others. The argument here is not that peacekeepers need only cross-cultural training, but rather to indicate one area where research has been done on training programmes which has direct relevance to the peacekeeper's situation, experience and effectiveness. Because of these similarities, cross-cultural training may provide some raw material and direction for the development of peacekeeping training programmes.

## 2.1 The Skills Necessary for Effective Intercultural Interaction

According to a recent review of cross-cultural literature, carried out by Hannigan, most research points to the importance of three basic factors which dictate success or failure in intercultural interaction. These are: skills or abilities, attitudinal factors, and personality traits.[5] The literature generally assumes that the first two factors, skills and attitudes, can be learned or changed and therefore are directly relevant to the training process, while the third factor, personality, is inherent and therefore related to the selection process.[6] For this reason, the training literature focuses largely on the acquisition and successful application of new skills and the change of attitudes which inhibit success.

Research in this field also indicates particular abilities and attitudes which have been found to relate to cross-cultural effectiveness. Abilities which have been found to be important are:

(1) interpersonal and communication skills including,
  – listening skills
  – ability to enter into dialogue
  – ability to initiate interaction
  – ability to deal with misunderstandings
  – ability to deal with different communication styles
  – linguistic ability
  – interaction management ability,
(2) organizational ability,
(3) competence in one's area of expertise,
(4) ability to effectively communicate one's knowledge to others,
(5) ability to deal with psychological stress.[7]

Of these ability factors research indicates that the most important skill area is communication.[8] It should be pointed out here that 'competence in one's area of expertise' is only one of a number of skills necessary for cross-cultural success. Indeed, some of the research cited in this review warns that technical skill and knowledge is 'only a small part of a complex multi-factor concept [of cross-cultural effectiveness]'.[9] Although an overseas worker may be highly technically qualified, lack of communication skills can lead to the problem of 'knowing a great deal but not being able to communicate the information'.[10] Finally, a significant point is made about what is termed the 'exposure/experience/expertise fallacy'. This argument counters the assumption that exposure and experience in a particular overseas environment automatically leads to expertise. Hannigan concludes that although more research in this area is necessary, 'an argument could be made that exposure and experience in a different culture is necessary but not sufficient to achieve intercultural effectiveness'.[11] This point relates to peacekeeping, where a similar belief prevails that experience automatically leads to expertise. As in the area of cross-cultural interaction, such an assumption can be misleading and deserves closer examination.

The review of literature also shows that particular attitudes relate positively to cross-cultural effectiveness. These attitudes are:

(1)  cultural empathy,
(2)  a relativist orientation to knowledge,
(3)  acceptance of others as people,
(4)  a non-judgemental attitude,
(5)  respect for the host culture,
(6)  interest in nationals,
(7)  appreciation of their culture,
(8)  a sense of politics,
(9)  flexibility.[12]

An attitude of flexibility is often mentioned in conjunction with persistence. It is suggested that it is a crucial aspect of intercultural interaction to be able to judge when it is best to be flexible and when it is better to be persistent.

Research has shown that certain personality traits correlate negatively with cross-cultural effectiveness. These research results have particular importance for the selection process for overseas workers. Traits found to correlate negatively are:

(1)  perfectionism,
(2)  rigidity,
(3)  dogmatism,
(4)  ethnocentrism,
(5)  dependent anxiety,

(6)  task-oriented behaviour,
(7)  narrow-mindedness,
(8)  self-centred role behaviours.[13]

Interestingly, the research also suggests two factors which appear to have relatively little effect on cross-cultural effectiveness: intelligence and authoritarianism.[14] It is possible that these two variables, intelligence and authoritarianism, do not have significant impact on an individual's ability to empathize or communicate effectively. However, it seems likely that this point would break down if taken to its extreme, i.e. a stupid dictator is unlikely to be an effective aid worker.

The skills, attitudes, and personality traits which research has indicated relate to cross-cultural effectiveness compare closely to those skills considered necessary for the effectiveness of third party intervention. As cited in Chapter 4, Deutsch suggests four skill areas which are important for effective third party intervention. These are:

(1)  the set of skills which relate to building an effective working relationship between the third party and each of the parties involved in the conflict, particularly communication and trust-building skills;
(2)  the set of skills needed to develop a cooperative problem-solving attitude amongst the antagonists;
(3)  the set of skills needed to contribute toward a creative group process and group decision-making;
(4)  general knowledge of the conflict including history and current issues.[15]

Deutsch goes on to suggest that,

many destructive conflicts between nations, groups and individuals result from their lack of skills related to the procedures involved in constructive conflict resolution, and... that training in these skills should be more widespread.[16]

Wehr gives ten skills he considers essential for effective intervention. These are:

(1)  conflict situation analysis/fact-finding,
(2)  empathy,
(3)  listening/active listening,

   (4)  sense of timing and appropriateness,
   (5)  trust and credibility development,
   (6)  mediation,
   (7)  communication,
   (8)  imagination,
   (9)  joint-costing,
  (10)  crisis management.[17]

These two lists of skills are very similar to the skills found important for cross-cultural effectiveness. In both cross-cultural interaction and third party intervention communication skills are pointed to as an essential contributor to effectiveness. Moreover, some of the third party intervention literature takes into account the importance of cultural factors in mediation, negotiation, etc.[18]

## 2.2 Techniques of Cross-Cultural Training

In order to increase cross-cultural effectiveness, training programmes are developed to teach skills and/or to develop and change attitudes. Six types of training for cross-cultural interaction make up the basic methodology of the field. These are: (1) *fact-oriented training*, a traditional approach where facts are presented through lectures, readings, case studies, discussion, etc; (2) *attribution training*, where the aim is for the trainee to internalize the values and norms of the host country by learning to explain events and behaviours from the host's point of view; (3) *cultural awareness training* is more conceptually oriented than other methods, approaching training by the examination of concepts of culture and cultural differences, often using the trainee's own culture as a starting point for study; (4) *cognitive-behaviour modification* 'applies certain principles of learning to the special problem of cross-cultural adjustment' by examining, for example, behaviours that are rewarded or punished in different cultural settings and then learning how to copy or avoid those behaviours; (5) *experiential learning*, aims at facilitating learning through actual experience by involving 'the trainees emotionally and physically as well as intellectually' in role plays, situation exercises, field trips, etc.; (6) *interactional learning* aims to familiarize trainees with the host through 'structured or unstructured interaction between the trainees on the one hand, and host nationals and/or "old hands" (experienced expatriates) on the other'.[19] All of these training programmes, utilized in a cross-cultural setting, attempt to create 'a balance of awareness, knowledge and skills'.[20]

Grove and Torbiorn outline a theory of adaptation which attempts to further understand intercultural adjustment (or effectiveness).[21] They begin by developing a theory of cross-cultural adjustment based on three variables: (1) applicability of behaviour, (2) clarity of the mental frame of reference, and (3) level of mere adequacy. Using these three 'psychological constructs', Grove and Torbiorn develop a four-phase model of an adjustment cycle. An individual goes through each phase of this adjustment cycle when adapting to a new culture.

> Stage I is characterized by a period of euphoria often experienced by people immediately after they enter a completely new culture.... Stage II...is characterized by culture shock.... Stage III is characterized by progressive recovery from culture shock.... Stage IV is characterized by completion of the process of adjustment.[22]

Stage II of the adjustment cycle is the period of most interest to Grove and Torbiorn. This is normally the longest and most difficult period of the cycle of adjustment and where the least amount of learning is possible. They argue that for an individual to operate effectively in another culture, she or he must get beyond Stage II. The aim of their work is to 'reduce the severity and shorten the duration of the newcomer's passage through Stage II', and they argue that training is the key to this process.[23]

Grove and Torbiorn apply their theoretical model to improving effectiveness through training. Their results suggest that particular types of training lead to greater adaptation or effectiveness (i.e. reduce the severity and shorten the duration of Stage II). From this analysis, Grove and Torbiorn conclude that fact-oriented training is important particularly at the beginning of a training programme. A great deal of information describing appropriate and inappropriate behaviour and the general characteristics of a different culture can be communicated utilizing the methodology of fact-oriented training.[24] However, Grove and Torbiorn argue that this type of preparation has definite limitations.

because mere knowledge of the inappropriateness of certain behaviors is unlikely to enable one to make sweeping modifications in his or her habitual patterns of activity, fact-finding training by itself is not sufficient.[25]

They conclude that experiential learning is the most promising method available at present because 'its emphasis on learning through actual experience carries the greatest potential for perfecting and/or developing needed skills'.[26]

The process of developing a training programme, according to Pederson, has five definitive stages.[27] The first stage is the needs assessment. At this stage the goal is to identify specific areas of knowledge, skills, and awareness for which a trainee will need preparation. This identification process is based on a realistic assessment by the trainer of the environment within which the trainees will be expected to function.

The second stage involves the development of objectives. Pederson notes that these objectives should,

be clearly stated and specific enough that their success or failure can be measured. The objectives should be described in terms of what the trainee will be able to do at the end of the training.[28]

The objectives should also balance the three areas of awareness, knowledge and skills.

The third stage is training programme design. An appropriate and comprehensive programme includes, according to Pederson, 'a balance of experiential approaches to increase awareness, lecture presentations, to transfer knowledge, and simulated opportunities to practise skills'.[29] Lederach argues that, in some circumstances, this design process should also take into account the potential input of the participants.[30]

The fourth stage is programme implementation. Several factors are especially significant during implementation. A positive group climate is considered important to enhancing learning. In addition, the role of the trainer is central. It is important that the trainers themselves have been trained not only in the areas they will be presenting but, equally important, in the skills of training. This is particularly true for trainers making use of experiential learning techniques since these techniques can be challenging and can provoke a mixture of reactions typified by general discomfort from the trainees.[31]

The final stage is programme evaluation. Pederson argues that an evaluation should take two forms. First is an internally focused formative evaluation. It asks 'how well and to what extent training objectives were reached and how well training activities related to the training objectives'.[32] The second type, called a summative evaluation, is external or outward looking. Its purpose is to find out 'whether training objectives were the right ones to eliminate performance discrepancies and change job performance'.[33]

The development of a comprehensive and effective training programme is a complicated task, particularly considering the large number of skills and attitudes which have been shown to relate to cross-cultural effectiveness. It is the importance of acquiring these skills and attitudes for effectiveness which makes training an essential part of cross-cultural interaction. The same can be said for the expansion and increasing complexity of peacekeeping operations and the need created by these changes for comprehensive and effective training.

## 2.3 The Case of Canadian Development Workers Overseas

Kealey recently produced a study on cross-cultural effectiveness, which looked at attributes and abilities necessary for success for Overseas Technical Advisors.[34] In this study, overseas success was defined as 'the ability to live and work effectively in the cross-cultural setting of an overseas assignment'.[35] The focus of the study was to

define the personal and behavioral characteristics that enhance overseas effectiveness, and to determine how those characteristics can be used to identify and select better candidates for overseas assignment.[36]

The results of Kealey's study of 277 Canadian technical assistance advisors working in 20 different developing countries yielded some interesting results.[37] Based on his research Kealey developed a profile of effectiveness for an overseas worker the main characteristics of which were:

(1) A professional commitment to the job and a desire to help.
(2) The necessary technical background and skills.
(3) Caring behaviour.

    (4)  Action orientation.
    (5)  Other-centredness.
    (6)  Low need for upward mobility.
    (7)  Low security needs (high tolerance of ambiguity)
    (8)  High self-monitoring.
    (9)  Social adroitness.
  (10)  Positive pre-departure expectations and a desire for contact with the local culture.[38]

A similar list is found in the work of Paige.[39] In addition, many of the same skills which Kealey found increase effectiveness in his study of overseas workers coincide with those listed in the preceding section.

Based on his results, Kealey concluded that

> More emphasis should be placed on training advisors for effectiveness, stressing the realities and difficulties of working overseas, and the need for establishing effective working relationships with national counterparts. Historically, pre-departure briefing programs have focused on assisting individuals and families to cope and adapt. To be effective overseas requires much more than successful adaptation and professional competence.[40]

The outcome of this research has direct relevance to peacekeeping. This research suggests that effectiveness is not necessarily tied to technical competence, but instead has more to do with positive and effective communication. The critical point here for peacekeeping is the need to establish a definition of effectiveness which includes technical competence but which goes beyond it. Moreover, a way to evaluate effectiveness is needed.

Kealey's study is a specific example of the utility and applicability to peacekeeping of a conceptual framework which produces testable hypotheses. This is not to say that Kealey's conclusions can be directly transplanted into the peacekeeping context. Such a conclusion is not warranted. The object of this discussion is, rather, to suggest the process by which concepts are tested and then translated into specific recommendations for training provision. It is this general cycle of events, not the specific outcomes of Kealey's research which are of most interest in the present discussion. Kealey's research, and the other work cited above, is based on theory, so that his conclusions about training are grounded within a testable conceptual context. Existing training provision for peacekeeping fails to utilize such a formula.

## 3. LINKING CROSS-CULTURAL INTERACTION RESEARCH WITH THE PRACTICE OF PEACEKEEPING

The relationship between cross-cultural interaction research and peacekeeping is unstudied. However, a sociological study of peacekeeping forces by Moskos provides a link which goes some way toward justifying the examination of information collected through cross-cultural research and utilizing it to enhance our understanding of peacekeeping.

Moskos's work focused on the UN Forces in Cyprus (UNFICYP). He examined 'the social factors that favor or hinder the peacekeeping role among the actual soldiers of a United Nations military force'.[41] The general aim of this study was to look at the adjustment of military forces to the peace-keeping role. Successful adjustment, according to Moskos, was defined by the development of a 'constabulary ethic' within the Force. The constabulary ethic was defined as 'minimum use-of-force and impartiality'.[42] Using the development of the constabulary ethic as a measure of successful adjustment from the purely military to the peacekeeping role, Moskos found that peacekeepers went through three phases of adjustment. It should be noted that adjustment from the military to the peacekeeping role could be viewed as adjustment from one 'culture' to another, i.e. from a 'military' culture to a 'third party' culture. The three phases of adjustment noted by Moskos compare well with the phases outlined by Grove and Torbiorn.

According to Moskos, the first phase of adjustment to a constabulary ethic was characterized by 'a preconceived and somewhat idealized norm of peacekeeping'.[43] This attitude was combined with a general perception of the peacekeeping role as that of a 'third force'. In practice this 'third force' utilized methods such as arbitration rather than negotiation to solve problems.[44] Grove and Torbiorn point out that Stage I of their model is characterized by a feeling of 'euphoria' combined with a high level of clarity on the part of the individual regarding expected roles and behaviours.[45]

The second phase in Moskos's adjustment cycle was characterized by the replacement of the 'idealized and active definition' of peacekeeping with 'an opposite cynicism'.[46] Here, peacekeepers often reported feelings of futility and powerlessness.[47] This phase, the longest of the three, generally persisted for one to two months. The corresponding phase in Grove and Torbiorn's model, Stage II, is characterized by culture shock. This phase is also the longest of the four-staged adjustment cycle.[48] According to Grove and Torbiorn, during this phase of 'deep confusion', individuals exhibit certain psychological symptoms including rationalization, projection, withdrawal, and overidentifying.[49]

In the final phase of adjustment identified by Moskos, 'The mood of peacekeeping cynicism gives way – though not consistently – to a realistic but somewhat positive evaluation [of peacekeeping].'[50] By the onset of this phase peacekeepers have adjusted to the constabulary ethic. According to Moskos, this final phase of adjustment was seen more often in peacekeepers beyond their first tour. In other words, the normal four to six month tour of a soldier was not necessarily long enough for the full adjustment to the constabulary ethic to take place. Grove and Torbiorn utilize two stages to Moskos's one. They distinguish between a period in which the individual progressively recovers from culture shock (Stage III), and a point where the individual is fully adjusted (Stage IV).

A serious limitation of Moskos's study is that it was completed in 1976. It does not take into account changes in peacekeeping since 1988. One result of this limitation is that Moskos defines peacekeeping and peacekeeping success through the limited conflict control role embodied in the constabulary ethic. It was argued earlier that conflict control is only one part of peacekeeping. Therefore, Moskos's conclusions regarding, for example, what constitutes successful peacekeeping, the utility of training, and the adaptability of standards of military professionalism to the peacekeeping role, must be re-evaluated in light of far more complex peacekeeping contexts such as in former Yugoslavia.

An interesting and more applicable aspect of Moskos's study is the cycle of adjustment. Although limited in the sense that it is based on adjustment to the constabulary ethic, the cycle offered by Moskos is useful in several ways. First, it provides a general indication of a peacekeeper's adjustment to the role of conflict control. While this is only one part of peacekeeping activity, it is an important part. Therefore, two outcomes of Moskos's study deserve further attention: (1) the second phase of the cycle normally takes one to two months, with the presumption that a peacekeeper is less effective during this time, and (2) it may take more than one four to six month tour for a peacekeeper to make the adjustment to the constabulary ethic. How these two points impact on the effectiveness of a peacekeeping force is an important question. Second, the adjustment cycle is useful in that it shows a remarkable similarity to Grove and Torbiorn's model. If this comparison is valid, and more research is needed to confirm this point, then one of the goals of training for peacekeeping should be the reduction of the severity and the duration of Stage II. According to Grove and Torbiorn, a broad approach to training which includes fact-oriented and experiential methods is necessary to accomplish this goal. Grove and Torbiorn's study also provides evidence which casts doubt on Moskos's conclusion that pre-departure training is not a factor in the adjustment process.

Moskos's work is significant in and of itself. It raises a number of important issues about peacekeeping effectiveness which deserve further attention. Although caution regarding the direct application of cross-cultural interaction research is necessary, Moskos's work suggests that such research would be a useful resource for the development of the theory and practice of peacekeeping. Of particular interest for future investigation is a more complete understanding of the adjustment cycle of peacekeepers and the impact of that adjustment on effectiveness. Accordingly, the development of training which addresses adjustment issues is needed.

## 4. CONCLUSION

The link between theory and practice should be characterized by an interactive process. The richness of the interaction relates directly to the applicability and effectiveness of methodology. Cross-cultural training offers not only an example of a rich interaction between theory and practice, but also a resource which can provide direction and information of further research on peacekeeping.

For peacekeeping, the development of an interactive process between theory and practice has been hindered by a lack of conceptualization. The development of a framework of conceptualization is crucial for the development of methodology. Training should play a key part in this process. As will be shown in the next chapter, however, training for peacekeeping, where it exists, is limited and fragmented and generally suffers from a lack of conceptual and practical direction from a central, institutionalized source. How important is this for peacekeeping? By way of conclusion Chapter 9 will look at this question in detail, bringing together the several strands of argument set out in this work.

# 8 Training for United Nations Peacekeepers

## 1. CURRENT TRAINING PROVISION

Where it exists, training for United Nations peacekeeping is fragmented. Many troop-contributing countries do not offer any peacekeeping training. This is not surprising considering the *ad hoc* approach taken to peacekeeping by the UN, coupled with the fact that 77 out of 184 Member States have participated in UN operations.[1] The fragmentation has its roots in the political situation which developed at the UN in the early 1960s (see Chapter 1). Between 1964 and 1988 the development of any institutions relating to peacekeeping did not occur for political reasons. In terms of training this has meant that no centralized, institutionalized training programme under the auspices of the UN specifically for peacekeeping has been developed. Peacekeeping has remained an '*ad hoc* institution' and training has been left to the countries contributing troops and a handful of international organizations. Even today the prospect that the UN might develop a centralized, institutionalized training programme is minimal. The Secretariat has neither the time nor resources to take on such a huge project, and in many logistical respects it would be inefficient. To carry out such a large-scale training programme, troops from countries all over the world would have to be transported to and from a central location. In addition, housing, food, and the materials and staff for the training programme would have to be provided. Not surprisingly, the Department of Peacekeeping Operations (DPKO) has no real interest in developing a centralized training system. Rather what is most often suggested in this context is the development of regional training centres (or national centres) around the world which would get information and direction from the DPKO.

Since 1988 there have been some signs of movement on the training issue. The work of the Committee of 34 was

179

mentioned in the previous chapter. In July 1992, DPKO appointed a 'focal point' for training. The job, in essence, is to provide briefing papers on specific missions and training information and guidelines to countries participating in peacekeeping operations. In the longer term the 'focal point' is responsible for developing specific training materials.[2] The impact these changes will have on the coordination and development of training for peacekeeping remains to be seen. Thus far, while there has certainly been more talk, concrete changes have been minimal.[3]

For both civilian or military peacekeepers, there are four possible types of training. *In-country training* is organized and carried out by and within either the country from which the peacekeepers originate or on a regional basis. *Mission-site training* is carried out once the peacekeepers have reached the mission area and can be organized by the peacekeepers' home country or by the United Nations Office of Human Resources Management (OHRM). Much of this type of training is carried out on-the-job. *Training at United Nations Headquarters* is organized and carried out in New York or at the main Duty Stations around the world (examples are Tokyo, Vienna or Geneva) by DPKO or OHRM. Finally a small group of *international agencies* offer training programmes for peacekeeping.

All peacekeeping training can be generally categorized as fact-oriented, although there is some on-the-job training which could, charitably, be characterized as interactional training. The only possible exception is the use of simulation exercises (categorized as experiential learning in the previous chapter) in military and international agency training. However, these are often better described as 'situation exercises' where role playing is limited and the object is to give the participants a feel for the mechanics of the situation. An interesting example of this difference was described by a reporter observing Dutch troops training for deployment to former Yugoslavia.[4] One part of a simulation exercise for the protection of aid convoys got 'out of hand' when the soldiers role-playing a paramilitary group dragged two young prospective peacekeepers from the back of an open truck and pushed them to the ground. An officer observing the simulation intervened saying the 'paramilitaries' had strayed too far from the script. Once back in their truck though, one of the young peacekeepers asked, 'Major, if they pull you out of the truck – what are you supposed to do?' There was no answer.

A simulation exercise tries to create situations as lifelike as possible and therefore the way a particular exercise develops cannot be predicted. The point is to teach a range of skills which can be applied and adapted to circumstances and then arrange a novel situation within which the trainee must apply and adapt those skills – perhaps coming up with a unique solution to a given problem. It is in testing those skills and finding the solution to such an unpredictable problem that experiential learning occurs. By having a carefully prepared script, with 'incidents' which have prearranged 'solutions', the soldier does not learn to adapt skills to new problems but only understands standard operating procedures for a set of proscribed incidents. Unfortunately, peacekeeping does not often offer 'by the book' incidents.

The remainder of this chapter will examine specific training provision focusing, in turn, on military, civilian and international agency training. The military training section looks at three training programmes – Canada, Ireland and the Nordic countries (Denmark, Finland, Norway and Sweden). Canada provides an example of a medium-sized professional military which sends formed units overseas. Ireland serves as an example of a country with limited resources and a small professional army. Prospective peacekeepers volunteer individually for UN service and are then formed into a unit. The Nordic countries provide examples of national service armies which rely on recruitment from a large reserve base (these are so-called 'non-professional' or 'conscript' armies). They also furnish the only example of training organized on a regional basis.

Civilian peacekeeping training is described with reference to the Namibian operation since this was the first mission for which UN personnel received formal training. Finally, training programmes offered by three international agencies – United Nations Institute for Training and Research (UNITAR), International Peace Academy (IPA), and the Austrian Study Centre for Peace and Conflict Resolution (ASPR), will be examined.

## 2. MILITARY TRAINING

Preparation for military elements of peacekeeping operations is far from uniform. In general, how well trained peacekeepers are depends on where they come from as well as whether they are officers or soldiers. The traditional troop contributors, Austria, Canada, Ireland and the Nordic Countries (excluding Iceland) have the best developed training programmes and the most experience with training and peacekeeping. Before 1990 these seven countries had contributed over 25 per cent of all peacekeeping troops and generally accounted for a similar proportion in each mission. Large operations in Cambodia, Somalia, and former Yugoslavia have reduced this percentage. Of this group of seven, the Nordics have the only regional training system (NATO is currently developing some inter-mural training programmes for peacekeping), as well as four of the six existing National Training Centres (the others are in Austria and Poland).[5] The other two countries, Ireland and Canada, have no institutionalized training system. Their training is on-demand, and targeted for specific missions.

For the rest of the troop contributors, with perhaps three or four exceptions, training for peacekeeping is not a priority. The justification for such an approach is usually that peacekeeping is essentially the same task as low-intensity warfare, and since, in professional armies at least, this is part of the curriculum, further training is not considered necessary. There is, of course, a crucial difference between low-intensity warfare and peacekeeping based on the fact that peacekeeping relies on consent and is therefore a peaceful third party intervention. Low-intensity warfare is not constrained in such a way.

As has been discussed at some length in previous chapters, violence control functions of peacekeeping, which are often but not always carried out by military peacekeepers, are only one part of peacekeepers' roles. And while training in these operational areas is important, the skills, knowledge and attitudes of conflict resolution which comprise another main part of peacekeeping activity, i.e. mediation and negotiation, are equally central. Indeed, even the violence control function must be carried with the consent of the parties to the dispute, and therefore relies, at least partially, on the peacekeepers' skills as negotiators and mediators.

Two final points should be made before continuing. First it should be noted that the programmes presented here represent the very best peacekeeping training available. Second, many troop-contributing countries developing training for peacekeeping rely heavily on the Nordic model. This presupposes that the Nordic model is sufficient and effective – a point which should not be taken for granted.

## 2.1 Canadian Forces (CF)

Canada's professional military has been contributing continuously to UN peacekeeping missions since 1947.[6] Service in a peacekeeping operation is not voluntary and selection is done on a battalion basis, not individually. Canada has no institutionalized training programme for peacekeepers. Their training for peacekeeping is managed on an *ad hoc* mission-by-mission basis. In a recent review of peacekeeping operations in the Canadian Forces, 'The Douglas Report', the section on training stated:

> The training of our personnel selected for UN operations is not well managed as a CF-wide task. Most training activities are *ad hoc* and, with few exceptions, occur only due to the initiative of field commanders.[7]

The major exception to this is a newly developed training programme for officers which began in 1991, and which is coordinated centrally by the Directorate of Peacekeeping Operations (CF-DPKO) in Ottawa. Overall training is conceptualized as a continuation of regular military training with refresher briefings and skills exercises augmented by briefings and skills exercises specific to the military aspects of UN procedures and the mission itself.

In general, there are three groups for whom training for peacekeeping is provided. These are: (1) units selected for rotation to an existing mission, (2) units which will become part of a new mission and, (3) officers who have been selected for Military Observers (UNMOs) or Staff Officers (UNSOs) positions.

Battalions selected for rotation to an existing mission receive pre-rotation, in-country training and mission-site training. Mission-specific training guidelines are issued to the battalion by CF-DPKO prior to rotation. These guidelines give a general synopsis of areas which should be covered in a training programme and it is then up to each unit commander to take responsibility for developing and carrying it out. Pre-rotation training can last as long as six to eight weeks but the actual specifics of the training schedule, timing, and quality depend on the particular commander. One particular problem of this method of training is lack of standardization and institutional learning.

Subjects covered in pre-rotation training include:

(1) socio-political briefings
(2) briefings on mission and UN organization
(3) information lectures including identifications and capabilities of the various forces of the parties to the conflict including leaders
(4) weapons handling
(5) biological and chemical warfare
(6) observer post duties
(7) crowd control techniques
(8) communications training [technical/electronic]
(9) UN incident report procedures
(10) first aid
(11) in-mission training plan and deployment plan
(12) administrative and financial arrangements in the mission area
(13) welfare plan including wives' travel arrangements in the mission area
(14) rear party support procedures
(15) family support arrangements.[8]

According to normal procedure at the end of the training period a simulation exercise of forty-eight hours duration is held 'covering company/battalion operational routine with simulated incidents'.[9] For example, in such an exercise a squadron would practise observation post duties, checkpoint procedures including searching vehicles, and foot patrols of a particular area. More in-depth training which might include cross-cultural training, conflict resolution skills training, and conflict analysis is not considered necessary and therefore is not part of regular training provision.

The normal overlap time between the arrival of a unit to the mission site and the departure of the current unit is two to three weeks. The mission-site training is, for the most part, on-the-job, where the incoming battalion goes through the same routines they practised in the simulation exercise at home, but this time at the mission site. In this case members of the incoming battalion are paired with those of the out-going battalion in patrols etc.

Preparation of units for a new mission is less thorough than preparation for planned rotations. Depending on how quickly mobilization can be achieved these units receive briefings for only a few hours or perhaps a few days. Briefings always include administrative information or 'house-keeping', and may also include socio-political briefings, and UN and mission organization briefings depending on time. This group of peacekeepers is by far the least prepared. Their training is on-the-job without the benefit of a two to three week overlap period with a more experienced battalion. If the battalion has previous peace-keeping experience this will help, but there is no guarantee that this will be the case.

Military Observers are now being trained together regardless of the particular mission assignment in an eight day programme run by CF-DPKO. The programme covers areas such as administrative material (compensation, benefits, travel and removal policy, passport and visa requirements, etc.), UN briefings, videos from different missions, geo-political briefings, weapons recognition, UN communication procedures and media relations.[10] In contrast, prospective Staff Officers receive two to five days of mission-specific briefings, usually at the CF-DPKO in Ottawa. These briefings cover a similar curriculum range as offered in the UNMO course but with an emphasis on the Staff Officer's particular job. Neither Military Observers nor Staff Officers receive more that a rudimentary introduction to cross-cultural interaction or mediation and negotiation concepts and skills.

The Douglas Report was critical of the preparation for UNMOs and UNSOs pointing out that,

the importance of friendly, and cooperative relationships with others must be stressed in training. Interpersonal relationships must be stressed as our reputation in this area is not of the best. We are seen by some as self-indulgent and not sensitive to the feelings, customs, and requirements of others.[11]

It is worth noting that in the pilot UNMO course one forty-five minute video approached the subject of cross-cultural relations, and no time was given to negotiation or mediation training.

The Douglas Report added that the selection process for UNMOs in particular was 'inadequate or absent'. Based on observations from the office of the Deputy Chief of Defence Staff and 'discussion with a large number of UNMOs' the report concluded that

> many individuals seem to have been selected more on the basis of their availability and desire to be employed as a UNMO than on their appropriateness to the task. Experience on ONUCA [United Nations Operation in Central America] indicated that, while part of the problem was a lack of preparation and training, there were several cases of individuals who should not have been selected for employment in any international organization.[12]

Two years later after the 'Douglas Report', a Canadian House of Commons report recommended that the Department of Defence conduct a 'complete evaluation' of peacekeeping training. The report argued that training should be more systematic, should 'make personnel more sensitive to the different cultures and practices of local populations' and should include training in conflict resolution.[13]

Two recent initiatives have had some impact on the prospects for improving peacekeeping training in Canada. A very public debate on the issue of peacekeeping training was initiated in 1991 with the publication of a report suggesting that a Canadian Peacekeeping Training Centre be established at CFB Cornwallis in Nova Scotia. The report cited the shortcomings of Canadian training provision particularly in view of new trends in peacekeeping. It suggested the goal of a training centre would be to 'facilitate the development of standardized training and operational procedures and... ensure that the necessary expertise and forces were readily available'.[14] The proposal envisioned the development of a regional training centre which would not only train military and civilian peace-keepers, but would 'facilitate important research and development in the field'.[15] In February 1994 the Canadian Department of Defence announced the establishment of an International Peacekeeping Training Centre located at CFB Cornwallis. Responsibility for setting up and running the new centre was delegated to the Canadian Institute of Strategic Studies (CISS). The Centre is mandated to provide research and education on peacekeeping and will not provide military training for peacekeeping missions. Training for UN operations will continue, as before, to be the responsibility of the home bases of units sent overseas. Given the broad scope of the original Cornwallis proposals, this new Centre is a disappointment. Its funding will be minimal: $5 million (Canadian dollars) for start-up costs and a further $1 million a year thereafter. In fact, given its limited mandate for peace-keeping training and its moderate funding, it would much more accurately be labelled a 'think tank', rather than an International Peacekeeping Training Centre.

Another recent initiative was begun by the last battalion to be sent to Cyprus which provided its officers with some mediation training. The initiative for this training came from within the regiment and was conducted during the six-week training period in preparation for deployment. The training included three lectures which were augmented by three practical exercises. Definitions for negotiation, mediation, etc. were provided along with a 'checklist of actions for investigation of incidents, preparation for, conduct of, and follow-up on negotiations'.[16] A follow-up evaluation of the training concluded that despite weaknesses it had been useful.[17] The training, while limited, was part of a larger research project conducted in Cyprus, directed by Major David Last, an officer in the regiment. This project aimed to

> identify mediation and negotiation strategies employed by Canadian troops in Cyprus, and relate the degree of success of these strategies to the nature of the dispute and the characteristics of the adversaries. The information will then be used to recommend negotiation techniques which could be taught to Canadian peacekeepers.[18]

With no institutionalized training base through which to feed such initiatives, there was little follow-up on the project. It is uncertain whether the results will be published and because each unit commander controls training curriculum, it is uncertain if the mediation training will be repeated.

## 2.2  Irish Defence Forces (IDF)

Ireland has a small professional army which, like Canada, has a long history of participation in peacekeeping. Unlike Canada, for Irish forces, peacekeeping duty is voluntary and organized outside the normal regimental structure. For Ireland's main peacekeeping contribution, a battalion in Lebanon (UNIFIL), individuals are selected from all over the country and form a new battalion prior to each re-deployment. Until 1994, they had no institutionalized, centralized training programmes.

The ethos for Irish Forces' preparation for peacekeeping extends from two prevailing circumstances. The first is that any peacekeeper needs basic military training in order to prepare for 'worst-case scenarios'. Training can then be augmented for peacekeeping based on that common level of preparation, and Irish soldiers have this training. The second is that Irish soldiers are involved in a large amount of internal security or 'Aid to the Civil Power' (ACP) duty which involves many of the same activities as peacekeeping. These two circumstances together mean, from the Irish point of view, that specific training in peacekeeping is not a matter of learning anything new, but rather of reviewing what is already well-trodden ground.

There are two categories of preparation for peacekeeping in the Irish Defence Forces: (1) training for service in UNIFIL (or other specified missions), all ranks, and (2) preparation for UNMOs and UNSOs. The details of the training programme for UNIFIL, all ranks, are set out in a training circular provided by the Irish Defence Forces, Director of Training. Although units are chosen for rotation on an *ad hoc* basis, there is a well-developed routine for the selection and training of this battalion. This is not surprising since Ireland has been contributing to UNIFIL since 1978. The training circular details the arrangements for training by specific timetabling, delegation of responsibility, and explication of training subject areas.[19]

There are four phases of training. Phase One takes place in the 'parent unit', where those in a particular unit who have been assigned to the UNIFIL battalion are given their initial training. The responsibility for initiating and overseeing this training period rests with each separate unit commander. This phase covers basic military training such as personal weapon skills, physical endurance and military communications. In all, Phase One requires approximately eighty-seven hours of training.[20]

In Phase Two, companies are formed at concentration areas, and training commences at the company level. A total of eighty-five hours of training includes areas such as UN orientation, and checkpoint and observation post training.

In Phase Three the companies which have been operating separately now come together for final preparation. This phase includes several simulation exercises, battle inoculation (a simulated battle which prepares soldiers for the sounds and atmosphere of real battle conditions) and separate training for several specialized units. The commander of the UNIFIL battalion has responsibility for the training in Phases Three and Four.

Phase Four training takes place in Lebanon and is supposed to be continuous throughout the six-month tour. Detailed specification of this training is not provided in the training circular except to say that 'there is significant emphasis in the first month on perfecting the tactics, techniques and skills, at all levels, that can only be developed in the operational area'.[21]

Although preparation for a six-month tour of UNIFIL takes approximately two months, within the training programme there are at most two hours on cross-cultural issues, one hour of which is an introduction to Lebanese culture, 'do's and don't's'. The other is a film. There is no time specifically set aside for instruction in such skills as mediation, negotiation and conciliation or in the conceptual issues of conflict and conflict analysis as they relate to the conflict in Lebanon or as they relate to a general *raison d'etre* for the peacekeeping operation beyond *status quo* measures.

Until 1994, there was no specific training course for UN Military Observers, Staff Officers, or Liaison Officers, although any officer selected to serve in one of these posts would have had at least one six-month tour in Lebanon.

Preparation for these positions, apart from the basic level of military training that all officers receive, was, in large part, left to individual initiative. Once the UNMO or UNSO had arrived in the mission area, there was an overlap period of approximately two weeks for orientation during which the officer was given on-the-job training.

In early 1994, the Irish Defence Forces set up a UN school at their Staff College at the Curragh. Not only will this school offer training for UN observers but it is also designated to provide training for units bound for service with UNIFIL. It is unlikely that the actual preparation of the UNIFIL units will change (apart from the venue) since their training was already well-established and semi-institutionalized. Training for UNMOs and UNSOs, though, constitutes a significant improvement on previous practice.

Another recent initiative which may have some impact on preparation in the future was started by the United Nations Veteran's Association in Ireland. This association funded a research project on Post-Traumatic Stress Syndrome (PTSS) in Irish peacekeepers.[22] The project was begun in response to what was seen as a growing problem of PTSS amongst peacekeepers returning from duty in Lebanon (a problem acknowledged by the IDF). The aim of the project was to identify better ways to treat the syndrome but also

> to develop improved training for military personnel before being sent on overseas missions. This training... would be designed to reduce to a minimum PTSS among troops confronted with war-like conditions and to improve the troops' effectiveness in carrying out their mission through a heightened psychological awareness of the many conflicts they will encounter as well as a more detailed understanding of the groups with whom they have to deal.[23]

The director of the research project pointed out that,

> there is a huge difference between the syndromes suffered by conflict troops and peacekeeping soldiers, and in many cases there is greater stress on the non-combatants because when they have come under attack they must exercise restraint and not return fire.[24]

This study could have major impact on how future peace-keepers are prepared. It may be that PTSS is the result of a lack of full adjustment first from a purely military role to a peace-keeping role, but also a similar lack of adjustment back to a purely military role once the peacekeeping tour is completed. Moskos's study, discussed in Chapter 7, argues that peacekeep-ers go through an adjustment period during which feelings of futility and powerlessness are common. Other researchers argue that reducing that difficult period of adjustment should be the main task of training. They reason that during such an adjustment phase an individual's ability to function effectively in the new environment is greatly inhibited. Moreover, these researchers present findings which indicate that fact-oriented training should be only a small part of a comprehensive train-ing package designed to reduce the severity and duration of this phase of adjustment.

### 2.3 The Nordic System: Regional Cooperation

The Nordic countries all provide special peacekeeping train-ing for their units in addition to the basic military training they receive. Each country has a conscript system of national service which lasts from eight months to two years after which most conscripts become reservists. Service for UN peacekeeping is voluntary and approximately 90 per cent of UN battalions are recruited from reservists while the remaining 8–10 per cent come from the small regular armies.

The ethos of training for peacekeeping in the Nordic coun-tries is based on the assumption that peacekeeping requires different skills and knowledge from those which regular mili-tary training provides, and therefore all peacekeepers receive special training before entering UN service. This specialized training ranges from two to seven weeks depending on the individual country, rank and particular job requirements of the trainee.

The Nordic attitude is markedly different to that found in either the Canadian or Irish forces. Both the Canadian and Irish forces argue that their peacekeepers do not need special-ized training because they are professionals who carry out the same tasks that they will face as peacekeepers every day of the year in their capacities as professional soldiers at home. This argument, of course, does not take into account several unique aspects of peacekeeping.

The Nordic approach is not *ad hoc* although Nordic Countries recruit for peacekeeping service utilizing an *ad hoc* method. The Nordic regional, cooperative training system is based on a conceptual proposition which provides specific direction for the training of UN personnel. The proposition is simply that UN peacekeeping, while requiring some basic military skills, is essentially different from regular military practice and therefore requires different training. Most significantly, there is the need to approach peacekeeping with a different attitude than one required for military tasks. A former Director of the Swedish UN Training Centre noted that of particular importance for good preparation is 'intercultural awareness'. He elaborated by pointing out that,

> If an understanding of these [cultural] differences is not put across, you will run into problems. This is because you can approach people in the wrong way particularly as a peace-keeper. A peacekeeper does not use a weapon, rather he uses his capacity to negotiate as a weapon, and, therefore, it is very important for him to know what kind of a person is on the other side of the table.... That understanding and knowledge will give them [peacekeepers] the right attitude.[25]

In 1964, Denmark, Finland, Norway, and Sweden agreed on the basic composition of the Nordic Stand-by Forces.[26] In addition to joint training arrangements which will be examined below, the Stand-By Forces agreement outlines the curriculum and timing of training for national units. Training for the stand-by forces is the responsibility of each country and is carried out separately although in accordance with the agreed training guidelines. These guidelines stipulate that UN training will consist of: information on the UN and peacekeeping; geo-political and cultural information; basic understanding of specific tasks of peacekeeping; conditions of service.[27] In addition to the training all ranks receive in preparation for peace-keeping (length and curriculum differ slightly for each country), there is a one-week 'refresher' training course during the call up and mobilization procedure for the Stand-By Forces. Mobilization from call up to arrival in the mission area takes approximately twenty days (this does not include the advance parties, the first of which arrives in the mission area within five to seven days of mobilization). Training during the mobilization period consists not only of basic military refresher training but covers the following peacekeeping topics:

- Manning of Checkpoints, Observation Posts and patrolling, emphasis laid on night patrolling.
- Knowledge concerning what to look for at a check point and how to search properly.
- Identification of various types of small arms, mortars, artillery, armoured cars, tanks, aircraft and naval boats, especially those in use in the area.
- Identification of the sound of small guns, especially distinguishing mortars from artillery.
- Knowledge of the ranges of weapons.
- Map reading.
- Construction of observation posts and shelters.
- Up-to-date information about the particular UN mission.
- Culture, habits, characteristics of local native population.
- Religion/s prevailing in the area.
- Medical checks, vaccinations.
- Transport preparations and transport training.[28]

This training is conducted at the National Training Centres (UNTCs) in each country and continues up until one to two days before the unit is transported to the mission area. It is in addition to the two to seven weeks of training all ranks have previously received in preparation for UN service.

National training is the responsibility of each individual country, and their arrangements differ slightly. Typically, training is carried out at a National Training Centre which is also responsible for recruiting personnel from the reserves. For example Finland rotates its troops three times a year, and so holds three recruiting and training rounds a year in preparation for rotation of troops to the various missions to which it contributes. Sweden's rotation is twice a year so their recruitment and training vary accordingly. Training covers the areas listed above in the previous section and is timed to be held just before troops are rotated to their UN assignment.

Along with the training programmes described above, the Nordic countries run a cooperative system of training for officers and NCOs in specialized areas of expertise. Denmark provides a UN Military Police Course (UNMILPOC), Finland provides a UN Military Observer's Course (UNMOC), Norway provides a UN Logistics and Movement Control Course (UNLOC), and Sweden provides a UN Staff Officer's Course (UNSOC). Each course runs for two to three weeks. While some military personnel from countries outside the Nordics can participate, the space is very limited.

While the Nordic system is the best example of training by countries participating in UN operations, the system has several shortcomings. Despite consistently pointing out the importance placed on intercultural relations, the peace-keepers' 'attitude' as well as the importance of conflict resolution skills, the Nordic training system has a surprisingly small number of hours devoted to these subjects. The UN Staff Officer's course is the only one which has time devoted to specific training in negotiation and mediation skills, but even this only takes up three lecture slots out of a total of 123 lectures (of 45 minute duration each). While it is positive that they have any specific training in the area at all, the time allotted is disproportionate to the stated and actual need. Of course, it is important to provide officers as well as rank and file with a good understanding of the UN system and the specific tasks that they will be expected to carry out. However, cross-cultural training and mediation and negotiation training are minimal, and conceptual teaching in conflict analysis and resolution is non-existent.

It should be reiterated that while it is possible and important to note the shortcomings of the Nordic system; in comparison to other countries, its training programme is excellent. This point underscores the most problematic aspect of training for UN peacekeeping. Because the demand for peacekeepers has increased there are fewer of the best trained peacekeepers to go around. When this situation is added to the fact that the nature of peacekeeping is expanding and becoming more complex and that it is not easy to discern how well prepared even the best prepared peacekeepers are, there must be increasing concern for both the safety of peacekeepers and for the effectiveness of their missions.

## 2.4 Secretariat: Briefings for Senior Military Staff

Very senior military staff in a peacekeeping operation including Force Commanders and Chief Military Observers normally receive about a week of briefings at the Department of Peacekeeping Operations in New York. The DPKO provides guidelines on how to manage the force, gives details about how the mandate will be translated into practice, and provides information and direction about the administrative and logistical aspects of the overall management of the operation. These briefings do not include specific training in mediation, negotiation, or cross-cultural interaction. Although they will cover the current conflict situation, they do not go further into conflict analysis nor do they provide an overall conceptual framework for the operation.


## 3. CIVILIAN TRAINING

Every UN operation involves the participation of civilians, since peacekeeping operations are directed by a civilian authority, i.e., the Secretariat under the overall control of the Security Council. The essential functions carried out by UN staff was noted in a 1990 UN report on civilian participation in peacekeeping:

> the core civilian functions of a peacekeeping operation, including the political direction and the administration of an operation in the field in all its facets, must be performed by United Nations staff members.[29]

The use of civilians in peacekeeping, while not a new phenomenon, has increased considerably in the last five years. However, with the exception of the training programmes of a small number of international agencies, civilian training is conducted on an *ad hoc* basis with little or no centralized coordination. Along with the increase in numbers has come an expansion of the roles civilian peacekeepers take on. Boutros-Ghali emphasized this point in *An Agenda for Peace*:

> Increasingly, peacekeeping requires that civilian political officers, human rights monitors, electoral officials, refugee

and humanitarian aid specialists and police play as central a role as the military.[30]

He went on to argue that given this increased participation more coordinated and comprehensive efforts in the area of training were necessary.

> I recommend that arrangements be reviewed and improved for training peacekeeping personnel – civilian, police, or military – using the varied capabilities of Member State Governments, of non-governmental organizations and the facilities of the Secretariat.[31]

There are four basic categories of civilian peacekeepers. First are the regular staff from the UN. One section of this group fulfils administrative and logistic functions directed in the field by a Chief Administrative Officer. The other main section of this group are UN staff working in the Special Representative's office. The second group are staff recruited and then 'seconded' from outside the UN to fill functions such as election supervision and police monitoring. The third group includes individuals brought in who have special areas of expertise (engineering or architectural consultants, for example). These individuals are normally hired on short-term contracts. The last group of civilians participating in peacekeeping operations is made up of those staff employed by companies who have service contracts with the UN. The first two categories, UN staff and 'seconded' personnel make up the largest percentage of civilians in peacekeeping missions and therefore are the primary focus here.

The participation of civilians in peacekeeping operations reached a watershed in Namibia during UNTAG. It was this operation that raised the profile of peacekeeping in general but also specifically for civilian involvement in peacekeeping. There were several novel aspects of civilian activity in this operation including the roles of both the political offices and the police monitors (see Chapter 3). In terms of training, Namibia was the first peacekeeping operation for which civilian peacekeepers were specifically trained by the UN. Training was coordinated by the UN Office of Human Resources Management (OHRM) which provided training for UN and seconded staff. The set-up and management of training aspects of UNTAG provided a blueprint for other similar peace-keeping missions with large civilian components such as Cambodia. For this reason training for UNTAG will be discussed in some detail.

The OHRM provided training for UN Staff at UN Head-quarters (and various UN duty stations such as Geneva and Vienna) and at the mission-site. It also provided mission-site training for seconded staff who, in some cases, also received in-country training prior to deployment to Namibia. A general overview of the training and deployment of the three separate waves of civilians sent to participate in UNTAG (except CIVPOL, which is dealt with separately) will be provided here.

The first wave was sent out at or around the beginning of April 1989, and was composed, largely, of UN Staff. This group received at most two and a half days of training which varied from a few hours of briefings with a large group to several days of training with smaller groups depending on the assignment and management level of the trainees. Two half-day briefings for all staff going to Namibia were held – one on 19 January 1989 and the other on 22 March 1989. The programme for both briefings included: (1) a video presentation, (2) a polit-ical and organizational analysis, (3) a discussion of typical assignments for UN staff and examples of day-to-day life, and (4) a presentation of personnel, administrative, and health and welfare-related issues.[32] A two and a half day workshop was held in New York for Regional Directors and Front Office Staff in early March 1989. The participants in this programme were briefed on administrative and operations aspects of the mission, and the current socio-political situation in Namibia. In addition participants were involved in a case-study where they were encouraged to work together to 'clarify operational objectives, their roles, and their relation to others who would be involved in the operation'.[33] Two further two-day workshops were held during March in New York and Geneva for Deputy Regional Directors, District Centre Heads, and Deputy District Centre Heads. The programme covered was similar though shorter than the programme for Regional Directors. It is interesting to note that whereas the job description for District Centre Heads specifically called for liaison (cross-cultural activity) and conflict resolution work, the preparation pro-gramme did not provide specific training for either role.[34]

Most UN staff who were part of the first wave and second waves later attended two to four days of election supervision training in Namibia.

The second wave was sent out to take part in the voter registration programme which started 3 July 1989. The second wave received one to three days of administrative and logistical briefings once they arrived in Namibia and before they were deployed throughout the country. This included a half-day briefing at UN Headquarters before deployment. Many of this group were UN personnel but some were seconded from governments.

The third wave was the largest (close to 1,200 in all). This group was made up of election supervisors, more than half of whom were seconded from governments. Some governments provided training for their personnel – many did not. The Swedish United Nations Training Centre, for example, provided a ten-day training programme for its contingent. Such pre-deployment preparation was the exception rather than the rule. Most of the personnel sent in the third wave arrived with little or no preparation. Once they arrived in Namibia they received three to four days of training focused on election supervision.[35] All of this training occurred during the six-week run-up to elections in early November 1989. There were three two-day workshops and two one-day workshops given during October for UN staff, military personnel and CIVPOL. For the third wave four training centres were set up around Namibia, each of which ran a single four-day workshop on election supervision for 100–600 people. These training programmes were all based on a 'Manual for UNTAG Election Supervisors' which gave details of the mechanics of each part of the electoral process, and provided written material which coincided with the presentations given during the three to four day training period.[36] Once training had been completed, election supervisors were dispersed to twenty-three election districts covering the territory of Namibia.[37] In all, 358 polling stations were established and supervised by UNTAG personnel.[38]

For the future, it is likely that training will benefit from more pre-planning, particularly in terms of fact-finding to determine training needs. It seems likely that such a development will have the most impact on preparation for UN staff rather than contingents from Member States. There are several reasons for this. First, as a matter of course, the Training Service of the OHRM will focus its energies on coordinating mission-site training, as opposed to looking to improve in-country pre-deployment training. Second, and probably more important are the limited financial resources available and the general financial crisis at the UN.

## 3.1 In-Country Training

In general, the OHRM has no part in this aspect of civilian preparation. Each contributing country is issued guidelines which provide a very general description of how a training programme can be set up.[39] In-country training in countries sending civilian contingents to participate in peacekeeping missions, is a purely *ad hoc* provision. It is difficult even to draw comparisons between countries. How good preparation is depends entirely on the will of the Member State involved to provide such preparation and to take the time and resources to set it up and run it. The example used here of in-country training for Namibia is of the Irish Garda contingent who were part of the civilian police force of UNTAG.

The Irish Garda contingent were given final confirmation of participation in UNTAG in late February 1989. It was at this time that preparations began on developing a training programme for the Irish police selected for duty in Namibia. They were expected to deploy as close to 1 April 1989 as possible. The contingent of 35 (with two alternates) was selected on a volunteer basis from a large pool of applications, and volunteers knew in advance that their posting would be for approximately one year. The training programme lasted eleven days in all, but was run in three parts spread over six weeks. Much of the information on Namibia and on the mission, as well as a large part of the actual training, was provided by the Irish military. Areas covered in the training programme included: UN task, geo-political briefings, cooking, driving, land mine recognition, and administrative details. During the last part of the training programme, a half-day session was presented by the Irish overseas voluntary agency, Agency for Personnel Service Overseas (APSO). This short programme tried to emphasize some of the psychological stresses of working overseas and provided practical ways to deal with them. As part of CIVPOL the Garda were expected to have everyday contact with SWAPOL and the people SWAPOL were policing. Creating an atmosphere of confidence among the Namibian people was considered a crucial part of CIVPOL's mandate, and that meant contact and liaison with a variety of organizations (some, such as SWAPOL, hostile to CIVPOL's intentions) and direct contact with as many ordinary civilians as possible.

Time pressures prevented more in-depth training which might have included conflict resolution skills and more cross-cultural training. However, even if more time had been available it is unlikely that these areas would have been augmented. The Garda are an unarmed constabulary and have experience of dealing with defusing violent situations non-violently. Whether this experience is, on the one hand, adequate, or whether it can be transferred to the peacekeeping arena, has not been studied.

The Irish Garda contingent arrived in Namibia on 15 April 1989. They stayed in the capital, Windhoek, for five days before being deployed. They received briefings which ran for two and a half days. These covered the geo-political situation, administration and logistics. The briefings were largely a repeat of the contingent's pre-deployment training.

## 4. TRAINING BY INTERNATIONAL AGENCIES

This type of training provides the only example of institutionalized training for civilian peacekeepers. The training is not targeted for one specific mission but for peacekeeping in general (although topics specific to a particular operation are covered in training sessions). The three institutions which will be examined here, United Nations Institute for Training and Research, the International Peace Academy, and the Austrian Study Centre for Peace and Conflict Resolution, carry out planned, institutionalized training. In the case of UNITAR and ASPR, this process has just begun; in the case of the IPA, peacekeeping training programmes have been running for over twenty years. A unique aspect of these programmes is that they bring together diplomats, military personnel, UN agency and NGO personnel and academics. This is rare in the area of peacekeeping training and is important for encouraging dialogue and cooperation and facilitating understanding of distinct operational areas.

### 4.1 United Nations Institute for Training and Research (UNITAR)

UNITAR's New York-based peacekeeping training programme began, officially, in November 1991 with a broad mandate 'to promote "peacekeeping literacy" among staff members of the United Nations system and Permanent Mission personnel' in the overall context of 'developing a longer-term integrated training programme'.[40]

It initially focused on developing monthly half-day seminars which dealt with the practical aspects of current peacekeeping missions, one-week training workshops for intensive orientation to peacekeeping, a series of instructional videos and simulation exercises. The programme's longer-term goals are to develop seminars on establishing regional and national peacekeeping training centres and to develop seminars for training trainers.

UNITAR in Geneva has developed a 'Fellowship Programme in Peacemaking and Preventive Diplomacy', held for the first time in 1993. While not explicitly for peacekeepers, its aim is to add to a cadre of international expertise in this area. Considering the connections between peacemaking, preventive diplomacy and peacekeeping, this is a positive development. Interestingly, the programme is co-sponsored by the IPA, and hosted by ASPR. Lack of secure financial support means that the future of this project is uncertain.

### 4.2 International Peace Academy (IPA)

An independent international institution, the IPA was founded in 1970 with the aim of promoting 'peaceful alternatives to the management and resolution of international as well as internal conflict'.[41] Much of IPA's work has been devoted to the enhancement of peacekeeping as a mechanism for the maintenance of international peace and security.

The IPA's training activity is fairly extensive. Since it was established, over 5000 people from 150 different countries have participated in IPA training seminars.[42] The programmes target middle-ranking diplomats and military officers, although others such as UN agency personnel, NGO personnel and academics may also be involved. Its yearly seminar schedule is anchored by four distinct programmes which culminate in the 'flagship' of the IPA's training programme, the Vienna Seminar on UN peacekeeping. Although the IPA is involved in a number of different activities related to promoting peaceful alternatives to conflict, its central device for facilitating such processes is the creation of a group of peacekeeping professionals whom the UN can call upon to serve in peacekeeping missions.

The Vienna Seminar hosts around thirty participants and runs annually for just under two weeks. Four main teaching techniques are utilized, including presentations and lectures, question and answer periods, case-studies, and simulation exercises. Three simulation exercises and two case-studies are the main organizing foci around which lectures are inserted.

The simulation exercises are developed based on one scenario of two fictional countries which share an island in the middle of the Pacific Ocean: Simulex One is a bilateral negotiation exercise between the two countries over a water dispute which is vital to each country's interests; Simulex Two is a multilateral negotiating exercise centred on the Security Council; Simulex Three involves the establishment of a peacekeeping force on the island.

For simulating the mechanics of bilateral and multilateral negotiations and increasing understanding of the requirements for setting up a peacekeeping force, the exercises have some benefit. However, apart from the lack of appropriate skills training, they are ineffective on a range of issues which are currently being explored with some vigour in academic circles – and which have been shown to have considerable impact on the success of conflict management initiatives. For example, the approach of a third party mediator would be significantly different from the approach of a bilateral negotiator, yet the two roles were not distinguished. The whole academic area of third party intervention exemplifies this point (see Chapter 4). Overall, basic conceptual issues are ignored and the nature of a peaceful third party role remains unexamined.

## 4.3  The Austrian Study Centre for Peace and Conflict Resolution (ASPR)

ASPR in Schlaining, Austria, is organized in association with the European University Centre for Peace Studies and is sponsored by the Austrian Government. It offered a pilot four-week training programme on peacekeeping and peacebuilding for civilians in late 1993. The ethos of the programme is based on the assumption that civilians trained in preventive diplomacy, peacekeeping and peacebuilding will be increasingly in demand to 'ensure a more pacific world under the new conditions that have followed the end of the Cold War'.[43]

The programme is organized to provide participants with a basic knowledge and understanding of conflict analysis, functions of civilians in peacekeeping and peacebuilding, organizations involved in peacekeeping and peacebuilding, and individual skills and needs in this general environment. The course provides cross-cultural and communications skills training, although it has no specific provision for negotiation and mediation. Because it clearly establishes the link between peacekeeping, peacemaking, and peacebuilding activities, and trains its participants in a number of contact skills and in cross-cultural relations, ASPR's project is particularly important. This approach could be very usefully expanded to include military peacekeepers.[44]

## 5.  CRITIQUE OF PEACEKEEPING TRAINING

### 5.1  Practical Critique

Chapter 7 briefly explored cross-cultural training as a potential source of raw material and direction for the development of peacekeeping training programmes. This practical critique of peacekeeping training will be based on the three factors generally considered important to cross-cultural effectiveness: skills or abilities, attitudes, and personality traits.

The skills which are thought to be related positively with effectiveness in cross-cultural interaction and in third party intervention are listed together in Chapter 7 (see also Chapter 4 for third party intervention skills). Teaching such skills would require expanding training programmes beyond the traditional fact-oriented approaches to include more of the six methods described in the previous chapter. Research in cross-cultural training suggests that experiential techniques may be the most useful for facilitating conflict resolution skills development. It is also apparent that these skills are needed.

Internal Canadian Forces reviews support the argument that the lack of preparation for peacekeeping is problematic:

> Military training – specifically Canadian army training – is far from the best means to prepare a soldier to be a negotiating peacekeeper. The young soldier at the 'problem' OP [observation post] in a foreign country is invariably neither socially nor mentally attuned to dealing with other military and civilians, in adversary relationships.[45]

'The Douglas Report' and 'The Report of the Director of Peacekeeping', both cited above, point out that it is not just a matter of adding some training in mediation or negotiation skills. Rather, the whole process of training lacks coherence and consistency as well as quality. As one Canadian Forces paper suggests, 'it is... negotiation by the individual peacekeeper which is at once the most fundamental, the most frequent, the most dangerous, and invariably the most unprepared for [role]'.[46]

Cross-cultural training too is important for peacekeeping. A study of peacekeeping in UNIFIL points out that experience in another culture does not necessarily lead to expertise or effectiveness in cross-cultural interaction. Heiberg examined the relations of peacekeepers with local populations in Lebanon. She argues that,

> the nature of the relationship a peacekeeping force achieves with the population within its area of control is a decisive element in determining the operation's success or failure.... Critically, however, the local population concerned [in Lebanon] is not a homogeneous, seamless or indeed self-evident entity. The human and political equations involved are multilayered, highly intricate, often contradictory and shifting, and not necessarily fully visible.[47]

She goes on to point out that 'only a small minority of UNIFIL personnel receive satisfactory political or cultural training about the area prior to their arrival'.[48] What Heiberg's study illustrates is that even the best prepared troops in Lebanon, of which the Irish Battalion is undoubtedly one, are not well prepared in areas which are critical for successful peace-keeping. In addition, these areas do not fall within the normal range of the military training curriculum. Moreover, many units and individuals sent on peacekeeping missions receive no preparation at all.[49]

Where training is provided for military peacekeeping skills, it appears to be relatively well-developed, utilizes a number of fact-oriented training techniques including situation exercises, and relates directly to training needs (within that limited context). In many cases skills overlap from regular duties and training to peacekeeping duties and training. This is often the case for both military and civilian personnel. The main problem for this type of training is that it does not prepare peacekeepers to carry out their third party role. A training programme may prepare a soldier in the correct techniques for foot or vehicle patrols, for correct operation of a check point including the details of filing reports, for routine radio procedures, or for vehicle searches. These skills are important for effective peacekeeping, but without reference to the third party role of peacekeeping, or the skills needed to carry out that third party role, they are inadequate. The inadequacy of preparation which covers only military peacekeeping skills should be apparent from the fact that peacekeepers are forced by the demands of the job to carry out third party roles without specialized training.

Civilian training also focuses almost exclusively on fact-oriented training, and while getting across the 'facts' of a situation is an important aspect of any training programme, unsupported by other methods it is not enough. This shortcoming aside, it is very difficult to properly train people in groups of between 100 and 600.[50] Even in the relatively problem-free implementation process in Namibia, the fact that individuals often worked in small teams of two or three and operated in remote areas points to the need to provide more comprehensive preparation. So too, does UNTAG's involvement through the political offices in the national reconciliation process.

Although some attention is paid to the importance of a shift in attitude, particularly from a military approach to a peacekeeping approach, very little training to effect such a shift is carried out. The experience of cross-cultural training suggests that to bring about real shifts in attitude, fact-oriented training is not sufficient. As Grove and Torbiorn note,

> because mere knowledge of the inappropriateness of certain behaviors is unlikely to enable one to make sweeping modifications in his or her habitual patterns of activity, fact-oriented training by itself is not sufficient.[51]

In other words it is not enough to tell a soldier that he/she is now a part of a peaceful third party intervention and not a war exercise. Since all of a soldier's training will have been focused on the latter, it should not be surprising that for professional soldiers in particular, the abrupt shift in job description and expectations is a difficult one to make. Of particular interest may be attribution-oriented training which has been shown to be particularly effective for helping individuals become aware of their own attitudes and those held by individuals in other cultures. A technique such as the general-culture assimilator might be usefully adapted for training potential peacekeepers.[52]

The attitudes necessary for effectively pursuing a third party role are unfamiliar not only to military personnel. The experience of cross-cultural training suggests that civilian peacekeepers are also likely to need training in this area. Thornberry described UNTAG as 'consciously a catalytic agent for political and attitudinal change in Namibia'.[53] It is ironic that while the peacekeepers themselves had no training in this area, they were expected to be the agents of such change through UNTAG.

Personality traits which impact negatively on effective cross-cultural interaction are listed in Chapter 7. They include, perfectionism, rigidity, narrow-mindedness and dogmatism. A selection process based on identifying personality traits in potential peacekeepers does not exist. Nor has research been carried out which identifies personality characteristics which impact negatively on effectiveness for peacekeepers. The importance of selection is suggested in cross-cultural interaction research, and, at least for officer ranks, by the Canadian review of peacekeeping mentioned above.

For political officers headed to Namibia (about 100 staff in all) there was a lengthy application and interview process. The applicants, especially at senior levels, were selected primarily for 'proven managerial skills'.[54] While this process was carefully conducted for key positions, a question mark remains on the criteria used for selection and how well they related to effectiveness in a peacekeeping environment. Moreover, for the large majority of civilian personnel in Namibia, selection was in the hands of contributing countries and outside of UN control. Given the inadequacy of much of the selection of military personnel, it is likely that selection processes for police monitors, election supervisors, etc. are similarly deficient.

## 5.2 Theoretical Critique

With the exception of the pilot ASPR course for civilians, existing training programmes all lack a sound theoretical basis. It is important to differentiate between the conceptual level argued for here and the concepts and practices upon which existing training programmes, particularly military ones, are based. In this work the conceptual base is derived from the assumptions and practices of conflict management and peaceful third party intervention, viewed through the application of contingency models. Existing training provision, based on a set of common practices and rules of engagement which over the years have come to be associated with the practice of peacekeeping, are used as a substitute for conceptualization. This is a crucial difference.

The rules which guide peacekeeping, whether they are called concepts, principles, or even theory, are not related to or derived from concepts about the causes of conflict. Whether these causes are subjective or objective, related to the role of basic human needs in conflict, or are the concepts inherent in settlement and resolution practices, etc., they have not been related to the practice of peacekeeping in any coherent fashion. Moreover, these rules do not provide a rationale for peacekeeping or for peacekeeping training which is testable, or which is anecdotally apparent. In other words, these rules do not constitute a theory of peacekeeping.

This brings us back to the argument posited by those who are opposed to developing a definition of peacekeeping. That is, that a specific definition of peacekeeping would render the technique inflexible, dogmatic, and eventually useless. This argument may be relevant with respect to defining peace-keeping through a set of rules as it is most often conceived. It is quite possible that such a development would limit the potential uses of peacekeeping. But it would not be relevant to peacekeeping which operated through the rationale of contingency theory, and which therefore, would be subject to the on-going re-evaluation, testing, and development process prescribed by contingency approaches.

The current provision for training is less than adequate, and the need to derive training provision from within a conceptual framework is pronounced. Training programmes, where they do exist, operate without reference to these points which results in the following: (1) a lack of standardization in train-ing, (2) a lack of coherence in training and in the develop-ment of training programmes, (3) a lack of evidence and research supporting training goals based on training needs, and (4) a lack of clear objectives and methodology which directly reflect a wider approach to the peaceful resolution of conflict and which are then related directly to peacekeeping activities.

## 6. CONCLUSION

Apart from the ASPR pilot programme, the Nordic countries provide the most teaching hours in their training programmes for conflict resolution skills and for cross-cultural orientation. To place this in perspective, though, it should be pointed out that at best only a small fraction of course time is spent on these two areas – approximately 5 per cent in any of the Nordic programmes, either national or regional.

For the best prepared UN peacekeepers training lasts from two weeks to two months. All of these programmes are very similar in content. Besides providing some specific mission-orientation information, such as command structure, mandate specifics, and geo-political information, they focus exclusively on non-contact skills. These are defined as the skills needed to carry out specific (normally military) tasks, such as check point and observation post operation, weapons firing, incident report forms, radio communication and operation, cooking, driving, first aid, etc. Training in these skills is almost exclusively fact-oriented although it may extend to interactional training as well. Current training programmes do not cover contact skills (there are two exceptions, but even in these cases the coverage is so minimal that the usefulness of the training is questionable). These contact skills are associated with negotiation, mediation, etc., or cross-cultural interaction. They constitute a substantial and integral part of many peacekeeping duties, particularly (but not exclusively) those activities involving direct contact with opposing armies, civilian populations, other parts of the peacekeeping force, etc.

Leaving aside the need for and current lack of training for contact skills, training military peacekeepers, where conscientiously provided, particularly for rotation, is relatively good. However, weaknesses become evident in several different areas: (1) training for initial contribution to a new mission is generally inadequate, unless it comes from one of the Nordic Stand-By battalions, (2) training for officers for specific UNMO and UNSO positions is generally inadequate, unless they have participated in the Nordic Courses or in the Canadian UNMO course, (3) training for any peacekeeper from outside the seven is, in some cases, at the same level as training for Canadian and Irish peacekeepers, but generally is either less adequate or non-existent. The most significant weakness of all perhaps is that there is no empirical research to confirm the usefulness of training. In addition, present training programmes are not based on conceptually driven methodology.

Civilian training is far less well planned and organized than military preparation for peacekeeping. All of the training of civilians is fact-oriented, mainly relying on briefing sessions. Where it exists it focuses on non-contact skills, such as the mechanics of election supervision, survival skills, first aid, and mission orientation information such as geo-political briefings. There is no training for contact skills for civilians beyond the cross-cultural training offered in the pilot ASPR programme. In general, specific training for civilian peacekeepers is significantly less adequate than military training, and for many civilian peacekeepers it is non-existent. Here again, there is no standardization of training or conceptually based empirical research needed to locate training needs or effectiveness.

If, as has been argued here, this knowledge and these skills are required at every stage and all levels of a peacekeeping mission (in varying degrees), then training programmes must be developed accordingly. A peacekeeping mission is based on a consensual relationship between all sides to the dispute and the UN. A peacekeeper cannot force peace or free and fair elections on anyone. Operational effectiveness is based on the strength of that consensual relationship which is facilitated by the UN and its peacekeepers on the ground through the application of peaceful third party intervention techniques. At present training does not reflect the dual reality of the peacekeeper's role – conflict control and conflict resolution. And while training may be good and appropriate for the actual task at hand – the conflict control role (although this too can be questioned), it is non-existent for a range of techniques which will most effectively facilitate not only short-term conflict control, but also long-term conflict resolution. Finally peacekeepers receive little or not re-entry support once they have returned from a mission.

Training and practice, without reference to these crucial points within the context of the expansion of peacekeeping roles and its growing complexity is, at best, irresponsible. At worst such deficiencies are dangerous for the peacekeepers, the civilians invariably caught in the middle, and the conflict process itself. In addition, lack of effectiveness has led to growing pressure to give peacekeepers enforcement powers. In the end, this last point is probably the most irresponsible and potentially dangerous result of continuing to ignore these points.

Ethical issues relating to intervention which were raised in Chapter 4 are again relevant. The ethics of putting individuals in positions for which they are unprepared is one side of the coin. The other side of the ethical problem is the unknown effect peacekeeping intervention has on the conflict process itself. It may be that by intervening as a third party and then lacking in the third party skills needed to facilitate settlement and resolution, peacekeeping prolongs conflict, further polarizes warring factions, and adds to economic and social problems by creating dependency.[55]

# 9 The Conceptualization of Peacekeeping: Implications for Training and Practice

## 1. COMPARING TRAINING AND PRACTICE: FINDING THE TRAINING GAP

Attitudes toward peacekeepers' roles and toward the training they should receive appear to be shifting in two directions. The first and less noticeable shift is toward the conclusion that increasing demands for micro-level peacemaking and peace-building activity on the part of peacekeepers necessitates specific preparation for this role. The second shift, based on a similar analysis of the increasingly complex interventions carried out by the UN, has led to a growing body of opinion which argues for the authorization of more military or enforcement powers for peacekeepers.[1] This second role should not be associated with third party peacekeeping. Boutros-Ghali makes a point of separating enforcement action from peacekeeping in *An Agenda for Peace*.[2] Ironically, the argument for this second role lends support to the claim here that military peacekeepers are trained for war but are asked to carry out a peaceful third party intervention which not only limits the applicability of their previous training but does not provide them with replacement skills or direction. This lack of knowledge and practice of the third party role has led some commentators to the conclusion that peacekeepers should, (1) continue with, or (2) rely solely on military doctrine, preparation and training. The point made by both interpretations is that the existing system of UN intervention is not functioning effectively and that changes are needed. The arguments presented here suggest an alternative to the reversion to a purely military doctrine for resolving these violent protracted conflicts.

It is asserted here that peacekeeping must be placed on a firm conceptual foundation directly congruent with its third party function. Such a grounding would provide direction and specific goals and activities relating to that conceptual framework. In addition, training appropriate to specific tasks and broad goals would not only lead to more effective facilitation of conflict resolution, but would promote attitude shifts away from military doctrine toward peaceful intervention and resolution. Current lack of effectiveness has led some to conclude that this third party role is not useful for resolving conflicts or that it is a 'soft' option. The counter argument to this is that peacekeepers have yet to take on fully this third party role with all its ramifications for practice and training. Moreover, contact skills should not be perceived as synonymous with giving in or getting pushed around. Skilled application of conflict resolution techniques, particularly in pressure situations, can and should be assertive and firm. It is certainly true that skillfully applying such techniques, especially in pressure situations, is difficult. More difficult but more effective for a peacekeeping force, it could be argued, than resort to military force. This point is made by a number of military peacekeepers.[3] The problem is that when these techniques are applied they are most often done so without appropriate knowledge and training. The result is that these techniques appear to be a soft option. The argument here is that we do not know the impact that conceptualization and training of the third party role would have on effectiveness and success. One reason we need to find this out is the reality that non-enforcement measures are often the only politically viable option at least until the crisis is so grave that any intervention, peaceful or otherwise, presents serious dilemmas (Bosnia is a depressing example of just such a situation). In addition, they are cheaper, in terms of money and lives (the Gulf War serves as a reminder of this fact) and in the long run, if practised properly, could be much less destructive and far more constructive than massive military intervention.

Attitudes toward peacekeeping are an important precursor to actual change and contribute to the growing body of evidence which suggests that peacekeeping is and should be much more than a symbolic gesture of the international community's collective will. Which way the UN will go, toward enforcement or toward a true third party role, is as yet undetermined. Support for the full implementation of the third party role is evident, and it is to an examination of part of this body of opinion that we will now turn.

## 1.1 Military View

The case studies in Chapter 3 and the training initiatives discussed in Chapter 8 show that peacekeeping roles go beyond traditional military ones and demand specialized training beyond traditional military programmes. The Canadian mediation research project in Cyprus is one example. The whole ethos through which Nordic training is conducted is another. There are numerous examples of officers, who point out the importance of bringing about a shift in attitude as well as providing cross-cultural training for peacekeepers. In these cases, however, there is a considerable difference between the stated need and the training provided.

In addition, a commonly presented view in the armed forces of these contributing nations, is that peacekeeping does not require special training at all. The argument is that training needs are adequately accommodated through the other military training programmes, especially low-intensity warfare and internal security activities. This argument relates to the point made above about calls for more enforcement powers for peacekeepers. For example, the British military establishment reasons that soldiers are already experienced peacekeepers if they have been in Northern Ireland. Canadian General Lewis MacKenzie has argued vigorously for combat trained and equipped troops for peacekeeping.[4] This kind of rationale is generally pervasive in the military, although much more apparent in large professional armies. It is a loud and often influential counterpoint to the development of a realistic empirical assessment of training for peaceful third party intervention.

Despite growing recognition that the third party peacekeeping role is qualitatively different from military activity, only rarely has this realization been translated into training and practice. In this context the Canadian mediation study could have significant impact. On the whole, training focused on military non-contact roles prevails, and even the more considered attitudes expressed most often by the Nordic countries have only resulted in minimal differences in preparation for peacekeeping.

Only a small number of experienced peacekeepers have argued that there are basic and crucial differences between normal military activity and UN peacekeeping. *In The Thin Blue Line*, Rikhye, Harbottle and Egge, all experienced military peacekeepers, write:

> plain military expertise, though a considerable asset, is not itself the only prerequisite for peacekeeping; there are other attributes that are not found in military textbooks nor learned on the barrack square. Whether the peacekeeper be of the lowest or the highest rank, his success will depend upon his ability to prevent conflict through every means other than force of arms. Tact, diplomacy, and quiet reasoning when negotiating or mediating between the contestants; complete self-restraint, infinite patience, and tireless effort regardless of provocation are the weapons of the peacekeeper's trade – not his self-loading rifle – and through judicious use of them he can defuse potentially dangerous situations, reduce tensions that could lead to violence, and thereby control and contain the conflict from escalating into something worse.[5]

They go on to argue that,

> possibly more important than anything else is the peacekeeper's understanding of the problem at the root of the conflict and of the human relationships involved; for this will determine his attitude and approach to the situations and problems that face him.[6]

Harbottle continues the line of reasoning that peacekeepers need specialized training for the third party role, by pointing to his experience in Cyprus (reconciliation work described in Chapter 3) as an example of how such third party skills can be utilized. He notes,

> Every day, members of peacekeeping forces are called upon to negotiate and mediate in situations of potential and manifest violence. It is their ability to fulfil this peacemaking role that determines their success as peacekeepers, not the

authority of the self-loading rifle that they may hold in their hands. Often in United Nations operations serious escalation in violence has been avoided through the mediatory efforts of a young non-commissioned officer or a junior commissioned officer.[7]

Suggesting that such peacemaking activities require special skills and training, Harbottle says,

The skill is not automatically acquired, but has to be developed in the individual through a process of awareness and training so that his attitude and approach to the problems with which he is confronted are such that he is able to achieve a de-escalation of tension and violence.[8]

This description of training needs, 'developed in the individual through a process of awareness', is very similar to descriptions of training needs for effective cross-cultural interaction. Harbottle also notes that fact-oriented methods are not designed to produce this type of change in the individual.

Canadian General Clayton Beattie also argues that training for peacekeeping should be considerably different from military training:

training, which could better prepare troops for their [UN] peacekeeping role, is more demanding and requires careful planning, familiarization, and practice [than military training]. The first of these involves the psychological change from an adversary to a pacific role, from confrontation to third party interposition. In peacekeeping, there is no enemy: the objective is to avoid hostilities, to improve communications between the parties, and advance the process of reconciliation. This necessitates a full understanding of the causes of the conflict – political, military, and economic – as well as the social and cultural environment. It demands a fair-minded and impartial approach while operating within an atmosphere of distrust and suspicion among the protagonists, often under difficult and provocative conditions.[9]

Beattie concludes his argument about training requirements by pointing out that the 'gap between what is needed and what is being accomplished is still very large. It would be preferable if the UN itself could coordinate these activities.'[10] On a more general level, Beattie notes that to improve peacekeeping's ability to take on the range of third party roles and operate effectively in conflict situations, more research is needed, particularly within a multi-national environment and through 'the development of common doctrine, instruction, and appreciation of the special political skills and requirements of peacekeeping'.[11]

These examples, along with those in the previous chapter, provide further support for: (1) the need to develop a conceptual basis for peacekeeping, (2) the central importance of contact skills for peacekeepers, and (3) the importance of providing specific training to effect a shift from a military to a peacekeeping attitude and to learn and practise contact skills.

### 1.2  Civilian View

Throughout this work a number of views regarding the basic task of peacekeeping have been noted. It was argued, and supported by sources in academia, the UN Secretariat, and elsewhere that peacekeeping needs a conceptual basis and that peacekeepers play a third party role which is essentially different from a military one and which requires the use of contact skills. As Skjelsbaek suggests,

> Soldiers in the peacekeeping forces face a double challenge. In order to have the respect of the armed forces of the adversaries they must demonstrate military competence. On the other hand, non-military methods like dissuasion, persuasion and negotiation constitute the essence of peacekeeping.[12]

The multiplicity of roles and the increased complexity of peacekeeping and wider peace processes led the Security Council to commission the report *An Agenda for Peace* from Boutros-Ghali in early 1992.

Boutros-Ghali points to unchecked population growth, debt burdens, poverty, famine, oppression and despair as both 'sources and consequences of conflict'.[13] To deal with these growing threats to international peace and security, the document proposes a four-part framework of peaceful intervention. Boutros-Ghali suggests that the integrated use of preventive diplomacy, peacemaking, peacekeeping and post-conflict peacebuilding 'taken together, and carried out with the backing of all Members, offer[s] a coherent contribution towards securing peace'.[14] The idea that these four areas offer a 'coherent contribution towards securing peace' is very similar to the approach put forward in contingency models. As such, *An Agenda for Peace* constitutes an initial step toward conceptualization of the UN's third party activities including peacekeeping. In a recent interview, Boutros-Ghali was more specific about the demands on peacekeeping and the tasks which peacekeeping operations are increasingly expected to carry out. According to the Secretary-General, the UN is called upon to conduct

> comprehensive peace operations: not merely to send peacekeeping forces to separate combatants, but to intervene in the whole national reconciliation process; in the restructuring of government; in the rehabilitation of the country; in the return of thousands and thousands of refugees; in the rebuilding of the bridges and the highways; in the restructuring of the political apparatus.[15]

Overall, *An Agenda for Peace* provides a much needed and important first step toward developing a broad framework for intervention. It does, however, reflect the present day conceptual limitations regarding peaceful third party intervention, and more specifically, stops some way short of a conceptual framework which could act to guide interventions at a number of levels.

Perhaps most troublesome, though, is that while the need for a much more fully conceptualized framework for UN intervention is acute, at many levels this need is not recognized. As Ruggie points out,

> UN civilian officials increasingly play the roles of human rights monitor, supervisor of electoral politics, aid specialist, administrator of a public agency, policeman. UN military personnel increasingly protect civilian populations, safeguard relief efforts, negotiate with local authorities or warlords the circumstances of their day-to-day functions, and cope with the constant threat of armed attack.... No new operational doctrines have been devised for the new peacekeeping mode, and training for it is virtually nonexistent....

It is a miracle that disaster has not yet befallen one of these peacekeeping missions.[16]

The gap between the day-to-day reality of peacekeeping and the concepts and training through which it is implemented is large. Although it is widely acknowledged that peacekeepers take on roles of peacemaking and peacebuilding at the micro-level, action to provide the needed concept of operations and training to guide this function is minimal. As Boutros-Ghali acknowledged recently, 'progress... has to be measured in very small doses'.[17]

### 1.3  Conclusion: Translating a Theory of Peacekeeping into Practice

*1.3.1  Two Essential Tasks*

By all accounts UN peacekeepers have from the start been involved in micro-level peacemaking and peacebuilding. The qualitative and quantitative increase in need since 1988 has brought these roles much more to the fore. The long list of peacekeeping roles provided in Chapter 2 combined with case-study and other evidence shows the evolution of peacekeeping away from largely but not exclusively passive operations toward much more active and pro-active operations. These roles are more pronounced as a result of need rather than design. It is the *ad hoc* evolution of an *ad hoc* institution. This approach, once crucial to the survival of peacekeeping, is no longer an appropriate response to the range and complexities of current conflict situations.

To understand the essential nature of peacekeeping it is important first to understand the theoretical basis of the third party role. As a third party function from within a contingency model of conflict intervention, peacekeepers perform three different tasks: (1) conflict control (which provides the base level of activity of peacekeeping preceding the application of either of the other two roles), (2) facilitation of an atmosphere conducive to negotiations and settlement, and in the long-term movement toward resolution, (3) facilitation of a previously negotiated settlement and resolution process. The question of particular relevance to training is how these roles translate into specific activities.

What are the actual skills that peacekeepers need? These skills can be divided into two categories: contact and non-contact skills. Non-contact skills are those abilities peace-keepers need, whether military or civilian, to carry out specific functions, from operating a radio, to running a polling station. As should be evident from the information provided in the previous chapters, peacekeepers need knowledge and ability in a range of non-contact skills depending on specific job require-ments. Two different types of contact skills have been discussed here. These are the skills of conflict resolution, i.e. mediation, negotiation, conciliation, and the skills important for effective cross-cultural interaction. In many cases these skills seem to overlap. It should be noted that it is not the point here to provide an exhaustive list of skill requirements. It is probable that empirical research will show that certain conflict resolu-tion skills or cross cultural interaction skills are inappropriate for peacekeeping or must be adapted to peacekeeping's unique needs. Much more research is needed. It will be sufficient here to note this possibility and to point out that however such skills might be utilized or adapted in the future, they are necessary in some form for the application of the third party role of peacekeeping.

Although non-contact skills are important for the function-ing of a peacekeeping operation, the essence of peacekeeping as a third party intervention must be contact skills. In a sense contact skills are the techniques of operationalization, com-mon for all peacekeepers (although it should be noted that different levels and jobs would require different levels of train-ing). It is through the use of communication skills, methods of negotiation, facilitation, mediation, and conciliation that peacekeepers de-escalate potentially violent or manifestly violent situations and facilitate movement toward conflict resolution. Non-contact skills are functional and differ depending on the specific mandate of the specific mission. It is also the case that contact skills require more time and effort on the part of the trainer and the trainee.

### 1.3.2 *The Training Gap*
The training gap exists at two levels. The first gap is one of basic provision, i.e., what training and how much? The second gap is one of content, i.e, within the existing programmes, what com-petence is training providing? This second gap relates to train-ing provision for contact and non-contact skills. These gaps in

preparation for peacekeeping mean first that many peacekeepers receive little or no training before deployment and second that the training they do receive prepares them to fulfil non-contact roles, but does not prepare them for their third party role. The daily activities of peacekeepers described in the case-studies and by the peacekeepers themselves, by the Secretariat, and by a number of academics amply supports the argument that the third party role constitutes the essence of peacekeeping. The training gap exists because this realization has not penetrated into existing training provision or peacekeeping practice, so that not only are many peacekeepers not trained at all, but those that are trained do not learn what they need to know to carry out their third party function.

It is the argument here that the reason for the existence of this training gap is directly related to the lack of an explicitly formulated conceptual framework for peacekeeping. The case of cross-cultural training provided in Chapter 8 gives an example of the interaction between theory and practice which is vital for the development of appropriate and effective preparation. This interaction is non-existent in peacekeeping. Moreover, without a conceptual framework through which intervention is carried out, through which research is conducted and through which training programmes are developed, a wealth of practical data and experience remains untapped. In such circumstances, peacekeeping as well as other UN interventions are relegated to dangerously *ad hoc*, inappropriate, and ineffective responses to extremely serious, complex conflict situations. The training gap is one visible outcome of this situation.

## 2. INCONSISTENCIES IN TRAINING AND PRACTICE

The purpose of this section is to highlight problems inherent in the current *ad hoc* system of peacekeeping and peacekeeping training. The examination of peacekeeping training and practice through the conceptual lens of a contingency framework reveals a number of issue areas. It is beyond the scope of this work to do more than point out and briefly discuss these dynamics of peacekeeping practice. Indeed, these inconsistencies add more weight to the argument for a conceptual framework because they highlight a number of complex issues which require further study.

## 2.1 Military Training and Peacekeeping Training

Taking military units which have been trained for war and placing them in situations which require peaceful third party intervention, can appear incongruous, particularly when it is apparent that they receive almost no training in the specialized skills of third party intervention or cross-cultural interaction. It is equally evident, however, that in many interventions it is necessary to use military units. The importance of an explicitly military presence for many peacekeeping operations is founded on the rationale that military force needs to counter military force. This is meant not in the sense of a 'head-to-head' clash of weaponry (although this is also increasingly called for), but in the sense of 'presence' There seem to be two corollaries to this reasoning. Perceived professionalism and military capability are important in gaining respect and compliance from opposing forces thereby adding weight to third party activities. In addition, it is apparent that there are military skills – non-contact skills – which are an important part of the functioning of a peacekeeping mission. For example, information gathering and reliable reporting are often mentioned as critical elements of effectiveness.[18] One such skill is the ability to recognize a range of different weaponry by sight and by sound. The UN guidelines for the preparation of military peacekeeping stress this point.[19] One peacekeeper eloquently expresses the importance of military skills and knowledge by pointing out that 'combat capability and protective "sandbagging" are more effective than blue paint in stopping bullets.'[20] Another source suggests that,

> The military expertise of a well-trained army has invaluable assets and through its well-tried and efficient operational and military procedures can make a considerable contribution to the smooth running of the overall operation of the whole force.[21]

The combination of such reasoning with an attitude toward training which regards peacekeeping as a military activity equivalent to low-intensity warfare is at least partially responsible for the lack of recognition given to negotiation and mediation as part of the peacekeeper's task. For example the UN guidelines state,

> Other forms of negotiation outside this formalized system [of liaison] exist: (a) military observers may be called to negotiate on a problem which has arisen on the ground; (b) junior leaders at the corporal or even private level may have to negotiate a sudden problem which has arisen in their area (e.g. a CHP [check point] dispute).[22]

The guidelines then state,

> The training for negotiation and liaison will of necessity be restricted. At the formal end of the scale, the selection of personnel with negotiating ability and experience is all important. As far as informal negotiation by UNMO's and junior leaders is concerned, some general training can be carried out.[23]

Both the selection process and general training in mediation and negotiation have been shown to be lacking. In addition, the UN guidelines recommend that general training cover 'diplomacy, tact, firmness, fairness, friendliness and flexibility', by using fact-oriented techniques. The usefulness of fact-oriented techniques in skills and attitude training has been shown in cross-cultural training to have limited effectiveness. But the most significant aspect of these passages in the Guidelines is the de-emphasis of these skills.

Another example of this incongruence appears in *The Thin Blue Line*. Here the authors argue that,

> whether the peacekeeper be of the lowest or highest rank, his success will depend upon his ability to prevent conflict through every means other than force of arms. Tact, diplomacy, and quiet reasoning when negotiating or mediating between the contestants..[24]

Later in the same chapter they argue,

> It might appear from what has been said that international peacekeeping requires special training on the part of the military. To an extent this may be true at the commander

and staff levels, but not so far as the junior commander and soldier levels are concerned.[25]

More specifically they point out that,

> The development of peacekeeping techniques at the junior level is a matter of adjustment rather than of re-orientation. The basic skills already exist – they need only to be adapted to meet a rather different form of soldiering.[26]

The contradiction shown here is pervasive. On the one hand, the argument goes that third party roles are taken on at all levels in a peacekeeping operation and that these roles require special skills. On the other hand, it is simultaneously argued that junior levels already have these skills and so do not need special training. As a coherent policy for training and practice such reasoning is not convincing.

A study by Galtung and Hveem examined the perception UN forces have of their own third party role and of the conflict itself. The study used a measure of distance and closeness to describe the contradiction inherent in the two basic role conceptions of keeping the belligerents apart, i.e. keeping distance, and the third party role of conflict resolution, i.e. facilitating closeness or cooperation. This study suggests one reason for the inconsistencies in training and practice of peacekeeping is that a basic contradiction exists in peacekeepers' roles.[27]

The conceptualization of peacekeeping as a third party activity provides the means to understand the differences and importance of the two basic roles of peacekeepers. The importance of military skills for military peacekeepers, carrying out military functions is obvious. It is equally obvious that all peacekeepers carry out another critical function based on their third party role using contact techniques.

### 2.1.1 Living with a Paradox

The basic paradox of peacekeeping in present day functioning is the fact that it is a peaceful third party intervention but is often carried out on the ground by military personnel. The military functions of peacekeeping are important and necessary, but the underlying *raison d'etre* of a peacekeeping force is the third party role. The fundamental contradiction is necessary. The problem arises from misunderstanding the responsibilities of a third party role and the undue emphasis placed on military functions. This is a direct result of lack of conceptualization. Although the paradox will continue to exist it could be mitigated by much better preparation as well as coherent and concerted application of peacekeeping through a conceptual framework.

A thorough examination of the use of military personnel to carry out the third party role versus the use of civilian police or other civilians would be an interesting area for future research. At the moment military forces are used because it is assumed that they will be more effective than civilian units, but research has not been carried out to test this assumption or to examine exactly what factors give military peacekeepers the edge. It could be that the use of military peacekeepers prolongs, legitimizes, or creates more conflict in some situations where the use of civilians would have a more beneficial effect.[28]

The contradiction can be seen not only in training but in specific aspects of practice like the perennial conundrum – the non-use of force. The complexity of this debate is evident in the Bosnian relief effort and in Croatia. Although it has been made clear that the forces involved in the relief effort will not use force except in self-defence, this restriction has been expanded slightly to include returning fire with equivalent force. According to one report, this expansion has been ineffective in stopping sniper fire and some peacekeepers are arguing for more forceful measures to be introduced.[29] The confrontation between Serb gunmen and Croatian refugees cited in Chapter 3 exemplifies this problem. One report, quoting senior UN officials, suggested that the peacekeepers had been authorized to use force. The commander in charge of the Russian troops, however, claimed that the UN troops 'did not have the right to open fire'.[30] In the hothouse atmosphere of bitter ethnic conflict, it is easy to see how complex the non-use of force issue has become.

The lack of emphasis on third party techniques may be part of the reason why so much emphasis is placed on the non-use of force issue. Military peacekeepers, with no training in any role other than the military one, do not have the knowledge or experience to consistently look for ways of utilizing contact skills to resolve problems. Their fall-back position is embodied in the self-loading rifle. Such deep-seated contradictions cannot be clarified by endless rules and regulations for the non-use of force or for limitations of military activity, etc. Rather the clarification must arise from a conceptual base which reflects long-term aims and which is testable. Ultimately, the problem is not living with a paradox, it is realizing that one exists and understanding the ramifications of its existence for training and practice.

## 2.2 The Profession of Peacekeeping

### 2.2.1 The Professional Soldier and the National Service Volunteer

An area frequently mentioned in peacekeeping literature is the influence the professional system and the national service system have on the effectiveness of peacekeepers. Some sources argue that the professional soldier is required to make a very significant adjustment from the military role to the peacekeeping one. Rikhye, Harbottle and Egge note that 'the professional career soldier is not automatically the best person for the peacekeeper's role in inter-community or intra-state conflicts'.[31] Rikhye argues,

> Whereas the professional has only his military background, his own character and personality to fall back upon, the 'amateur' from the factory bench, the farm, the school house or the motor garage, immediately has a mutual point of interest and common ground of understanding with his counterpart in the local community in which he is stationed. Where the needs are for good relations, patience and the ability to reason and persuade, a common bond of interest is an invaluable asset and can mean the difference between success and failure in settling a dispute. The usefulness of the civilian soldier is one of the strengths of a United Nations Peace Force and these natural attributes should not be smothered but encouraged.[32]

Harleman points out that,

> In Sweden, as well as in the other Nordic countries, there are no significant difficulties to [sic] transfer a soldier to a peacekeeper.... However, to transfer a professional soldier to a peacekeeper must be given much more consideration particularly regarding the use of arms. The difficulties are

understandable as a professional soldier has been trained to use his arms as a means to solve a conflict but a peacekeeper only can rely on his/her ability in negotiation to find a peaceful solution.[33]

The UN Guidelines for military preparation seem to take a different point of view:

> The level of training requirement will vary from one contributing country to another. Full-time professional soldiers will require less grounding than reserves. Full-time professionals with experience in aid to the civil power or internal security will have encountered the techniques before but will be required to direct them towards peacekeeping, which may involve a less aggressive mode.[34]

Beattie suggests that the national service system produces, 'a younger, perhaps less experienced soldier' but that this problem can be made up for in pre-deployment training.[35]

The most significant contradiction evidenced here is seen in the differing opinions about whether the professional career soldier or a national service volunteer 'civilian' soldier makes a better peacekeeper, as well as what training is needed for each. Do civilian soldiers need military training or do professional soldiers need 'peacekeeping' training? The answer probably lies somewhere between these poles.

Two points should be made regarding this debate. First, those who receive some kind of peacekeeping training, both professional and civilian soldiers receive training in non-contact skills. Neither, however, receive any significant amount of training in contact skills. Second, the debate over which type of military personnel makes a better peacekeeper would have more currency if they were all receiving training appropriate to their third party role.

### 2.2.2 *Independent Initiative*

The impact of non-contact skills training, which for military peacekeepers means nearly exclusive emphasis on translating military skills into the peacekeeping context, leads to another contradiction in the practice of peacekeeping. The demands of military skills and operations require, among other things, discipline, particularly in following orders, organization, and a well defined and used chain of command. Although some initiative and independent action are called for, they are within the tactical and operational limits of the military objective. The demands of peacekeeping require a different kind of initiative and independent action carried out largely through contact skills, and require them at all levels of the mission. As Harbottle notes,

> Unconventional or unorthodox situations call for unconventional methods to deal with them. This is what the peacekeeping role is all about, requiring as it does a more flexible approach than that required in standard type military warfare. Stereotyped solutions to problems and tactical concepts have no place in third party operations.[36]

Military personnel are not trained in this type of initiative, particularly at the rank-and-file level. It has already been observed that appropriate, independent action at the lowest level can defuse a situation which otherwise might escalate dangerously. The independent action of a third party peacekeeper calls for the use of contact-skills. But a list of 'do's and don't's' is in no way sufficient. Rather, this type of initiative asks the individual peacekeeper to apply general knowledge and ability to an analysis of a new situation which may require a totally unique solution. This is the art of negotiation and mediation. This kind of knowledge and skill requires a different type of training from traditional fact-oriented approaches and points again to the significant difference between 'situation' and 'simulation' exercises. The lessons from cross-cultural training and conflict resolution support this point. Military tradition and training do not seek to develop this type of initiative and independence because it is contradictory to the effective functioning of a military unit. The problem and contradiction for military peacekeepers is that while discipline, organizational machinery, and strict hierarchy are important for effectively fulfilling their military functions, or non-contact role, the third party contact role requires initiative and independence which can clash with the purely military ethos and the military milieu.

### 2.2.3 *Developing a New Profession*
The conceptualization of peacekeeping as a third party role suggests the need for a concept of a peacekeeping profession

which is significantly different from a purely military one. Harbottle makes this point when he says,

> in the sphere of UN peacekeeping, common sense, patience and an understanding of people and their point of view is every bit as important as intelligence, while professionalism is of another kind – the uninhibited professionalism of the amateur using his common sense, patience, understanding and sympathy to prevent a war from starting or re-starting. This form of professionalism is not found in text books or taught at military staff colleges – nor is it learnt on the parade ground or on the field of battle.[37]

The peacekeeping profession deserves as much attention and professionalism as the military profession. The development of a professional peacekeeper is impeded by a military attitude which sees peacekeeping as a 'temporary deviation from the norm and an interruption of their primary function to train for war'.[38] This attitude is less obvious in countries with national service, but can still be perceived in the almost exclusive emphasis on military techniques or non-contact skills in their training programmes. The lack of a conceptualization of peacekeeping delineating its distinctive characteristic as a third party intervention inhibits the development of a peacekeeping profession. For example, a specific positive outcome of the development of a peacekeeping profession would be an examination of the ethical issues of peacekeeping as a third party intervention.[39]

## 2.3 The Experience/Expertise Fallacy

The problem here derives from the assumption that experience in peacekeeping leads to expertise in peacekeeping. It should be noted that this point is perhaps more applicable to contact skills than non-contact skills. Research in cross-cultural training and practice lends support to this point.

Equating experience with expertise can lead to several practical repercussions. First, experience is substituted for training. For example, the experience of having been to Lebanon inevitably leads some peacekeepers to conclude that they know what they need to know about Lebanese culture and the complexities of effective cross-cultural interaction and do not need training. Similar examples can be taken from the civilian side of peacekeeping. Yet cross-cultural research does not support such an assumption. In addition, much of the research points to the need and usefulness of on-going training. These points are likely to be especially valid for the application of contact skills. It is highly probable that experience contributes greatly to training, but it should not necessarily be considered a substitute for it. A second related point is the selection and training of trainers. This point may not be as relevant for non-contact skills; but for contact skills and for the techniques used to teach those skills, it is essential that trainers be trained appropriately.

## 2.4 Culture Variables

The significance of the impact of cultural variables on the process of conflict resolution and third party intervention is a difficult, complex and controversial subject. Debates in the academic field of conflict resolution focus largely on theoretical issues centered around the universality of human needs theory.[40] Several recent studies suggest that resolving conflict in different cultures requires a modification of intervention techniques.[41] In addition, the field of cross-cultural relations provides us with a large amount of data and theoretical material which contributes to the general conclusion that intercultural interaction is a complex and often difficult activity.

For peacekeeping, cross-cultural interactions occur at two levels: between the peacekeeping force and disputants and between different contributors within the force. Little is known about how the strengths or weaknesses of either of these types of interactions enhance or diminish the effectiveness of a peacekeeping intervention. Only a few studies have approached these issues. Galtung and Eide concluded, for example, that acceptance of a UN force by the local population was an important factor to its overall effectiveness. They found eleven factors which contributed to lack of acceptance, including: no contact at all with the local population or highly unpopular fraternization; conspicuous demonstration of power; and no engagement in good deeds (peacebuilding activity).[42] Another example is found in a study of peacekeepers and local populations which looked at the relationship between different troop contributors and the local population. This study also examined some of the problems which occur in intra-force relations because of cultural differences.[43]

Two other variables may contribute to the impact of cultural differences and cultural interaction on the effectiveness of peacekeeping. These variables can be described as a conflict culture and a military culture. It has just been noted that the task of conflict resolution appears to be significantly complicated by the addition of cross-cultural interaction. The existence of a military culture, the differences in military cultures between and among troop-contributing countries, and the application of military methods as part of a peaceful third party intervention, all deserve examination for the effects they may have, positive or negative on the conflict resolution process.[44] For example, how does the military culture help or hinder the cultural adaptation process for soldiers in peacekeeping missions? What are the implications for training?

In general, the culture question is given only minimal attention in existing training programmes and certainly deserves more serious consideration both in training and in research.

## 3. FUTURE DIRECTIONS: RECOMMENDATIONS FOR RESEARCH

### 3.1 Development of Training Programmes and Curricula

If implemented, a conceptual framework for peacekeeping discussed here would benefit training. Two areas need attention. First there is the need to begin the process of pushing for the establishment of regional or national training centres. Second, a model and curriculum for such centres should be developed. Both should come about through close consultation with the Secretariat, the DPKO, and the OHRM, and should relate to a conceptual framework. A model similar to the proposed Canadian Peacekeeping Training Centre which combines a regional training facility for both civilian and military peacekeepers along with a research agenda seems most appropriate.[45] It should be noted, though, that if, as in the case of the Canadian proposal, research will be part of a

UNTC, the issue of the appropriateness and validity of the military conducting evaluations and research should be examined closely. Interaction between the Secretariat and such regional centres would need to be frequent and characterized by a close working relationship. This arrangement, which puts research and training facilities in a regional centre, has the benefit of facilitating the interactive development of theory, training and practice.

## 3.2 Improving the Conceptual Framework

A framework which defines a specific third party role for peacekeeping within a contingency model of conflict resolution provides a starting point for research and analysis which should expand the current limits of knowledge in two distinct directions. First, research work should focus on the applicability and development of the meta-contingency model, which posits the sequential and simultaneous use of different intervention strategies based on an assessment of conflict escalation. Much more evidence supporting the efficacy of this approach needs to be accumulated which differentiates and targets particular intervention strategies for particular stages in an escalation process. The escalation process itself requires further examination, possibly taking into account different levels of escalation for different aspects of the same conflict – a type of horizontal escalation.

The second direction research in this area should take is the development of a contingency model specifically for peacekeeping (see Figure 6.2). This research might be best approached along the lines of the study by Bercovitch *et al.*, which develops a contingency model for mediation, and the study by Diehl which suggests how a contingency model might be applied to peacekeeping.[46] There are two areas of particular interest for a researcher undertaking such a project. One would be the potential resource provided from analogous data from fields like cross-cultural interaction and conflict resolution and the applicability of the theories and practices in these fields to peacekeeping. A second would be the utility of data from past peacekeeping operations, and the potential problem of applicability to current circumstances.

Research possibilities and needs are only one part of the problem of conceptualization. The other major problem comes from the UN itself. Initial steps toward conceptualization have been offered in *An Agenda for Peace*. The UN must now take the next steps to establish a more comprehensive intervention framework which is based specifically on and supports empirical research. Post-Cold War conflict must be addressed though the development of viable peaceful third party strategies operated from within a broad conceptual framework of peaceful third party intervention. It is time to take a long-term view of conflict management, recognize the serious limitations of military intervention, and begin work to improve and develop other more viable options.

# Appendix 1: UN Peacekeeping Operations 1948 to 1993

**Nascent Period: 1945–56**

1948–  **UNTSO**
United Nations Truce Supervision Organization
Operates in Egypt, Israel, Jordan, Lebanon, and Syria

1949–  **UNMOGIP**
United Nations Military Observer Group in India and Pakistan

**Assertive Period: 1956–66**

1956–67  **UNEF I**
United Nations Emergency Force
Operated in Egypt and Israel

1958  **UNOGIL**
United Nations Observation Group in Lebanon

1960–64*  **ONUC**
United Nations Operation in the Congo

1962-63*  **UNTEA/UNSF**
United Nations Temporary Executive Authority
United Nations Security Force
Operated in West New Guinea (West Irian)

1963–64  **UNYOM**
United Nation Yemen Observation Mission

1964–*  **UNFICYP**
United Nations Peacekeeping Force in Cyprus

1965–66  **DOMREP**
Representative of the Secretary-General in the Dominican
Republic

1965–66  **UNIPOM**
United Nations India-Pakistan Observer Mission

## Dormant Period: 1966–73

## Resurgent Period: 1973–78

1973–79 **UNEF II**
United Nations Emergency Force
Operated in Egypt and Israel

1974– **UNDOF**
United Nations Disengagement Observer Force
Operates in the Syrian Golan Heights

1978–* **UNIFIL**
United Nations Interim Force in Lebanon

## Maintenance Period: 1978–88

## Expansion Period: 1988–92

1988–91 **UNIIMOG**
United Nations Iran-Iraq Military Observer Group

1989–92 **UNAVEM I**
United Nations Angola Verification Mission

1989–90* **UNTAG**
United Nations Transition Assistance Group
Operated in Namibia

1989–91 **ONUCA**
United Nations Observer Group in Central America

1989–90* **ONUVEN**
United Nations Observation Mission for the Verification of
Elections in Nicaragua

1990–91* **ONUVEH**
United Nations Observer Group for the
Verification of Elections in Haiti

1991–* **ONUSAL**
United Nations Observer Mission in El Salvador

1992–* **UNAVEM II**
United Nations Angola Verification Mission

1991–* **MINURSO**
United Nations Mission for the Referendum in Western Sahara

1992–* **UNTAC**
United Nations Transitional Authority in Cambodia

1992–*    **UNPROFOR 1**
United Nations Protection Force
Operates in Croatia

1992–*    **UNPROFOR 2**
United Nations Protection Force Bosnia-Herzegovina

1992–93*    **UNOSOM 1**
United Nations Operation in Somalia

1992–*    **ONUMOZ**
United Nations Operation in Mozambique

1993–*    **UNAMIR**
United Nations Assistance Mission in Rwanda
Subsumed UNOMUR, United Nations Observer Mission in
Uganda/Rwanda

1993–    **UNOMIG**
United Nations Observer Mission in Georgia

1993–    **UNOMIL**
United Nations Observer Mission in Liberia

## Are These Missions Peacekeeping?

1988–90    **UNGOMAP/OSGAP**
United Nations Good Offices in Afghanistan and Pakistan Office
of the Secretary-General in Afghanistan and Pakistan

1991–    **UNIKOM**
United Nations Iraq-Kuwait Observation Mission

1991–*    **UNHUC**
United Nations Humanitarian Centers (in Iraq) under the
authority of UNDRO, Office of the United Nations Disaster
Relief Coordinator

1993–*    **UNOSOM 2**
United Nations Operation in Somalia

* can be characterized as multidimensional operations

# Appendix 2: Summary of Contrasting Conflict Management Approaches

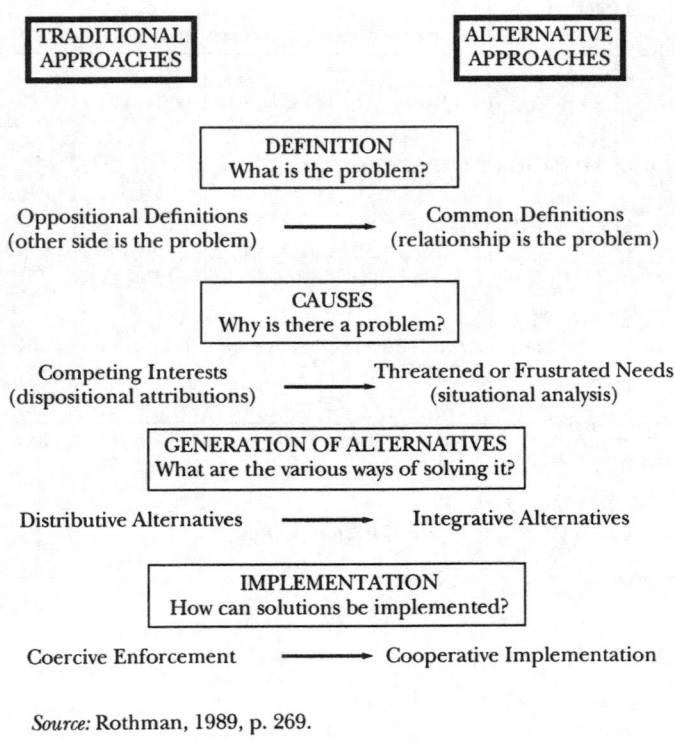

TRADITIONAL APPROACHES

ALTERNATIVE APPROACHES

**DEFINITION**
What is the problem?

Oppositional Definitions
(other side is the problem)

Common Definitions
(relationship is the problem)

**CAUSES**
Why is there a problem?

Competing Interests
(dispositional attributions)

Threatened or Frustrated Needs
(situational analysis)

**GENERATION OF ALTERNATIVES**
What are the various ways of solving it?

Distributive Alternatives

Integrative Alternatives

**IMPLEMENTATION**
How can solutions be implemented?

Coercive Enforcement

Cooperative Implementation

*Source:* Rothman, 1989, p. 269.

# Appendix 3: Effects of Escalation on Conflict

| Escalation Stage | Issues | Communication/ Interaction | Perceptions/ Images | Perceived Possible Outcomes | Preferred Method of Conflict Management |
|---|---|---|---|---|---|
| Discussion | Substantive Issues | Discussion/ Debate | Relatively Accurate/ Benign | Win – Win | Joint Decision- making |
| Polarization | Concerns over Relationship | Reliance on interpretations of actions/ less direct | Rigid/ Simplified Stereotypes | Mutual Compromise | Negotiation |
| Segregation | Needs/ Values | Use of Threats | Good versus Evil | Win – lose | Defensive/ Competition |
| Destruction | Ultimate Survival | No Direct Communication/ Attacks of Violence | Other Party as Non-Human | Lose – Lose (minimize loss – inflict maximum costs) | Outright Attempts at Destruction |

*Source*: Adapted from Fisher 1990, pp. 234–5.

# Appendix 4: Contingency Model of Third Party Intervention

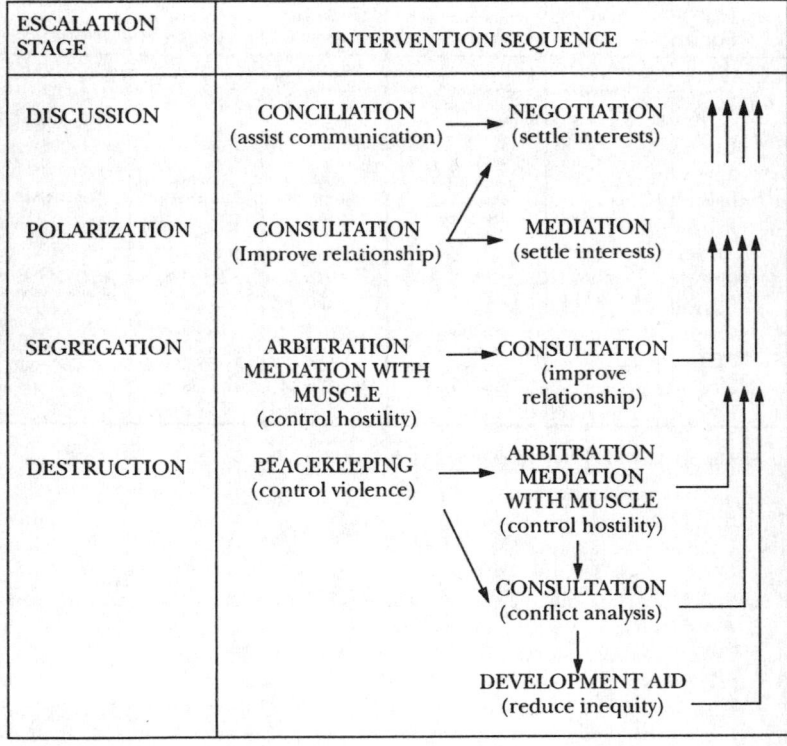

| ESCALATION STAGE | INTERVENTION SEQUENCE |
|---|---|
| DISCUSSION | CONCILIATION (assist communication) → NEGOTIATION (settle interests) |
| POLARIZATION | CONSULTATION (Improve relationship) → MEDIATION (settle interests) |
| SEGREGATION | ARBITRATION MEDIATION WITH MUSCLE (control hostility) → CONSULTATION (improve relationship) |
| DESTRUCTION | PEACEKEEPING (control violence) → ARBITRATION MEDIATION WITH MUSCLE (control hostility) → CONSULTATION (conflict analysis) → DEVELOPMENT AID (reduce inequity) |

*Source:* Fisher, 1990, p. 237.

# Notes and References

## 1 A Brief History of United Nations Peacekeeping, 1945–87

1.  A.L. Bennett (1988), *International Organizations: Principles and Issues*, Englewood Cliffs, NJ: Prentice-Hall, 4th edn., p. 43.
2.  United Nations Charter, Preamble.
3.  The total number of participating states does not include Poland because it did not participate in the UNCIO, although it subsequently signed the Charter as a founding state.
4.  See Bennett, 1988, p. 50; G. Goodwin (1966), 'The General Assembly of the United Nations', in E. Luard (ed.), *The Evolution of International Organizations*, London: Thames & Hudson, pp. 43–6.
5.  For an account of the complex workings of the specialized agencies of the UN system and their interrelationships, see D. Williams (1987), *The Specialized Agencies and the United Nations: The System in Crisis*, London: C. Hurst & Company.
6.  I.L. Claude (1966), 'The Security Council', in Luard (ed.), p. 72.
7.  The Gulf War and the protection of Kurds in Northern Iraq, the establishment of the humanitarian mission in Bosnia followed by the establishment of the mission in Somalia are all examples of shifts in how we understand the principle of sovereignty. For further discussion, see Chopra and Weiss, 1992; Weiss and Campbell, 1991; Formuth, 1993; Camilleri and Falk, 1992.
8.  Originally the SC had 11 members, including the permanent five. A majority was seven for all votes except an absolute majority of six for electing jurists to the International Court of Justice.
9.  UN Doc. *Provisional Rules of Procedure of the Security Council*, Chap. 4, rule 18.
10. In practice, abstention by a permanent member is considered a 'concurring' vote, for a permanent member to block a substantive vote, that country would have to register a veto or 'no' vote.
11. UN Charter, Chapter V, Art. 24(1) and Art. 25.
12. UN Charter, Chapter VII, Art. 42.
13. See G.R. Berridge (1991), *Return to the UN: UN Diplomacy in Regional Conflicts*, London: Macmillan, pp. 3–11.
14. In practice this restriction is often ignored by the GA.
15. Figures quoted from William Pace from the Center for Development of International Law, Washington, DC, 21 September 1993.
16. For a more lengthy discussion of how these precedents came about, see N. Elaraby (1987), 'The office of the Secretary-General and the maintenance of international peace and security', in United Nations Institute for Training and Research (UNITAR), *The United Nations and the Maintenance of International Peace and Security*, Dordrecht: Martinus Nijhoff, pp. 177–209.
17. Elaraby, in UNITAR, 1978, p. 187.

18. Before March 1992 the name of the DPKO was the Office of Special Political Affairs, its current U-S-G is Kofi Annan.
19. E.B. Haas (1987), 'The collective management of international conflict, 1945–1984,' in UNITAR, p. 7.
20. B. Urquhart (1981), 'International peace and security: thoughts on the twentieth anniversary of Dag Hammarskjold's death', *Foreign Affairs*, 60(1):7.
21. This section follows the argument set out in H. Scheltema (1988), 'Transformations within the United Nations', in J. Harrod and N. Schrijver (eds), *The UN Under Attack*, Aldershot: Gower, pp. 1–7.
22. Scheltema, in Harrod and Schrijver, 1988, p. 4.
23. J. Kaufman (1988), 'Developments in decision-making in the United Nations', in Harrod and Schrijver, p. 17.
24. The Soviet Union had been boycotting the Security Council meetings since January 1950 over the issue of representation of China.
25. UN Doc. SCR 1501, 25 June 1950.
26. UN Doc. SCR 1588, 7 July 1950.
27. UN Doc. GAR 377 (v ) 3 November 1950.
28. For a more detailed description of the UN involvement in Korea, see R. Higgins (1970), *United Nations Peacekeeping, 1946–1967: Documents and Commentary, Vol. 2*, London: Oxford University Press, pp. 153–314.
29. Haas, in UNITAR, 1987, pp. 9–10.
30. H. Miall (1992), *The Peacemakers: Peaceful Settlement of Disputes Since 1945*, London: Macmillan.
31. H. Wiseman (1987), 'The United Nations and international peace-keeping: a comparative analysis', in UNITAR, p. 265.
32. James, in UNITAR, 1987, p. 219.
33. Urquhart, 1981, p. 8.
34. Wiseman offers the following definitions of the different types of peacekeeping operations: observer missions function 'to observe, investigate and report on the compliance of the parties to a cease-fire. The size of these missions is generally very small, about 100 personnel, but not over 1,000.' Force-level missions function as 'interposition of military forces between belligerents to ensure the maintenance of a cease-fire and such other matters as detailed in a mandate. The numbers employed on such operations have generally ranged from 3,000 to 20,000, which is an indication of the magnitude of their tasks' (in UNITAR, 1987, p. 263–4).
35. These missions were the United Nations Truce Supervision Organiza-tion (UNTSO) set up in 1948 and the United Nations Military Observer Group in India and Pakistan (UNMOGIP) set up in 1949. Both of these observer missions are still active.
36. Rikhye, 1984, p. 1.
37. For a detailed description of the Suez Crisis, see *The Blue Helmets*, 1990; Urquhart, 1987; James, 1990a.
38. A. James (1990a), *Peacekeeping in International Politics*, London: Macmillan, p. 212.
39. B. Urquhart (1987), *A Life in Peace and War*, New York: Harper Row, p.133.
40. Urquhart, 1987, p. 133.

41. G. Abi-Saab (1978), *The United Nations Operation in the Congo 1960–1964*, Oxford: Oxford University Press, p. 6.
42. Urquhart, 1981, pp. 6–7.
43. F.T. Liu (1990), 'United Nations peacekeeping: management and operations', *Occasional Papers on Peacekeeping, No. 4*, New York: International Peace Academy, p. 7.
44. Urquhart, 1981, p. 6.
45. Wiseman, in UNITAR, 1987, pp. 264–99.
46. Wiseman, in UNITAR, 1987 p. 288.
47. Wiseman, in UNITAR, 1987, p. 289.
48. G.L. Sherry (1990), 'The United Nations reborn: conflict control in the post-cold war world', *Critical Issues, No. 2*, New York: Council on Foreign Relations, pp. 7–10.

## 2 UN Peacekeeping in the Post-Cold War World

1. W. Eckhardt (1989), 'Civilian deaths in wartime', *Bulletin of Peace Proposals*, 20(1):97.
2. Eckhardt, 1989, p. 90.
3. Stockholm International Peace Research Institute, (SIPRI) (1993), *SIPRI Yearbook 1993: World Armaments and Disarmament*, Oxford: Oxford University Press, p. 86.
4. P. Wallensteen and K. Axell (1993), 'Armed conflict at the end of the Cold War, 1989–92', *Journal of Peace Research*, 30(3):333.
5. Wallensteen and Axell, 1993, p. 333. Further recent work on conflict finds that 'enduring rivalries' account for '...about half of the militarized disputes, violent territorial changes, and wars in the international system'. G. Goertz and P.F Diehl (1993), 'Enduring rivalries: theoretical constructs and empirical patterns', *International Studies Quarterly*, 37:167; further evidence of the protracted nature of these conflicts, Ted Gurr notes that 'eighty-eight of the 230 communal groups surveyed in the Minorities at Risk study have been engaged in serious political or intercommunal conflict sat some time between 1945 and 1989', in T.R. Gurr (1992), 'The internationalization of protracted communal conflicts since 1945: which groups, where, and how ', in M. Midlarsky (ed.), *The Internationalization of Communal Strife*, London: Routledge, pp. 3–26.
6. R.L. Sivard (Annual 1974–), *World Military and Social Expenditures*, Leesburg, Va.: World Priorities; SIPRI Annual.
7. C. Nordstrom (1992), 'The backyard front', in C. Nordstrom and J. Martin (eds), *The Paths to Domination, Resistance, and Terror*, Berkeley, CA: University of California Press, p. 261.
8. UN Doc. A/48/1, 10 September 1993.
9. SIPRI, 1993, p. 20.
10. Sivard, 1991, p. 36.
11. Sivard, Annual; SIPRI, 1993; The World Commission on Environment and Development (1987), *Our Common Future*, Oxford: Oxford University Press.

12. Eckhardt, 1989, p. 97. He defines structural violence as '...those deaths caused by the way wealth and power are distributed in any society or any world, so as to reduce the life chances of those with less money and power' (p. 96).

13. 'Adhockery' describes a situation where decisions and behaviours are focused exclusively on the problems and crises of the present moment, disregarding effects or goals over the long term. This typifies much of the UN's peacemaking and peacekeeping activity. It could also be called 'crisis management'.

14. M. Renner (1993), 'Critical juncture: the future of peacekeeping', *Worldwatch Paper, No. 114*, Washington, DC: Worldwatch Institute, p. 29.

15. SIPRI, 1993, p. 49.

16. B. Boutros-Ghali (1993), 'An agenda for peace: one year later', *Orbis*, 37(3):327.

17. UN Doc. DPI/1399-93527, *United Nations Peacekeeping*, 31 May 1993, p.9.

18. Boutros-Ghali, 1992a.

19. UN Doc. A/48/1.

20. UN Doc. A/47/965 S/25944, 15 June 1993; UN Doc. A/48/1.

21. Sherry, 1990, pp. 22–3.

22. P. Formuth (1993), 'The making of a security community: the United Nations after the Cold War', *Journal of International Affairs*, 46(2):351–2.

23. See Holiday and Stanley, 1993; 'El Salvador's reborn death squads', *The Economist*, 13 November 1993; UN Doc. S/25812, 21 May 1993 and S/26581, 14 October 1993.

24. UN Doc. SCR 696, 30 May 1991; UN Doc. S/22627, 20 May 1991.

25. UN Doc. S/25140, 21 January 1993, provides details of the re-start of the civil war in Angola; UN Doc. S/25840, 25 May 1993 and S/26434, 13 September 1993, provide details of the UN's peacemaking efforts as well as details of the worsening humanitarian crisis and UN efforts in that area; G. Marion, 'Angola in the grip of despair', *The Guardian Weekly*, 3 October 1993.

26. UN Doc. S/21360, 18 June 1990; UN Doc. SCR 658, 27 June 1990.

27. UN Doc. S/26185, 28 July 1993; UN Doc. A/48/426, 27 September 1993; Durch, 1993.

28. For claims about UNTAC's successes, see UN Doc. S/26529, 5 October 1993 on the 'successful' completion of the UN's mandate in Cambodia. For a general overview of the problems still facing Cambodia and its future prospects, see UN Doc. S/26360, 26 August 1993; UN Doc. S/26546, 7 October 1993.

29. UN Doc. SCR 794, 3 December 1993.

30. UN Doc. SCR 814, 26 March 1993; for a good overview of the UN's involvement in Somalia, see UN Doc. UNDPI, 'The United Nations and the situation in Somalia', *Reference Paper*, 30 April 1993.

31. On activities outside of Mogadishu, see UN Doc. S/26317, 17 August 1993.

32. UN Doc. S/26385, 30 August 1993; UN Doc. SG/T/1821, 18 October 1993; 'UN threatens to withdraw from Mozambique', *Reuter News Service*, 18 October 1993.

33. UN Doc. SCR 872, 5 October 1993.
34. UN Doc. SCR 866, 22 September 1993.
35. UN Doc. SCR 858, 24 August 1993.
36. UN Doc. S/26646, 27 October 1993.
37. UN Doc. SCR, 23 September 1993; UN Doc. S/26352, 25 August 1993.
38. S. Tisdall, 'Horror's Homeland', *The Guardian*, 30 October 1993.
39. UN Doc. SCR 689, 9 April 1991.
40. UN Doc. SCR 687, 3 April 1991, para. 5.
41. UN Doc. SCR 689, 9 April 1991, para. 2.
42. Formuth, 1993, p. 348.
43. H. Wiseman (1990), 'Peacekeeping in the international context: historical analysis and future directions', in I.J. Rikhye and K. Skjelsbaek (eds), *The United Nations and Peacekeeping: Results, Limitations and Prospects*, London: Macmillan/IPA, p. 35.
44. See Rikhye, 1989; Diehl and Kumar, 1991; Prins, 1991; Pugh, 1992; Harbottle, 1991.
45. For more extensive discussions on this and other management issues, see Jonah, in Rikhye and Skjelsbaek, 1990; Liu, 1990; Rikhye, 1984; *Peacekeeper's Handbook*, 1984.
46. UN Doc. A/48/1, para. 300.
47. A.R. Norton and T.G. Weiss (1990b), 'UN peacekeepers: soldiers with a difference', *Headline Series, No. 292*, New York: Foreign Policy Association, pp. 27–8.
48. UN Doc. A/48/1, para. 301.
49. Jonah, in Rikhye and Skjelsbaek, 1990, p. 86.
50. Jonah, in Rikhye and Skjelsbaek, 1990, p. 86.
51. G. Evans (1993), *Cooperating for Peace: The Global Agenda for the 1990s and Beyond*, St. Leonards, NSW, Australia: Allen & Unwin, p. 121.
52. For further discussion on financial issues, see UN Doc. A/45/582, 10 October 1990; Mills, 1989; Durch, ed., 1993; UN Doc. PS/DPI/15/Rev.5, October 1993; UN Doc. DH/1505, 22 October 1993.
53. UN Doc. A/46/1, September 1991.
54. Boutros-Ghali, 1992a, p. 41.
55. *USIS Wireless File EPF410, United Nations Report*, 5 August 1993; UN Doc. DH/1505, 22 October 1993; UN Doc. PS/DPI/15/Rev.5, October 1993; B. Rudolph, 'United Nations: Running on Empty', *Time Magazine*, 4 October 1993, p. 47.
56. UN Doc. A/48/1, para. 306.
57. Mackinlay, 1989, p. 216.
58. B. Urquhart (1987), 'United Nations peacekeeping operations and how their role might be enhanced', in UNITAR, p. 254.
59. See Chapter 3 for more details on this particular incident.
60. Urquhart, 1987, p. 336.
61. Mackinlay, 1989, pp. 219–20.
62. 'Italy to seek transfer of troops in Mogadishu', *Reuter News Service*, 12 August 1993; 'Italy blasts "Rambo" UN command in Somalia', *Reuter News Service*, 13 August 1993; 'Italy denies failing to help Nigerians in Somalia', *Reuter News Service*, 6 September 1993;
63. Urquhart, in UNITAR, 1987, p. 258; see also, Urquhart, 1990.

64. Evans, 1993, pp. 109–14.
65. Heiberg, in Rikhye and Skjelsbaek, 1990, pp. 147–60; J. Galtung and I. Eide (1976), 'Some factors affecting local acceptance of a UN force: a pilot project report from Gaza', in J. Galtung, *Peace, War and Defence: Essays in Peace Research, Vol. 2*, Copenhagen: Christian Ejlers.
66. Heiberg, in Rikhye and Skjelsbaek, 1990 p. 148.
67. Galtung and Eide, in Galtung, 1976, Vol. 2, p. 256.
68. P.F. Diehl (1989), 'A permanent UN peacekeeping force: an evaluation', *Bulletin of Peace Proposals*, 20(1):27–36.
69. Diehl, 1988, pp. 502–3.
70. Haas, in UNITAR, 1987, p. 32.
71. Haas, in UNITAR, 1987, p. 33.
72. C.C. Moskos (1976), *Peace Soldiers: The Sociology of a United Nations Military Force*, Chicago: University of Chicago Press, p. 129.
73. Moskos, 1976, p. 133.
74. Simon Tisdall, 'Cover story – horror's homeland', *The Guardian*, 30 October 1993, offers a haunting account of the succession of failures in Haiti. See also, Sommerville, 1993.
75. See Africa Rights (1993), *Somalia: Human Rights Abuses by the United Nations Forces*, London: Africa Rights; Human Rights Watch, 1993; 'UN orders corruption inquiry', and 'The soldiers are out of control: they are feasting on a dying city', *The Guardian Weekly*, 5 September 1993; 'Torture used to treat patient', *The Canberra Times*, 12 September 1993; 'Mozambique: Portuguese UN troops accused of misconduct', *Reuter News Service*, 8 October 1993; E. Luce, 'UN blamed for sex boom', *The Guardian Weekly*, 14 November 1993.
76. As of April 1994 the level of staffing at the DPKD was 267. (128 professional officers, 139 general service officers, and 80 military officers).
77. See Ross, 1992.

## 3 Case-Studies: United Nations Peacekeeping in Cyprus, Namibia and Former Yugoslavia

1. R. MacDonald (1988/9), 'The problem of Cyprus', *Adelphi Paper* No. 234, London: Brassey/IISS, p. 7.
2. UN Doc. SCR 186, 4 March 1964.
3. UN Doc. SCR 186, 4 March 1964, para. 5.
4. Higgins, 1981, provides a detailed description of the early financial difficulties and debates over the issue in the Security Council, pp. 286–301.
5. UN Docs. S/5679, 2 May 1964 and S/5764, 15 June 1964.
6. Reasons for the redrawing and redeployment are given in Stegenga, 1969, pp. 97–101, and seemed, at least in part, due to embarrassing breaches of discipline by some UNFICYP troops, who, acting out of sympathy for the Turkish Cypriots, were caught gun-running.
7. M. Harbottle (1971), *The Blue Berets*, London: Leo Cooper, pp. 65–6. Harbottle quotes his own work here taking a passage from (1970), *The Impartial Soldier*, London: Oxford University Press.
8. Harbottle, 1970, pp. 63–8.

9. UN Doc. *aide-mémoire* dated 10 April 1964; UN Doc. S/5671, 29 April 1964, Annex I.
10. UN Doc. S/5950, 10 September 1964.
11. UN Doc. S/5950, 10 September 1964, para. 7(b).
12. Harbottle, 1970, p. 69.
13. UN Doc. S/5672, 2 May 1964, para. 4.
14. I.J. Rikhye, M. Harbottle and B. Egge (1974), *The Thin Blue Line: International Peacekeeping and Its Future*, New Haven: Yale University Press, p. 109.
15. *The Blue Helmets*, 1990, p. 295.
16. *The Blue Helmets*, 1990, p. 296; Harbottle, 1970, pp. 30–1.
17. See Harbottle, 1970 and (1980), 'The strategy of third party interventions in conflict resolution', *International Journal*, 35(1):118–31.
18. Harbottle, 1980, p. 118.
19. Harbottle, 1970, p. 119.
20. Harbottle, 1970, p. 118.
21. Harbottle gives the number of meetings as sixteen in *The Impartial Soldier* and fourteen in his 1980 article.
22. Harbottle, 1970, p. 120.
23. Harbottle, 1980, p. 120.
24. Harbottle, 1970, pp. 116–20.
25. See UN Doc. S/6228, 11 March 1965 for examples of the importance of negotiation in avoiding escalation of the conflict.
26. M. Harbottle (1979), 'Cyprus: an analysis of the UN's third party role in a "small war"', in P. Worsley, and P. Kitromilides (eds), *Small States in a Modern World: The Conditions of Survival*, Cyprus: New Cyprus Association, p. 218.
27. James, 1989, p. 482.
28. James, 1989. pp. 482–3.
29. UN Doc. SCR 353, 20 July 1974, para. 5.
30. Higgins, 1981, p. 371.
31. N. McQueen (1983), 'Ireland and the United Nations Peacekeeping Force in Cyprus', *Review of International Studies*, 9(2):100–1.
32. UN Doc. SCR 831, 27 May 1993.
33. UN Doc. GAR/47/236, 14 September 1993; see also, UN Doc. A/47/1004, 26 August 1993.
34. See UN Doc. S/26777, 22 November 1993 for full details of the new arrangements for UNFICYP.
35. For more details on the peacemaking effort, particularly the confidence building measures including re-opening Nicosia Airport, see UN Doc. S/26438, 14 September 1993; UN Doc. SG/SM/5180, 15 December 1993; UN Doc. S/26777, 22 November 1993.
36. R.S. Jaster (1990), 'The 1988 Peace Accords and the future of Southwestern Africa', *Adelphi Papers* No. 253, London: International Institute for Strategic Studies, p. 6.
37. G. Bender and W. Schneidman (1988), 'The Namibia negotiations: multilateral versus bilateral approaches to international mediation', *Case No. 422*, University of Southern California: Center for International Studies of the School of International Relations, p. 2; See also

*UN Chronicle*, March 1989, p. 47.

38.  Jaster, 1990, p. 5.
39.  Bender and Schneidman, 1988, p. 2.
40.  Jaster, 1990, p. 7.
41.  Jaster, 1990, pp. 5–6.
42.  For more information see Berridge, 1989, 1990; Crocker, 1990; Jaster, 1990; Legum, 1988.
43.  UN Docs. S/12827 and SCR 435, 29 September 1978; further refined in subsequent documents, see, UN Docs. S/12636 (1978), S/12827 (1978), S/12841 (1978), S/12867 (1978), S/15287 (1982), S/17658 (1985), S/20345 (1988), S/20412 (1989), S/20635 (1989), etc.
44.  UN Doc. SCR 632, 16 February 1989.
45.  UN Doc. SCR 385, 30 January 1976.
46.  *The Blue Helmets*, 1990, p. 360.
47.  *The Blue Helmets*, 1990, p. 360.
48.  *The Blue Helmets*, 1990, pp. 354–5.
49.  *The Blue Helmets*, 1990, p. 365; more information about aspects of the civilian component can be found in pp. 354–7.
50.  The following documents provide a description the reasons for the delay: UN Doc. SCR 629, 16 January 1989; UN Doc. S/20412, 23 January 1989, especially sect II, para. 50–53; UN Doc. SCR 632, 16 February 1989; UN Doc. S/20457, 9 February 1989, para. 2; UN Doc. S/12827, 29 September 1978, sect III, para. 26.
51.  Jaster, 1990, p. 35.
52.  Jaster, 1990, p. 38.
53.  *UN Chronicle*, June 1989, p. 6.
54.  Jaster, 1990, p. 36.
55.  *UN Chronicle*, September 1989, p. 6.
56.  Jaster, 1990, p. 41.
57.  *UN Chronicle*, March 1990, p. 43.
58.  Private interview with author.
59.  *The Blue Helmets*, 1990, p. 368.
60.  Address given by Cedric Thornberry, Director of the Special Representative's Office, in Johannesberg, South Africa, UN Doc. UNTAG *Press Release*, 5 December 1989, p. 4.
61.  Address given by Thornberry, 1989, p. 4.
62.  *UN Chronicle*, December 1989, p. 8.
63.  *UN Chronicle*, December 1989, p. 9.
64.  Jaster, 1990, p. 43.
65.  Jaster, 1990, p. 42.
66.  *The Blue Helmets*, 1990, p. 385.
67.  Jaster, 1990, p. 41.
68.  UN Doc. 'Statement By the SRSG for Namibia', 14 November 1989.
69.  Jaster, 1990, p. 45.
70.  *UN Chronicle*, March 1990, p. 45. For a lengthier study of Namibia's economic and political progress a year after independence, see Simon, 1991.
71.  The Republic of Bosnia-Herzegovina will be referred to as 'Bosnia'.
72.  J. Gow (1991), 'Deconstructing Yugoslavia', *Survival.* 33(4):293.

73. Gow, 1991, p. 293.
74. Gow, 1991, pp. 296, 298–303.
75. M. Glenny (1992), *The Fall of Yugoslavia: The Third Balkan War,* London: Penguin, pp. 12–14.
76. L. Basta-Posavec *et al,* (1992), *Inter-ethnic conflict and war in former Yugoslavia,* Belgrade: Institute for European Studies, p. 7.
77. Glenny, 1992, p. 143.
78. 'Serbian militants blockade Sarajevo', *International Herald Tribune,* 3 March 1992.
79. UN Doc. SCR 713, 25 September 1991.
80. UN Doc. SCR 724, 15 December 1991. The concept and plan were outlined in a document prepared by the Secretary-General, UN Doc. S/23280, 11 December 1991.
81. UN Doc. SCR 743, 21 February 1992. Delays were caused by opposition to UN involvement – particularly from the leader of Krajina's Serbian communities, Milan Babic; 'News Digest for January 1992', *Keesing's Record of World Events,* p. 38704; 'UN pressure on Yugoslavs grows', *The Guardian,* 8 February 1992.
82. UN Doc. S/23280, 11 December 1991.
83. Lord Carrington held his position on behalf of the EC (Council of Ministers) Presidency.
84. UN Doc. S/24795, 11 November 1992, provides details on the structure and organization of the new conference.
85. Figures from a 1991 census show that Sector East had a population of 200,000, of which 80,000 were Serbs. Sector West had a population of 100,000 of which 40,000 were Serbs. Sector North had a population of 77,000 of which 55,000 were Serbs. Sector South had a population of 117,000 of which 89,000 were Serbs, see, J. Gow and J.D.D. Smith (1992), 'Peacemaking, peacekeeping: European security and the Yugoslav wars', *London Defence Studies,* No. 11, London: Brassey's/Centre for Defence Studies, p. 73.
86. UN Doc. S/23488, 24 April 1992.
87. Human Rights Watch, 1993, p. 91.
88. UN Doc. 23844, 24 April 1992, paras. 9 and 13.
89. UN Doc. S/ 23900, 12 May 1992, para. 24; 'Fresh fighting rules UN out of Bosnia', *The Independent,* 8 May 1992.
90. UN Doc. S/23900, 12 May 1992, para. 18.
91. UN Doc. S/23844, 24 April 1992, para. 23.
92. UN Doc. S/23900, 12 May 1992, para. 34.
93. UN Doc. S/ 24333, 21 July 1992, para. 13.
94. UNIC, UK, Doc. NS/21/92, 28 May 1992.
95. UN Doc. SCR 762, 30 June 1992, based on S/24188, 26 June 1992, para. 16.
96. UN Doc. SCR 769, 7 August 1992, based on S/24353, 27 July 1992.
97. UN Doc. S/24848, 24 November 1992.
98. 'Peace troops stop Croatian clash', *The Guardian,* 1 October 1992.
99. 'Serbs "violating UN plan"', *The Guardian,* 1 October 1992.
100. UN Doc. S/24600, 28 September 1992, para. 5.
101. UN Doc. S/24600, 28 September 1992.

102.  'Thin blue line of Russians halt march of angry Croats', *The Times*, 1 October 1992; 'Peace troops stop Croatian clash', *The Guardian*, 1 October 1992; UN Doc. S/24848, 24 November 1992, para. 20.

103.  UN Doc. S/24600, 28 September 1992 and S/24848, 24 November 1992, paras. 15–16.

104.  'Yugoslav commander threatens to halt Croatian withdrawal', *The Times*, 20 October 1992; 'Overland relief convoys suspended by UN', *The Financial Times*, 21 October 1992. On withdrawal from the Prevlaka peninsula, see UN Doc. SCR 779, 6 October 1992; 'Peace pact for Dubrovnik wins favour at the UN', *The Guardian*, 6 October 1992; 'Warship talks clear way to end Dubrovnik siege', *The Independent*, 6 October 1992.

105.  UN Doc. SCR 802, 25 January 1993; UN Doc. S/26470, 20 September 1993.

106.  From its inception until mid-September 1993, the peacekeeping force in Croatia sustained 347 casualties, 31 of them fatal; UN Doc. S/26470, 20 September 1993.

107.  UN Doc. S/25993, 24 June 1993, para. 3.

108.  Summary of outbreak of violence is found in, 'News Digest for March 1992', *Keesings Record of World Events*, p. 38832; 'Bosnia claims independence poll victory', *The Financial Times*, 2 March 1992; 'Serbian militants blockade Sarajevo', *International Herald Tribune*, 3 March 1992.

109.  On 28 April 1992, the Council agreed in principle to extend its involvement into Bosnia, 'News Digest for April 1992', *Keesing's Record of World Events*, p. 38848.

110.  UN Doc. SCR 757, 30 May 1992; 'News Digest for May 1992', *Keesing's Record of World Events*, p. 38918.

111.  UN Doc. S/24000, 26 May 1992.

112.  UN Doc. S/24000, 26 May 1992.

113.  UN Doc. SCR 758, 8 June 1992.

114.  'UN paves way for troops in Sarajevo', *The Financial Times*, 11 June 1992; 'UN convoy heads for Sarajevo', *The Independent*, 11 June 1992.

115.  UN Doc. S/24075, 6 June 1992.

116.  'Nato forces to help Sarajevo airlift', *The Guardian*, 17 June 1992; 'UN halts attempt to relieve siege airport', *The Daily Telegraph*, 22 June 1992.

117.  'French planes deliver supplies to Sarajevo after the UN takes tenuous control of airport', *The Wall Street Journal*, 30 June 1992.

118.  'Carrington gloomy over Bosnia talks', *The Guardian*, 16 July 1992; 'Upsurge in fighting racks Bosnia', *The Independent*, 14 July 1992; 'Victims of European diplomacy', *The Independent*, 16 July 1992; 'Refugees "trail of misery"', *The Independent*, 20 July 1992; 'Truce in Sarajevo fails to take hold', *International Herald Tribune*, 20 July 1992.

119.  UN Doc. S/24333, 21 July 1992.

120.  'Bosnia factions agree ceasefire', *The Guardian*, 18 July 1992; 'Bosnia – the unfinished agenda', *The Guardian*, 20 July 1992.

121.  'Boutros-Ghali attacks EC plan', *The Financial Times*, 22 July 1992; 'Carrington and UN fall out over Bosnian peace plan', *The Times*, 22 July 1992.

122.  'Boutros-Ghali rebuffs UK in call for new talks on Bosnia', *The*

*Independent*, 24 July 1992; 'Keeping the UN peace', *International Herald Tribune*, 27 July 1992; 'Conference agrees basis for Bosnian peace deal', *The Financial Times*, 28 August 1992; 'Sanctions could last for years, says Owen', *The Times*, 3 September 1992.

123. 'Boutros-Ghali attacks EC peace plan', *The Financial Times*, 22 July 1992.
124. 'UN demands cash for peace', *The Guardian*, 29 August 1992.
125. 'Ogata tries to persuade world to face the facts', *The Financial Times*, 29 July 1992; 'Europe facing refugee crisis not seen for half a century', *The Daily Telegraph*, 30 July 1992.
126. UN Doc. S/23900, 12 May 1992, para. 6.
127. UN Doc. S/23900, 12 May 1992, para. 34.
128. 'Ambush blocks UN aid convoy in Bosnia', *The Independent*, 27 July 1992; 'US consults allies on military escort to protect Bosnia relief', *The Times*, 29 July 1992.
129. 'Nato may send in 100,000 troops to cover aid convoy', *The Independent*, 7 August 1992; Margaret Thatcher, 'Stop the excuses: Serbia should get ultimatum', *International Herald Tribune*, 7 August 1992; David Owen, 'When it is right to fight', *The Times*, by 4 August 1992.
130. UN Doc. SCR 770, 13 August 1992.
131. UN Doc. SCR 771, 13 August 1992.
132. 'Italy suspends further aid flights to Sarajevo', *The Financial Times*, 5 September 1992; 'French peacekeepers killed in Yugoslavia', *The Times*, 9 September 1992.
133. UN Doc. S/24540, 10 September 1992.
134. UN Doc. S/24848, 24 November 1992.
135. UN Doc. SCR 776, 14 September 1992.
136. UN Doc. S/24848, 24 November 1992.
137. 'Peacekeeping force to increase fivefold', *The Times*, 16 September 1992.
138. Ibid.
139. 'UN fights time as Bosnia winter nears', *International Herald Tribune*, 25 September 1992; 'Vance attacks British delay in sending troops', *The Times*, 15 October 1992; 'In Ex-Yugoslavia, UN spins its wheels', *International Herald Tribune*, 21–22 November 1992.
140. 'UN intends to open all Bosnia roads without a fight', *International Herald Tribune*, 23 September 1992.
141. 'UN fights time as Bosnia winter nears', *International Herald Tribune*, 25 September 1992.
142. 'What is in store for them?', *The Daily Telegraph*, interviewing John Mackinlay, 11 September 1992.
143. W. Pfaff, 'No salvation in sight for the damned of Sarajevo', *International Herald Tribune*, 24 September 1992.
144. Ibid.
145. 'Peacekeepers at war: British troops leaving for Bosnia would find themselves under fire from all sides', *The Times*, 11 September 1992; 'Crisis of confidence afflicts UN in Bosnia: the peacekeeping operation in Sarajevo is rapidly falling apart', *The Independent*, 21 September 1992.
146. UN Doc. SCR 781, 9 October 1992.
147. Human Rights Watch, 1992, p. 94.

148. UN Doc. SCR 816, 31 March 1993; Human Rights Watch, 1992, pp. 94–5.
149. Human Rights Watch, 1992, p. 95.
150. UN Doc. S/24923, 9 December 1992 provided a plan for the mission to Macedonia which was authorized by SCR 795, 11 December 1992.
151. Human Rights Watch, 1992, p. 97.
152. Human Rights Watch, 1992, p. 98.
153. UN Doc. SCR 819, 16 April 1993.
154. UN Doc. SCR 824, 6 May 1993.
155. UN Doc. SCR 836, 4 June 1993, para. 4.
156. UN Doc. S/25939, 14 June 1993.
157. UN Doc. S/25939, 14 June 1993.
158. UN Doc. HR/CN/459, 30 July 1993.
159. 'UN orders corruption inquiry', and 'The soldiers are out of control: they are feasting on a dying city', *The Guardian Weekly*, 5 September 1993; 'Torture used to treat patient', *The Canberra Times*, 12 September 1993.
160. K. Schork, 'Swedes set new standard for peacekeeping in Bosnia', *Reuter News Service* , 6 November 1993; K. Schork, 'Moslem looting sparks UN intervention in Bosnia town', *Reuter News Service* , 4 November 1993.
161. Ibid.
162. Ibid.
163. K. Schork, 'Swedish UN troops say they led into a trap in Bosnia', *Reuter News Service*, 8 November 1993; K. Schork, 'UN hostages freed in Bosnia', *Reuter News Service* , 7 November 1993.
164. A. Boadle, 'Canada to review peacekeeping role in Bosnia', *Reuter News Service*, 4 January 1994; 'UN Chief, Canadian Premier discuss Bosnia', *Reuter News Service*, 9 January 1994.
165. K. Schork, 'Bosnia fighting shadows Vienna peace pledge, Bonn Summit', *Reuter News Service*, 5 January 1994.
166. F. Langan and R. Fox, 'International – double blow to Bosnia peacekeeping effort', *The Daily Telegraph*, 5 January 1994; 'Belgian UN Commander wants to quit', *Reuter News Service*, 4 January 1994.
167. 'Belgian UN Commander wants to quit', *Reuter News Service*, 4 January 1994.
168. 'Delay in deployment puts UK troops at grave risk', *The Times*, 11 September 1992.
169. 'British troops confident they can deliver aid', *The Independent*, 3 November 1992; 'British troops launch diplomatic offensive', *The Daily Telegraph*, 4 November 1992.

# 4 Outlining a Theoretical Approach

1. For a more detailed discussion of these perspectives see: Pearson and Rochester, 1992; Smith *et al.*, 1981; Light and Groom, 1985; Klare and Thomas, 1991; Banks, 1984; Gaddis, 1993.
2. H. Morganthau (1948), *Politics Among Nations*,. New York: Knopf. *Politics Among Nations* has been through six editions, the last one pub-

lished in 1985 following Morganthau's death. See also, Waltz, 1959, 1979.

3. Examples of neo-realist perspectives: Small and Singer, 1979; Keohane, 1986.

4. Gaddis, 1993, offers an interesting discussion on the predictive capability of international relations theory given the end of the Cold War.

5. R. Falk (1991), 'Theory, realism and world security', in Klare and Thomas, p. 22; see also, Banks, in Burton and Dukes, Vol. 3, 1990; Tickner, 1992.

6. A.J.R. Groom (1990), 'Paradigms in conflict: the strategist, the conflict researcher and the peace researcher', in Burton and Dukes, Vol. 3, p. 76.

7. See Falk, Kim and Mendolvitz, 1982; Walker, 1988; Miller, 1990; Soroos, 1986.

8. Groom, in Burton and Dukes, Vol. 3, 1990, p. 76.

9. See Burton and Sandole, 1986; Burton, 1984; Burton, Vol. 1, 1990.

10. Falk, in Klare and Thomas, 1991, p. 23.

11. For more on 'transformation' see Vayrynen, in Vayrynen, 1991; Falk *et al.*, 1991.

12. N. Young (1987), 'The peace movement, peace research, peace education and peace building', *Bulletin of Peace Proposals*, 18(3):334.

13. P. Wallensteen (1988), 'The origins of peace research', in P. Wallensteen (ed.), *Peace Research: Achievements and Challenges*, Boulder, CO: Westview, p. 10.

14. Young, 1987, p. 335.

15. Young, 1987, pp. 336–7.

16. Galtung, Vol. 1, 1975.

17. A. Rapoport (1982), 'Various conceptions of peace research', in G. Pardesi (ed.), *Contemporary Peace Research.* Brighton: Harvester, p. 43.

18. Galtung, Vol. 1, 1975, p. 256.

19. For an interesting discussion of the 'structuralist'/'evolutionist' debate within the field, see Boulding, 1977.

20. Galtung, Vol. 1, 1975, p. 29.

21. A. Curle (1971), *Making Peace*, London: Tavistock, p. 1.

22. Curle, 1990, outlines Curle's approach to peace research and to creating positively peaceful societies.

23. Galtung, Vol. 1, 1975, p. 29.

24. Galtung, Vol. 1, 1975, p. 111.

25. J. Galtung (1985), 'Twenty-five years of peace research', *Journal of Peace Research*, 22(2):145.

26. A. Curle (1990), *Tools for Transformation: A Personal Study*, Stroud, UK: Hawthorne Press, p. 22–3.

27. K. Boulding (1987), 'Peace and the evolutionary process', in R. Vayrynen (ed.), *The Quest for Peace*, London: Sage, p. 52.

28. Burton, Vol. 1, 1990, pp. 36–48.

29. For more detailed discussion of human needs theory, see Burton, 1979; Burton, Vol. 2, 1990; Sites, 1973.

30. G. Sorensen (1992), 'Utopianism in peace research: the Gandhian her-

itage', *Journal of Peace Research*, 29(2):135–44, provides an interesting discussion of contradictions inherent in different conceptions of peace. Of particular relevance to this discussion is his critique of Galtung's definition of violence as it is embedded in human needs theory, pp. 136–8.

31. K. Avruch and P.W. Black (1987), 'A generic theory of conflict resolution: a critique', *Negotiation Journal* 3(1):87–96.

32. Avruch and Black, 1987, p. 91.

33. This refers to attempts to resolve conflicts through the application of problem-solving workshops or consultancy approaches. See Rothman, 1992; R.J. Fisher, 1983, 1990; Hill, 1982; Burton, 1969; Doob, 1970; Cohen *et al.*, 1977.

34. Groom, in Burton and Dukes, Vol. 3, 1990, p. 96.

35. Burton, Vol. 1, 1990, p. 3, defines provention as, 'deducing from an adequate explanation of the phenomenon of conflict, including its human dimensions, not merely the conditions that create an environment of conflict, and the structural changes required to remove it, but more importantly, the promotion of conditions that create cooperative relationships.'

36. See Soroos, 1990a.

37. Some examples of work on the causes of conflict are, Cashman, 1993; R.J. Fisher, 1990; Waltz, 1959; Small and Singer, 1989; Gurr, 1993; Horowitz, 1985; Burton, 1984; Mitchell, 1981b.

38. M. Deutsch (1991), 'Subjective features of conflict resolution: psychological, social and cultural influences', in Vayrynen, p. 31.

39. Burton, Vol. 1, 1990, p. 2.

40. Burton, Vol. 1, 1990, p. 2.

41. E.E. Azar (1990), *The Management of Protracted Social Conflict: Theory and Cases*, Aldershot, U.K.: Dartmouth, especially pp. 1–17.

42. Azar, 1990, p. 12.

43. Azar, 1990, p. 2.

44. Mitchell, 1981b, p. 16 shows the model. Explanation of the three parts of the model follows, pp. 19–34.

45. Mitchell, 1981b, p. 29

46. Mitchell, 1981b, pp. 47–68.

47. Deutsch, in Vayrynen, 1991, p. 27.

48. F. Glasl (1982), 'The process of conflict escalation and roles of third parties', in G.B.J. Bomers and R.B. Peterson (eds), *Conflict Management and Industrial Relations*, Boston: Kluwer Nijhoff, p. 122.

49. H. Eckstein (1980), 'Theoretical approaches to explaining collective political violence', in T.R. Gurr (ed.), *Handbook of Political Conflict: Theory and Research*, New York: Free Press, p. 138.

50. J.W. Burton (1972c), *World Society*, London: Cambridge University Press, pp. 137–8.

51. Eckstein, in Gurr, 1980, p. 139.

52. Banks, in Burton and Dukes, Vol. 3, 1990, p. 56.

53. Banks, in Burton and Dukes, Vol. 3, 1990, p. 68.

54. For an excellent discussion of this debate see C. Mitchell (1991),

'Recognising conflict', in T. Woodhouse (ed.), *Peacemaking in a Troubled World*, New York: Berg, pp. 209–25.

55. C. Mitchell (1981a), *Peacemaking and the Consultant's Role*, Westmead: Gower, p. 22.
56. C. Mitchell (1973), 'Conflict resolution and controlled communication: some further comments', *Journal of Peace Research*, 10:128.
57. Mitchell, 1981a, p. 31.
58. Burton, 1972c, p. 149.
59. Mitchell, 1981b, pp. 15–34.
60. Fisher, 1990, pp. 234–8.
61. Deutsch, in Vayrynen, 1991, p. 28.
62. J. Bercovitch (1986), 'International mediation: a study of the incidence, strategies and conditions of successful outcomes', *Cooperation and Conflict*, 21:155.
63. J. Bercovitch, J.T Anagnoson and D.L. Willie (1991), 'Some conceptual issues and empirical trends in the study of successful mediation in international relations', *Journal of Peace Research*, 28(1):7.
64. Mitchell, 1981b, p. 278.
65. Conflict management will be used here as a generic term to encompass all types of strategies employed to reduce or end conflict.
66. J.W. Burton (1987), *Resolving Deep-Rooted Conflict: A Handbook*, Lanham MD: University Press of America, p. 21.
67. Azar, 1990, pp. 1–17.
68. Mitchell, 1981b, p. 253.
69. Burton, Vol. 1, 1990, p. 3.
70. J. Laue (1990), 'The emergence and institutionalization of third-party roles in conflict', in Burton and Dukes, Vol. 3, p. 258.
71. Laue, in Burton and Dukes, Vol. 3, 1990, p. 258.
72. See note 33 for references on problem-solving.
73. A discussion of the development of the field of conflict intervention is offered by Laue, in Burton and Dukes, Vol. 3., 1990. Laue describes the influences, roles, expectations of this emerging field.
74. Mitchell, 1981b, pp. 274–5.
75. Laue, in Burton and Dukes, Vol. 3, 1990, p. 260.
76. Laue, in Burton and Dukes, Vol. 3, 1990, pp. 260–1.
77. This point is discussed more fully by Burton, Vol. 1, 1990, pp. 188–210, especially the model used to distinguish between third party roles, pp. 196–7.
78. Bercovitch *et al.*, 1991, p. 8.
79. Bercovitch *et al.*, 1991, p. 8.
80. R. Fisher and L. Keashly (1991), 'The potential complementarity of mediation and consultation within a contingency model of third party intervention', *Journal of Peace Research*, 28(1):30.
81. For a general overview of mediation see Wall and Lynn, 1993; Wall, 1981; Fisher and Keashly, 1988; Bercovitch, 1991, 1992; Bercovitch and Lamare, 1993.
82. See note 33 for references on consultancy (problem-solving).
83. Fisher and Keashly, 1991, p. 30.

84. Wehr, 1979, p. 45.
85. van der Merwe *et al.*, in Burton and Dukes, Vol. 3, 1990, p. 233.
86. Burton, 1987b, p. 7.
87. For further discussion of negotiation, see Pruitt and Carnavale, 1993; Druckman, Kidd and Saks, Vol. 2, 1983; Druckman, 1993; Kriesberg, 1988; Saunders, 1985; Stein, 1989c; Touval, 1989; Rubin, 1989.
88. G. Tillett (1991), *Resolving Conflict: A Practical Approach*, Sydney/ Melbourne: Sydney University Press/Oxford University Press Australia, p. 45.
89. van der Merwe *et al.*, in Burton and Dukes, Vol. 3, 1990, p. 218.
90. R. Fisher and W. Ury (1981), *Getting to Yes: How To Negotiate to Agreement Without Giving In*, London: Arrow.
91. van der Merwe *et al.*, in Burton and Dukes, Vol. 3, 1990, p. 224.
92. Fisher and Keashly, 1991, p. 33.
93. A useful discussion of conciliatory gestures is offered in Mitchell, 1991.
94. Deutsch, in Vayrynen, 1991, p. 49.
95. Deutsch, in Vayrynen, 1991, p. 49.
96. Wehr, 1979, pp. 50–52.
97. C. Honeyman (1988), 'Five elements of mediation', *Negotiation Journal*, 4(2):152–55.
98. N. Katz and J. Lawyer (1985), *Communication and Conflict Resolution Skills*, Dubuque, Iowa: Kendall/Hunt, pp. 11–12.
99. Katz and Lawyer, 1985, pp. vii–ix.
100. Burton and Dukes, Vol. 4, 1990, pp. 187–8.
101. The field of peace research, in particular, has focused on this problem and there have been numerous approaches and positions put forward. For a range of arguments see Boulding, Brigagao and Clements, 1991; Curle, 1990; Dumas and Thee, 1989.
102. See Avruch, Black and Scimecca, 1991; Wehr and Lederach, 1991.
103. M.H. Ross (1992), 'The language of success and failure in ethnic conflict management', paper prepared for the First International Conference of the Ethnic Studies Network, Northern Ireland, 8–10 June 1992, pp. 6–7.
104. The main arguments of this framework are summarized in J. Laue (1982), 'Ethical considerations in choosing intervention roles', *Peace and Change*, 8(2/3):29–41.
105. Laue, 1982, pp. 35–6.
106. Wehr, 1979, p. 50.
107. Burton, Vol. 1, 1990, p. 159.
108. Burton, Vol. 1, 1990, p. 160.
109. Burton, Vol. 1, 1990, p. 160.
110. N. Lewer and O. Ramsbotham (1993), 'Something must be done: towards and ethical framework for humanitarian intervention in international social conflict', *Peace Research Report*, No. 33, Bradford, UK: Department of Peace Studies, University of Bradford, p. 98.
111. See Prein, 1984; Bercovitch *et al.*, 1991; Haas, 1986.
112. See Bercovitch *et al.*, 1991. This paper provides a good example of analysis of third party intervention yielding empirical evidence which is then applied to a contingency model.

113. See Wehr and Lederach, 1991. This is a good example of a case-study approach which could yield useful evidence for a contingency model. Examples of the data-set approach can be found in Bercovitch *et al*., 1991, and Miall, 1992.

114. Bercovitch *et al*., 1991, p. 9.

115. Gaddis, 1993, p. 58.

116. For example Haas, 1987, did a very similar study to that of Bercovitch *et al*., 1991, covering a very similar data set, and came up with somewhat different conclusions. Based on his results, Haas suggests that mediation is more successful in intense, violent conflicts, while relatively unsuccessful in relatively less intense ones. Bercovitch *et al*., on the other hand, find the opposite to be the case. They argue that mediation is more successful if a conflict has not escalated into violence.

117. Prein, 1984, p. 82.

118. Laue, 1982, p. 35.

119. The results of Prein's 1984 study seem to indicate that such an approach is valid. His research suggests that process or contingency approaches offer a general strategy combined with other approaches operating at a more specific level, p. 100.

120. Q. Wright (1965), 'The escalation of international conflicts', *Journal of Conflict Resolution*, 4(4):434–5.

121. Glasl, in Bomers and Peterson, 1982, pp. 119–40.

122. Fisher and Keashly, 1991, pp. 35–9.

123. For a further explanation of this approach and its development, and the theory behind it, see R.J. Fisher, 1990; Fisher and Keashly, 1988.

124. See Glasl, in Bomers and Peterson, 1982.

125. Fisher and Keashly, 1991, p. 42.

126. Rothman, 1989, p. 274.

127. W. L. Ury (1987), 'Strengthening international mediation', *Negotiation Journal*, 3(3): 226–7.

128. van der Merwe *et al*., in Burton and Dukes, Vol. 3, 1990, p. 232.

129. Mitchell, 1981b, p. 279.

130. Azar, 1990, p. 127.

131. Azar, 1990, p. 127.

132. Bercovitch *et al*., 1991, pp. 7–17.

133. Wehr and Lederach, 1991.

134. See Wehr and Lederach, 1991.

# 5 Peacekeeping, Peacemaking and Peacebuilding: Definitions and Linkages

1. G. Sherry (1986), 'The United Nations, international conflict, and American security', *Political Science Quarterly*, 101(5):759.

2. Sherry, 1990, p. 30.

3. Norton and Weiss, 1990b, p. 31.

4. J.J. Holst (1990), 'Support and limitations: peacekeeping from the

point of view of troop-contributors', in Rikhye and Skjelsbaek, p. 111.

5. B. Russett and J.S. Sutterlin (1991), 'The United Nations in a new world order,' *Foreign Affairs*, 70(2):70–3.

6. R.A. Coate and D.J. Puchala (1990), 'Global policies and the United Nations system: a current assessment', *Journal of Peace Research*, 27(2):127.

7. Scheltema, in Harrod and Schrijver, 1988, p. 4.

8. Simonia, in Weiss, 1990, pp. 60–1.

9. Haas, in UNITAR, 1987, p. 29.

10. K. Skjelsbaek (1986), 'Peaceful settlement of disputes by the United Nations and other international bodies', *Cooperation and Conflict*, 21(3):146.

11. Rikhye *et al.*, 1974, pp. 9–10.

12. Rikhye *et al.*, 1974, p. 268.

13. International Peace Academy (1984), *Peacekeeper's Handbook*, New York: Pergamon, p. 22.

14. In March 1992 as part of a broader reform package, the Office of Special Political Affairs became the Department of Peacekeeping Operations. In March 1993, Marrack Goulding became Under-Secretary-General for the Department of Political Affairs (DPA), and was replaced as U-S-G at the DPKO by Kofi Annan.

15. M. Goulding, 'The evolving role of United Nations peacekeeping operations', *Conference Proceedings: The Singapore Symposium on the Changing Role of the UN in Conflict Resolution and Peacekeeping*, 13–15 March 1991, New York: UNDP1 (UN Doc. DP1/1141, September 1991), p. 25.

16. M. Goulding (1993), 'The evolution of United Nations peacekeeping', *International Affairs*, 69(3):455.

17. Simonia, in Weiss, 1990, pp. 60–1.

18. Malitza, in UNITAR, 1987, p. 238.

19. P. Formuth (ed.)(1988), *A Successor Vision: The United Nations Of Tomorrow*, Lanham: University Press of America, pp. 40–1.

20. Boutros-Ghali, 1992a, p. 11.

21. UN Charter, Chapter VI, Art. 33, p. 19.

22. United Nations Office of Legal Affairs (1992), *Handbook on the Peaceful Settlement of Disputes Between States*, New York: United Nations (UN Doc. OLA/COD/2394).

23. Malitza, in UNITAR, 1987, p. 247; see also the *Handbook on Peaceful Settlement of Disputes* for a discussion of the Secretariat and S-G's legal basis for preventive activity, pp. 128–33.

24. Evans, 1993, pp. 61–80, provides a good discussion on options to enhance preventive capability.

25. M. Goulding, presentation to the International Peace Academy's Vienna Seminar, 'Establishing UN Peacekeeping Operations', 7–18 July 1991, Vienna, Austria.

26. *Peacekeeper's Handbook*, 1984, p. 1.

27. Malitza, in UNITAR, 1987, p. 250.

28. UN Doc. A/43/1, p. 5.

29. UN Doc. A/45/1, p. 6.
30. See 'Expansion Period' in Chapter 2 for more details on the problems encountered by these UN missions.
31. Boutros-Ghali, 1992a, p. 11.
32. Boutros-Ghali, 1992a, p. 8.
33. Evans, 1993, p. 9.
34. International Conference on Peacebuilding (1986), 'Summary of Conference Proceedings', Shannon International Airport, Ireland, 28 April–3 May 1986, p. 14.
35. Malitza, in UNITAR, 1987, p. 250.
36. Coate and Puchala, 1990, pp. 127–8.
37. Galtung and Hveem, in Galtung, Vol. 2, 1976, p. 264.
38. J. Rosenau (1992a), 'The United Nations in a turbulent world', *IPA Occasional Paper Series*, Boulder, CO: Lynne Rienner, p. 13; see also, Rosenau, 1992b.
39. Boutros-Ghali, 1992a, p. 32.
40. Williams, 1987, offers an interesting discussion of the reasons behind coordination problems; in particular he notes the 'inter-agency rivalry, especially in the competition for funds from such sources as the UNDP and the World Bank' (p. 23).
41. 'Albright accuses UN aid agencies of turf wars', *Reuter News Service*, 2 November 1993.
42. Interview with Adel Khalifa, Deputy Resident Representative, UN Development Programme, Nicosia, Cyprus, 26 April, 1991.
43. 'Peacemaking in Cambodia: a disillusioning experience', *International Herald Tribune*, 23 September 1992.
44. 'UN chief under pressure to reappoint famine envoy', *The Guardian*, 30 October 1992.
45. 'Peacemaking in Cambodia: a disillusioning experience', *International Herald Tribune*, 23 September 1992.
46. F. Bouchet-Saulnier, 'How aid can abet a war', *The Independent*, 22 November 1993; 'Aid doctors say UN failed in Bosnia and Somalia', *Reuter News Service*, 22 November 1993; I. Traynor, 'Medical charity attacks "dithering" UN missions', *The Guardian*, 8 November 1993; 'Albright accuses UN aid agencies of turf wars', *Reuter News Service*, 2 November 1993.
47. F. Bouchet-Saulnier, 'How aid can abet a war', *The Independent*, 22 November 1993.
48. Ibid.
49. J. Power, 'Militarization of relief missions sparks debate', *Arab News*, 30 November 1993.
50. S. Ogata (1993), 'The UN response to the growing refugee crisis,' *Japan Review of International Affairs*, 7(3):214.
51. J. Power, 'Militarization of relief missions sparks debate', *Arab News*, 30 November 1993.
52. CF Doc, 'Negotiation in peacekeeping', (1990), in *The Central American Handbook: A Guide to Service with ONUCA*, CF-DPKO, p. 3.
53. Norton and Weiss, 1990b, p. 47.
54. Boutros-Ghali, 1992a, p. 34.

## 6 Developing a Conceptual Framework for Peacekeeping

1. UN Doc. SG/SM/5159, 18 November 1993.
2. Boutros-Ghali, 1992a, pp. 24–7; B. Boutros-Ghali (1992b), 'Empowering the United Nations', *Foreign Affairs*, 72(5):89–102.
3. UN Doc. SG/T/1822, 18 October 1993.
4. UN Doc. SG/SM/5145/Rev.1, 29 October 1993.
5. This point is made in Boutros-Ghali, 1992a.
6. UN Doc. A/44/1, p. 5.
7. UN Doc. DPI/1141 (40708), September 1991, p. 21.
8. Harbottle, 1991, pp. 7–8.
9. On regional cooperation particularly, see Evans 1993; UN Doc. S/25944, 15 June 1993; UN Doc. S/25996, 15 June 1993 and Add.1, 14 July 1993; for coordination at other levels, see Formuth, 1988; Coate and Puchala, 1990; Greindl, in Rikhye and Skjelsbaek, 1990; Malitza, in UNITAR, 1987.
10. *Peacekeeper's Handbook*, 1984, p. 2.
11. Bercovitch *et al*, p. 8–9.
12. Bercovitch *et al.*, 1991; Fisher and Keashly, 1991.
13. See Prein, 1984; Glasl, 1982; Bercovitch *et al.*, 1991; R.J. Fisher, 1990; Fisher and Keashly, 1991; Wehr and Lederach, 1991.
14. K. Skjelsbaek (1990), 'UN peacekeeping: expectations, limitations and results: forty years of mixed experience', in Rikhye and Skjelsbaek, pp. 61–2.
15. Bercovitch *et al.*, 1991, p. 15.
16. Bercovitch *et al.*, 1991, p. 15.
17. Haas, in UNITAR, 1987, pp. 12–19.
18. Bercovitch *et al.*, 1991, pp. 12–13.
19. Azar, 1990.
20. Miall, 1992, p. 185, and table 7.1, pp. 112–113.
21. This conclusion is also reached by Diehl, 1988, p. 505.
22. P.F. Diehl (1993), *International Peacekeeping*, Baltimore: Johns Hopkins University Press, p. 171.
23. Diehl, 1988, p. 507.
24. T. Weber (1989), 'The problems of peacekeeping', *Interdisciplinary Peace Research*, 1(2):15.
25. Galtung, Vol. 2, 1976, p. 284.
26. Galtung and Hveem, in Galtung, Vol. 2, 1976, p. 280.
27. See Miall, 1990; Bercovitch *et al.*, 1991; Azar, 1990; Burton, 1987 and Vol 1, 1990.
28. For examples of the kinds of activities peacekeepers could become involved in former-Yugoslavia, see Duffy, 1993; Kusmanic and Truger, 1993.
29. Stein, 1989c; Zartman, 1989.
30. See R.J. Fisher, 1989; Rothman, 1989; Kelman, 1978.
31. Interview in *The Guardian*, 23 May 1992.
32. For example, a data-set might be all multidimensional operations carried out by the UN. Alternately, a data-set might include all UN peacekeeping operations.

33. Bercovitch *et al.*, 1991, pp. 13 and 17.
34. Bercovitch *et al.*, 1991, p. 16.
35. Bercovitch *et al.*, 1991, p. 16.
36. Diehl, 1993, p. 40; see also Diehl, 1988.
37. Diehl, 1993, pp. 169–75.
38. See Bercovitch *et al.*, 1991; Fisher and Keashly, 1991.
39. For more discussion of this integration in UNTAG see Chapter 3.
40. K. Skjelsbaek (1989), 'United Nations peacekeeping and the facilitation of withdrawals', *Bulletin of Peace Proposals*, 20(3):261.
41. See UN Doc. A/45/502; Wiseman, 1991.
42. See Prein, 1984; Glasl, in Bomens and Peterson, 1982; R.J. Fisher, 1989, 1990; Fisher and Keashly, 1988, 1991; Wehr and Lederach, 1991; Coate and Puchala, 1990.
43. Wehr and Lederach, 1991, p. 98.
44. Coate and Puchala, 1990, p. 133.
45. Coate and Puchala, 1990, p. 133.
46. Diehl and Kumar, 1991, p. 375.

# 7 Training as a Critical Link between Theory and Practice

1. This view is supported in the recent reports presented by the Committee of 34 to the Special Political Committee (now the 4th Committee); see UN Docs. A/48/173, 25 May 1993, A/48/403/Add.1, 2 November 1993, A/SPC/46/L.9, 1991, refers to C-34 Report A/46/254, 18 June 1991. A survey of early Committee documents suggests that training was not then an issue. This is hardly surprising considering the much larger problems associated with Cold War politics which effectively sidelined the Committee from 1965 until 1988.
2. UN Doc. A/46/254, 18 June 1991, p. 12, item 76.
3. The culture question is also an important one for third party intervention research and training, see Lederach, 1990; Avruch, Black and Scimecca, 1991.
4. R.D. Albert (1986), 'Conceptual framework for the development and evaluation of cross-cultural orientation programs', *International Journal of Intercultural Relations*, 10(2):200.
5. T.P. Hannigan (1990), 'Traits, attitudes, and skills that are related to intercultural effectiveness and their implications for cross-cultural training: a review of the literature', *International Journal of Intercultural Relations*, 14:89.
6. Hannigan, 1990, pp. 89–90.
7. Hannigan, 1990, pp. 93–107.
8. Hannigan, 1990, pp. 93–4.
9. Hannigan, 1990, pp. 101–2.
10. Hannigan, 1990, p. 102.
11. Hannigan, 1990, p. 101.
12. Hannigan, 1990, pp. 93–107.

13.  Hannigan, 1990, pp. 93–107.
14.  Hannigan, 1990, pp. 104–5.
15.  Deutsch, in Vayrynen, 1991, p. 49.
16.  Deutsch, in Vayrynen, 1991, pp. 27–8.
17.  Wehr, 1979, pp. 50–2.
18.  See Lederach, 1990; Wehr and Lederach, 1991; Avruch and Black, 1991; Avruch, Black and Scimecca, 1991.
19.  C.L. Grove and I. Torbiorn (1985), 'A new conceptualization of intercultural adjustment and the goals of training', *International Journal of Intercultural Relations*, 9:222.
20.  P. Pederson (1983), 'The transfer of intercultural training skills', *International Journal of Psychology*, 18:334.
21.  Grove and Torbiorn, 1985, pp. 205–33.
22.  Grove and Torbiorn, 1985, pp. 214–15.
23.  Grove and Torbiorn, 1985, p. 217.
24.  Grove and Torbiorn, 1985, p. 223.
25.  Grove and Torbiorn, 1985, p. 223.
26.  Grove and Torbiorn, 1985, p. 223.
27.  Pederson, 1983, pp. 333–4.
28.  Pederson, 1983, p. 337.
29.  Pederson, 1983, p. 341.
30.  J.P. Lederach (1990), 'Training on culture: four approaches', *Conciliation Quarterly*, 9(1):12–13, especially the 'adapt-a-process' approach and the 'create-a-model' approach.
31.  Katz and Lawyer, 1985, p. 4.
32.  Pederson, 1983, p. 342.
33.  Pederson, 1983, p. 342.
34.  D.J. Kealey (1990), *Cross-Cultural Effectiveness: A Study of Canadian Technical Advisors Overseas*, Hull, Quebec: Canadian International Development Agency (CIDA); see also, D.J. Kealey (1988), 'Explaining and predicting cross-cultural effectiveness: a study of Canadian technical advisors overseas', Hull, Quebec: CIDA.
35.  Kealey, 1990, p. 5.
36.  Kealey, 1990, pp. 3–4.
37.  Kealey, 1990, p. 25.
38.  Kealey, 1990, pp. 53–4.
39.  R.M. Paige (1986), 'Trainer competencies: the missing conceptual link in orientation', *International Journal of Intercultural Relations*, 10(2):137.
40.  Kealey, 1990, p. 66.
41.  Moskos, 1976, p. 1.
42.  Moskos, 1976, p. 129.
43.  Moskos, 1976, p. 93.
44.  Moskos, 1976, p. 93.
45.  Grove and Torbiorn, 1985, p. 214.
46.  Moskos, 1976, p. 94.
47.  Moskos, 1976, p. 94.
48.  Grove and Torbiorn, 1985, p. 215.
49.  Grove and Torbiorn, 1985, p. 215.
50.  Moskos, 1976, p. 94.

## 8 Training for United Nations Peacekeepers

1. Australian Parliament Doc. Joint Standing Committee on Foreign Affairs, Defence and Trade, Defence Sub-Committee, *Inquiry into Australia's Participation in Peacekeeping.* Submission and Incorporated Documents, Vol. 3, Annex II, 28 September 1993.
2. Interview with appointee, Christian Harleman, New York, 2 September 1992.
3. For example, see UN Docs. A/48/173, 25 May 1993 and A/48/403/ Add.1, 2 November 1993; NATO Press Service, *Press Release*, M-NACC-2(93)73, 'Progress Report to Ministers by the NACC *Ad Hoc* Group on Cooperation in Peacekeeping', 3 December 1993; Canadian House of Commons Doc., 'The Dilemmas of a Committed Peacekeepers: Canada and the Renewal of Peacekeeping', *Standing Committee on National Defence and Veterans' Affairs,* June 1993, esp. pp. 21–6; Canadian House of Commons Doc., *Proceedings: Standing Committee on National Defence and Veterans' Affairs,* Issue No. 42, 30 March 1993.
4. H. Moleman, 'Bosnia for beginners', *The Guardian,* 19 December 1993.
5. Australia, Hungary, Nigeria, Thailand and the US are 'developing' training centres.
6. CF-DPKO Doc. Memorandum, 4500-1, February 1991, p. 2.
7. CF Doc. Brigadier-General Douglas, 'Peacekeeping Operations Review – Interim Report', 26 November 1991, p. 10 (Interim 'Douglas Report').
8. CF-DPKO Doc. briefing paper.
9. CF-DPKO Doc. Report 4500-1, 12e Regiment blinde du Canada, 28 February 1991, p. 3.
10. CF-DPKO Doc. 4640-1, 'Peacekeeping Briefing Session – Officers, Pilot Course', Annex C, 25 April 1991.
11. CF Doc. Interim 'Douglas Report', 1991, pp. 11–12.
12. Ibid, p. 8.
13. Canadian House of Commons Doc., 'The Dilemmas of Committed Peacekeepers: Canada and the Renewal of Peacekeeping', *Standing Committee on National Defence and Veterans' Affairs,* June 1993, p. 25.
14. P. Langille and E. Simpson (1991), *CFB Cornwallis: Canada's Peacekeeping Training Centre,* Annapolis Royal, Nova Scotia: Common Security Consultants, p. 3. See also, P. Langille and E. Simpson (1992), *A Blueprint for a Peacekeeping Training Centre of Excellence,* Annapolis Royal, Nova Scotia: Common Security Consultants and Stratman Consulting Inc.
15. 'CFB Cornwallis', p. 10.
16. D.M. Last (1992), 'Training Officers to Mediate', draft, article prepared for *Peacekeeping and International Relations,* National Press Building, Ottawa, Ontario, Canada, p. 1.
17. D. Last (1993), 'Negotiating skills for peacekeepers', *Peace Magazine,* 9(4/5):17.
18. CF Doc. Draft proposal, 'Design for research on mediation by peacekeepers', 1st Regiment, Royal Canadian Horse Artillery, Commanding Officer L.Col. M.D. Capstick, 22 May 1991, p. 1.

19. IDF Doc. 'Preparation and Training for UNIFIL', *Training Circular*, Office of Director of Training, Defence Forces Headquarters, Dublin, Ireland, October 1991.
20. Ibid, Appendix B, p. 2.
21. Ibid, Appendix D, p. 1.
22. 'Peace troops who suffer in silence', *Irish Independent*, 1 July 1992, p. 10.
23. Ibid, p. 10.
24. Ibid, p. 10.
25. Interview with Harleman, 30 October 1990, at the IPA in New York.
26. Nordic Doc. *Information Circular*, 'Nordic Stand-By Forces and Training System'.
27. Ibid, p. 3.
28. Ibid, p. 6.
29. UN Doc. A/45/502, p. 2.
30. Boutros-Ghali, 1992a, pp. 30–1.
31. Boutros-Ghali, 1992a, pp. 30–1.
32. UN Doc. OHRM Training Service, 'So You Think You Want To Go To Namibia', 19 January 1989, p. 1.
33. UN Doc. OHRM Training Service, 'Report of Briefing and Training Programs for Staff Assigned to UNTAG Namibia, January–March 1989', p. 2.
34. UN Doc. SRO, Namibia, 'Job Description, Post Nos. 46–85', paragraphs 1 and 4.
35. UN Doc. OHRM Training Service, 'Outline for Training For Peace-keeping Missions'.
36. UN Doc. UNTAG, 'Manual for UNTAG Election Supervisors', November 1989.
37. *UN Chronicle*, December 1989, p. 8.
38. UN Doc. 'UNTAG Namibia: Description and Analysis of the Mission's Operational Arrangements', 9 September 1991 (draft copy), p. 179 (para. 372).
39. UN Doc. OHRM Training Service 'Operational Plan for In-Country Mission Training'.
40. UN Doc. *Press Release*, UNITAR/626, 8 November 1991.
41. IPA Doc. Information Sheet.
42. Harleman, 1990, p. 3.
43. 'International Civilian Peacekeeping and Peacebuilding Training Program', Austrian Study Centre for Peace and Conflict Resolution (ASPR), Stadtschlaining, Austria.
44. Ibid.
45. CF Doc. 'Negotiation in Peacekeeping', 1991, p. 13.
46. Ibid, p. 11.
47. Heiberg, in Rikhye and Skjelsbaek, 1990, p. 148.
48. Heiberg, in Rikhye and Skjelsbaek, 1990, p. 150.
49. This point is made in Heiberg, in Rikhye and Skjelsbaek, 1990, p. 162, in reference to the preparation of the Ghanaian and Nepalese battalions. The article points out difficulties that both battalions have with their peacekeeping duties which can be directly attributed to lack of training.

50. Several UNTAG election supervisors seconded from their governments pointed out the negative aspects of the UNTAG on-site training programme. One complaint was directed at the large numbers of trainees which meant that they could not actually practise the polling techniques themselves. Another complaint was directed at the trainers for having poor English language skills.

51. Grove and Torbiorn, 1985, p. 223.

52. See Brislin, 1986.

53. Thornberry, in Hay, 1991, p. 19.

54. UN Doc. 'UNTAG Namibia: Description and Analysis of the Mission's Operational Arrangements', 9 September 1991 (draft copy), p. 271 (para. 692).

55. For further discussion of these ethical issues, see Burton and Dukes, Vol. 4, 1990, ; Webb, in Mitchell and Webb, 1988; Laue, 1982.

# 9 The Conceptualization of Peacekeeping: Implications for Training and Practice

1. See Mackinlay and Chopra, 1992; Boutros-Ghali, 1992a (proposal for peace enforcement units); Pugh, 1992; special issue of *Survival*, 1990, 32(3).

2. Boutros-Ghali, 1992a, p. 26.

3. Beattie, in Wiseman, 1983; Harbottle, 1980, 1990; Harleman, 1990, 1992; Boutros-Ghali, 1992a; Rikhye and Skjelsbaek, 1990; UN Doc. A/46/254; See also Last, in *Peace Magazine*, 1993; CF Doc. 'Negotiations on Peacekeeping', 1991.

4. L. MacKenzie (1993), 'Military realities of United Nations peacekeeping operations', *RUSI Journal*, 138(1):21–4.

5. Rikhye *et al.*, 1974, pp. 267–8.

6. Rikhye *et al.*, 1974, p. 268.

7. Harbottle, 1980, p. 119.

8. Harbottle, 1980, p. 119.

9. Beattie, in Wiseman, 1983, p. 209.

10. Beattie, in Wiseman, 1983, p. 216.

11. Beattie, in Wiseman, 1983, p. 216.

12. Skjelsbaek, 1989, p. 261.

13. Boutros-Ghali, 1992a, pp. 6–7.

14. Boutros-Ghali, 1992a, p. 12.

15. Interview in *The Guardian*, 23 May 1992.

16. J.G. Ruggie, 'No, the world doesn't need a United Nations army', *International Herald Tribune*, 26–7 September 1992.

17. 'In a world of trouble', *The Guardian*, 6 October 1992.

18. Hagglund, 1990, p. 235.

19. UN Doc. *Training Guidelines For National or Regional Training Programs*, Part 5, 'Training in UN Operating Techniques', pp. 38–53.

20. Beattie, in Wiseman, 1983, p. 214.

21. Rikhye *et al.*, 1974, p. 267.

22. UN Doc. *Training Guidelines For National or Regional Training Programs*, p. 50.

23. Ibid, p. 50.
24. Rikhye *et al.*, 1974, p. 267.
25. Rikhye *et al.*, 1974, p. 272.
26. Rikhye *et al.*, 1974, p. 273.
27. Galtung and Hveem, in Galtung, Vol. 2, 1976, pp. 264–81.
28. Moser, for example, argues that the use of military peacekeepers in 'a situation where the local population has just been victimized by regular and irregular militias.... runs counter to the immediate social need of building trust and confidence in place of fear and suspicion'. In Y. Moser (1992), 'United Nations warriors or peacekeepers: examining the logic of combating war with soldiers', *Nonviolence International Papers*, Bangkok: Nonviolence International, p. 3.
29. W. Pfaff, 'No salvation is sight for the damned of Sarajevo', *International Herald Tribune*, 24 September 1992; J. Burns, 'UN fights time as Bosnia winter nears', *International Herald Tribune*, 25 September 1992.
30. I. Traynor, 'Peace troops stop Croatian clash', *The Guardian*, 1 October 1992.
31. Rikhye *et al.*, 1974, p. 267.
32. I.J. Rikhye (1970), 'Training for peacekeeping', paper presented to the Institute of Vredesvraagstikken, Holland, December 1970, p. 2.
33. C. Harleman (1991), 'Education and training of Swedish UN Troops at the United Nations Training Centre (UNTC), Almnaes, Sweden', unpublished paper, 20 January 1992.
34. UN Doc. *Training Guidelines For National or Regional Training Programs*, p. 38.
35. Beattie, in Wiseman, 1983, p. 213.
36. Harbottle, 1991, p. 10.
37. Harbottle, 1970, pp. 191–2.
38. Harbottle, 1991, p. 3.
39. A discussion of the ramifications for ethical considerations for the professionalization of conflict resolution can be found in Burton and Dukes, Vol. 4, 1990, pp. 186–8.
40. For more detailed discussions of the theoretical debate, see Avruch and Black, 1987, 1991; Burton, Vol. 1, 1990; Burton and Sandole, 1986, 1987.
41. See Wehr and Lederach, 1989, 1991; Lederach, 1990; van der Merwe *et al.*, in Burton and Dukes, Vol. 3, 1990; Avruch, Black and Scimecca, 1991.
42. Galtung and Eide, in Galtung, Vol. 2, 1976, p. 256.
43. Heiberg, in Rikhye and Skjelsbaek, 1990, pp. 147–69.
44. See Moskos, 1976, for an early study on military culture; see Nordstrom and Martin, 1992, for an anthropological view of cultures of conflict and violence; see Fetherston and Nordstrom, forthcoming, 1994, for a discussion of peacekeeping and the enthography of warzones.
45. 'A Blueprint for a Peacekeeping Training Centre of Excellence', 1992.
46. Bercovitch *et al.*, 1991; Diehl, 1988, 1993.

# Bibliography

Abi-Saab, G. (1978). *The United Nations Operation in the Congo 1960–1964*. Oxford: Oxford University Press.

Adolph, R.B. (1992). 'Peacekeeping: our least understood mission', *Military Intelligence*. (July–September):17–19.

Akashi, Y. (1993). 'The challenges faced by UNTAC', *Japan Review of International Affairs*. 7(3):185–201.

Albert, R.D. (1986). 'Conceptual framework for the development and evaluation of cross-cultural orientation programs', *International Journal of Intercultural Relations*. 10(2):197–214.

Alevy, D.I. *et al.* (1974). 'Rationale, research, and role relations in the Stirling Workshop', *Journal of Conflict Resolution*. 18(2)(June):276–84.

Anstey, M. (1991). *Negotiating Conflict: Insights and Skills for Negotiators and Peacemakers*. Kenwyn, SA: Juta and Company.

Assefa, H. (1992). 'Mediation in internal wars: the Ethiopia/Eritrea conflict', *Security Dialogue*. 23(3):101–106.

Attalides, M.A. (ed.)(1977). *Cyprus Reviewed*. Nicosia:Jus Cypri Association

Avruch, K. and P.W. Black (1987). 'A generic theory of conflict resolution: a critique'. *Negotiation Journal*. 3(1)(January):87–96.

Avruch, K. and P.W. Black (1991). 'The culture question and conflict resolution', *Peace and Change*. 16(1):22–45.

Avruch, K., P.W. Black and J.A. Scimecca (eds)(1991). *Conflict Resolution: Cross-Cultural Perspectives*. New York: Greenwood Press.

Axelrod, R. (1984). *The Evolution of Cooperation*. New York: Basic Books.

Axelrod, R. and R.O. Keohane (1985). 'Achieving cooperation under anarchy: strategies and institutions', *World Politics*. 38(1):226–54.

Azar, E.E. (1990). *The Management of Protracted Social Conflict: Theory and Cases*. Aldershot: Dartmouth.

Azar, E.E. and J.W. Burton (eds)(1986). *International Conflict Resolution: Theory and Practice*. Sussex: Wheatsheaf Books.

Baev, P.K. (1993). 'Peacekeeping as a challenge to European borders', *Security Dialogue*. 24(2):7–20.

Bailey, S.D. (1964). *The Secretariat of the United Nations*. London: Dunmow.

Bailey, S.D. (1975). *The Procedure of the UN Security Council*. Oxford: Clarendon Press.

Banks, M. (ed.)(1984). *Conflict in World Society: A New Perspective on International Relations*. Brighton: Wheatsheaf Books LTD.

Barnaby, F. (ed.)(1991). *Building a More Democratic United Nations: Proceedings of CAMDUN-1*. London: Frank Cass.

Baratta, J.P. (1989). 'International peacekeeping: history and strengthening', *Monograph No. 6*. Washington, D.C.: The Center for UN Reform Education.

Basta-Posavec *et al.* (1992). 'Inter-ethnic conflict and war in former Yugoslavia', Belgrade: Institute of European Studies.

Belonogov, A.M. (1990). 'Soviet peace-keeping proposals', *Survival* 32(3):206–11.

Bendana, A. (1991). 'Conflict resolution in Central America: the Nicaraguan experience', *Bulletin of Peace Proposals.* 22(2):211–16.

Bender, G. and W. Schneidman (1988). 'The Namibia negotiations: multilateral versus bilateral approaches to international mediation', *Case No. 422* . Center for International Studies of the School of International Relations, Univ. of S. California.

Bennett, J.M. (1986). 'Modes of cross-cultural training: conceptualizing cross-cultural training as education', *International Journal of Intercultural Relations.* 10(2):117–34.

Bennett, M.J. (1986). 'A developmental approach to training for intercultural sensitivity', *International Journal of Intercultural Relations.* 10(2):179–96.

Bennett, A. Leroy (1988). *International Organizations: Principles and Issues.* London: Prentice Hall.

Berat, L. and Y. Shain (1992). 'Provisional governments in democratization', *Coexistence.* 29(1):19–40.

Bercovitch, J. (1986). 'International mediation: a study of the incidence, strategies, and conditions of successful outcomes', *Cooperation and Conflict.* 21:155–68.

Bercovitch, J. (1991). 'International mediation and dispute settlement: evaluating the condition for successful mediation', *Negotiation Journal.* 7(1): 17–30.

Bercovitch, J. (1992). 'Mediators and mediation strategy in international relations', *Negotiation Journal.* 8(2):99–112.

Bercovitch, J., J.T. Anagnoson and D.L. Willie (1991). 'Some conceptual issues and empirical trends in the study of successful mediation in international relations', *Journal of Peace Research.* 28(1):7–17.

Bercovitch, J. and J.W. Lamare (1993). 'The process of international mediation: an analysis of the determinants of successful and unsuccessful outcomes', *Australian Journal of Political Science.* 28:290–305.

Bercovitch, J. and R. Wells (1993). 'Evaluating mediation strategies: a theoretical and empirical analysis', *Peace and Change.* 18(1):3–25.

Berridge, G.R. (1989). 'Diplomacy and the Angolan/Namibian accords', *International Affairs.* 65(3):463–79.

Berridge, G.R. (1991). *Return to the UN: UN Diplomacy in Regional Conflicts.* London: Macmillan.

Bertrand, M. (1991). 'The difficult transformation from 'arms control' into a "world security system"', *International Social Science Journal.* 127(February): 87–102.

Birnbaum, R. (1984). 'The effects of a neutral third party on academic bargaining relationships and campus climate', *Journal of Higher Education.* 55(6)(Nov-Dec):719–34.

Blodgett, J.Q. (1991). 'The future of UN peacekeeping', *The Washington Quarterly.* 14:207–20.

Bloomfield, L.P. (1964). *The Power to Keep Peace.* Berkeley, CA: World Without War Council.

Boehringer, G.H. *et al.* (1974). 'Stirling: the destructive application of group techniques to a conflict', *Journal of Conflict Resolution.* 18(2)(June):257–75.

Bokhari, I.H. (1991). 'Evolution of a dual negotiation process: Afghanistan', *The Annals, AAPSS.* 518:58–68.

Bomers, G.B.J. and R.B. Peterson (eds) (1982). *Conflict Management and Industrial Relations*. Boston: Kluwer Nijhoff.

Boulding, E. (ed.) (1992). *New Agendas for Peace Research: Conflict and Security Reexamined*. Boulder, CO: Lynne Rienner.

Boulding, E., C. Brigagao and K. Clements (eds) (1991). *Peace Culture and Society: Transnational Research and Dialogue*. Boulder, CO: Westview.

Boulding, K. (1977). 'Twelve friendly quarrels with Johan Galtung', *Journal of Peace Research*. 14(1):75–86.

Boutros-Ghali, B. (1992a). *An Agenda for Peace: Preventive Diplomacy, Peacemaking and Peacekeeping*. New York: UN Department of Public Information.

Boutros-Ghali, B. (1992b). 'Empowering the United Nations', *Foreign Affairs*. 72(5):89–102.

Boutros-Ghali, B. (1993). 'An agenda for peace: one year later', *Orbis*. 37(3):323–32.

Boyd, J.M. (1966). 'Cyprus: episode in peacekeeping', *International Organization*. 20(1):1–17.

Brett, J.M., S.B. Goldberg and W. Ury (1980). 'Mediation and organizational development: models for conflict management', Proceedings of the 33rd Annual Meeting of the Industrial Relations Association:195–202.

Brislin, R.W. (1986). 'A culture general assimilator: preparation for various types of sojourns', *International Journal of Intercultural Relations*. 10(2):215–34.

Brock-Utne, B. (1989). *Feminist Perspectives on Peace and Peace Education*. New York: Pergamon.

Brookfield, S.D. (1986). *Understanding and Facilitating Adult Learning: A Comprehensive Analysis of Principles and Effective Practices*. Milton Keynes, UK: Open University Press.

Brown, G., B. Barker and T. Burke (1984). *Police as Peacekeepers*. Victoria, Australia: UNCIVPOL (Vic) Club.

Brown, N. (1984). 'Palme and Brandt: the world perspective', in Howe, J.O. (ed.), *Armed Peace: The Search for World Security*. London: Macmillan.

Bunche, R.J. (1965). 'The United Nations operation in the Congo', in Cordier, A. and W. Foote (eds), *The Quest for Peace*. New York: Colombia University Press.

Burton, J.W. (1969). *Conflict and Communication*. London: Macmillan.

Burton, J.W. (1972a). 'Resolution of Conflict', *International Studies Quarterly*. 16(1):5–29.

Burton, J.W. (1972b). 'Some further comments – in reply to criticism', *International Studies Quarterly*. 16(1):41–52.

Burton, J.W. (1972c). *World Society*. London: Cambridge University Press.

Burton, J.W. (1979). *Deviance, Terrorism and War*. Oxford: Martin Robertson.

Burton, J.W. (1984). *Global Conflict*. Brighton: Wheatsheaf.

Burton, J.W. (1986). 'The theory of conflict resolution', *Current Research on Peace and Violence*. 9(3):125–30.

Burton, J.W. (1987). *Resolving Deep-rooted Conflict: A Handbook*. Lanham, MD: University Press of America.

Burton, J.W. (1989). 'Conflict resolution as a political system', *Peace in Action*. 5(1):4–6.

Burton, J.W. (1990). *Conflict: Resolution and Provention, Vol. 1.* London: Macmillan.

Burton, J.W. (ed.)(1990). *Conflict: Human Needs Theory, Vol. 2.* London: Macmillan.

Burton, J.W. and F. Dukes (eds)(1990). *Conflict: Readings in Management and Resolution, Vol. 3.* London: Macmillan.

Burton, J.W. and F. Dukes (1990). *Conflict: Practices in Management, Settlement and Resolution Vol. 4.* London: Macmillan.

Burton, J.W. and D.J.D. Sandole (1986). 'Generic theory: the basis of conflict resolution', *Negotiation Journal.* 2(4)(October):333–44.

Burton, J.W. and D.J.D. Sandole (1987). 'Expanding the debate on generic theory of conflict resolution: a response to critique', *Negotiation Journal.* 3(1)(January):97–100.

Camilleri, J.A. and J. Falk (1992). *The End of Sovereignty: The Politics of a Shrinking and Fragmenting World.* Aldershot: Edward Elgar.

Camp, G.D. (1980). 'The Greek-Turkish conflict over Cyprus', *Political Science Quarterly.* 95(1):43–70.

Caradon, H. (1985). 'The Security Council as an instrument for peace', in Lall, A.S. (ed.), *Multilateral Negotiation and Mediation.* New York: Pergamon Press.

Carlsson, I. (1992). 'A new international order through the UN', *Security Dialogue.* 23(4):7–11.

Carment, D. (1993). 'The international dimensions of ethnic conflict: concepts, indicators, and theory', *Journal of Peace Research.* 30(2):137–50.

Carnevale, P.J. (1992). 'The usefulness of mediation theory', *Negotiation Journal.* 8(4):387–90.

Cashman, G. (1993). *What Causes War? An Introduction to Theories of International Conflict.* New York: Lexington.

Childers, E.B. (1990). 'The future of the United Nations: the challenges of the 1990's', *Bulletin of Peace Proposals.* 21(2):143–52.

Chopra, J. and T.G. Weiss (1992). 'Sovereignty is no longer sacrosanct: codifying humanitarian intervention', *Ethics and International Affairs.* 6:95–117.

Clawson, P. (1993). 'Sanctions as punishment, enforcement, and prelude to further action', *Ethics and International Affairs.* 7:17–37.

Coate, R.A. and D.J. Puchala (1990). 'Global policies and the United Nations system: a current assessment', *Journal of Peace Research.* 27(2):127–40.

Cohen, S.P. and E.E. Azar (1981). 'From war to peace: the transition between Egypt and Israel', *Journal of Conflict Resolution.* 25(1)(March):87–114.

Cohen, S.P., H.C. Kelman, *et al.* (1977). 'Evolving intergroup techniques for conflict resolution: and Israeli-Palestinian pilot workshop', *Journal of Social Issues.* 33(1):165–89.

Cooper, R. and M. Berdal (1993). 'Outside intervention in ethnic conflicts', *Survival.* 35(1):118–42.

Cot, Jean-Pierre (1972). 'Critical remarks on John Burton's paper on resolution of conflict with special reference to the Cyprus conflict', *International Studies Quarterly.* 16(1):31–9.

Cox, D. (1993). 'Exploring *An Agenda for Peace*: issues arising from the Report of the Secretary-General', *Aurora Papers, No. 20.* Ottawa: Canadian Center for Global Security.

Cremin, C. (1984). 'United Nations peacekeeping operations: an Irish initiative, 1961–1968', *Irish Studies in International Affairs.* 1(4):79–84.

Crocker, C.A. (1990). 'Southern African peace-making', *Survival.* 32(3):221–32.

Curle, A. (1971). *Making Peace.* London: Tavistock Publications.

Curle, A. (1986). *In the Middle: Non-Official Mediation in Violent Situations.* Leamington Spa: Berg Publishers.

Curle, A. (1990). *Tools for Transformation: A Personal Study.* Stroud, UK: Hawthorne Press.

de Reuck, A. (1974). 'Controlled communication: rationale and dynamics', *The Human Context.* 6(1):64–80.

Deeb, M-J. and Deeb, M.K. (1991). 'Regional conflict and regional solutions: Lebanon', *The Annals, AAPSS.* 518:82–94.

Denktash, R.R. (1988). *The Cyprus Triangle.* London: K. Rustem and Brother

Deutsch, M. (1991). 'Subjective features of conflict resolution: psychological, social and cultural influences', in Varyrnen, R. (ed.), *New Directions in Conflict Theory.* London: Sage.

Diehl, P.F. (1987). 'When peacekeeping does not lead to peace: some notes on conflict resolution', *Bulletin of Peace Proposals.* 18(1):47–53.

Diehl, P.F. (1988). 'Peacekeeping operations and the quest for peace', *Political Science Quarterly.* 103(3):485–507.

Diehl, P.F. (1989). 'A permanent UN peacekeeping force: an evaluation', *Bulletin of Peace Proposals.* 20(1):27–36.

Diehl, P.F. (1992). 'What are they fighting for? The importance of issues in international conflict research', *Journal of Peace Research.* 29(3):333–44.

Diehl, P.F. (1993). 'Institutional alternatives to traditional UN peacekeeping: an assessment of regional and multinational options', *Armed Forces and Society.* 19(2):209–30.

Diehl, P.F. (1993). *International Peacekeeping.* Baltimore: Johns Hopkins.

Diehl, P.F. and C. Kumar (1991). 'Mutual benefits from international intervention: new roles for United Nations peacekeeping forces', *Bulletin of Peace Proposals.* 22(4):369–75.

Diehl, P.F. and S.R. Jurado (1993). 'United Nations election supervision in South Africa: lessons from the Namibian peacekeeping experience', *Studies in Conflict and Terrorism.* 16(1):61–74.

Donnelly, J. (1983). 'Human rights, humanitarian intervention and American foreign policy: law, morality, and politics', *Journal of International Affairs.* 37:311–28.

Donnelly, J. (1990). 'Global policy studies: a skeptical view', *Journal of Peace Research.* 27(2):221–30.

Doob, L.W. (1974). 'A Cyprus workshop: an exercise in intervention methodology', *Journal of Social Psychology.* 94:161–78.

Doob, L.W. (ed.)(1970). *Resolving Conflict in Africa: The Fermeda Workshop.* New Haven: Yale University Press.

Doob, L.W. and W.J. Foltz (1973). 'The Belfast Workshop: an application of group techniques to a destructive conflict', *The Journal of Conflict Resolution.* 17(3)(September):489–512.

Doob, L.W. and W.J. Foltz (1974). 'The impact of a workshop upon grass-roots leaders in Belfast', *Journal of Conflict Resolution.* 18(2)(June):237–56.

Doob, L.W. (1976). 'A Cyprus Workshop: intervention methodology during a continuing crisis', *Journal of Social Psychology.* 98:143–4.

Druckman, D. (1983). 'Social psychology in international negotiations', in Kidd, R.F. and M.J. Saks (eds), *Advances in Applied Social Psychology, Vol. 2.* Hillsdale, NJ: Erlbaum, pp. 51–81.

Druckman, D. *et al.* (1988). 'Value differences and conflict resolution: facilitation or delinking?', *Journal of Conflict Resolution.* 32(3)(September):489–510.

Druckman, D. (1993). 'The situational levers of negotiating flexibility', *Journal of Conflict Resolution.* 37(2):236–76.

Duffy, T. (1993). 'Peace activism in a conflict zone: building a culture of peace in former-Yugoslavia', *Journal of International Studies.* No. 30 (January):97–116.

Dumas, L.T. and M. Thee (eds)(1989). *Making Peace Possible: The Promise of Economic Conversion.* Oxford: Pergamon.

Durch, W.J. (1993). 'Building on sand: UN peacekeeping in Western Sahara', *International Security.* 17(4):151–71.

Durch, W.J. (ed.)(1993). *The Evolution of UN Peacekeeping: Case-Studies and Comparative Analysis.* New York: St. Martin's Press.

Eckhardt, W. (1989). 'Civilian deaths in wartime', *Bulletin of Peace Proposals.* 20(1):89–98.

Eckstein, H. (1980). 'Theoretical approaches to explaining collective political violence', in Gurr, T.R. (ed.) *Handbook of Political Conflict: Theory and Research.* New York: Free Press.

Evans, G. (1993). *Cooperating for Peace: The Global Agenda for the 1990s and Beyond.* St. Leonards, NSW, Australia: Allen & Unwin.

Falk, R.A. *et al.* (eds)(1991). *The United Nations and a Just World Order.* Boulder, CO: Westview Press.

Fetherston, A.B. (1993a). 'Toward a Theory of United Nations Peacekeeping', *Peace Research Report, No. 31.* Bradford, UK: Department of Peace Studies, University of Bradford.

Fetherston, A.B. (1993b). 'Making United Nations peacekeeping more peaceful: relating concepts of "success"to field reality', *Working Paper, No. 139.* Canberra: Peace Research Centre, The Australian National University.

Fetherston, A.B. and C. Nordstrom (forthcoming, 1994). 'Overcoming conceptual *habitus*: UN peacekeeping and warzone ethnography', *Working Paper No. 147.* Canberra: Peace Research Centre, The Australian National University.

Fisher, R. and S. Brown (1988). *Getting Together: Building a Relationship That Gets to YES.* Boston: Houghton Mifflin Company.

Fisher, R. and W. Ury (1981). *Getting to Yes: How to Negotiate Without Giving In.* London: Arrow Books.

Fisher, R.J. (1980). 'A third-party consultation workshop on the India-Pakistan conflict', *Journal of Social Psychology.* 112:191–206.

Fisher, R.J. (1983). 'Third party consultation as a method of intergroup conflict resolution: a review of studies', *Journal of Conflict Resolution.* 27(2):301–34.

Fisher, R.J. (1989). 'Prenegotiation problem-solving discussions: enhancing the potential for successful negotiation', *Negotiation Journal.* 44:442–74.

Fisher, R.J. (1990). *The Social Psychology of Intergroup and International Conflict Resolution*. New York: Springer-Verlag.

Fisher, R.J. and L. Keashly (1988). 'Third party interventions in intergroup conflict: consultation is not mediation', *Negotiation Journal*. 4(4):381–93.

Fisher, R.J. and L. Keashly (1991). 'The potential complementarity of mediation and consultation within a contingency model of third party intervention', *Journal of Peace Research*. 28(1):29–42.

Fisher, T. (1993). 'Mediating theory and practice', *Interdisciplinary Peace Research*. 5(1):74–88.

Fitzduff, M. (1988). *Community Conflict Skills: A Handbook for Anti-Sectarian Work in Northern Ireland*. Cookstown, N. Ireland: Community Conflict Skills Project.

Formuth, P. (ed.)(1988). *A Successor Vision: The United Nations of Tomorrow*. Lanham, MD: University Press of America.

Formuth, P. (1993). 'The making of a security community: the United Nations after the Cold War', *Journal of International Affairs*. 46(2):341–66.

Frydenberg, P. (ed.)(1964). *Peacekeeping: Experience and Evaluation*. Oslo: Norwegian Institute of International Affairs.

Gaddis, J.S. (1992/3). 'International relations theory and the end of the Cold War', *International Security*. 17(3):5–58.

Galtung, J. (1975). *Essays in Peace Research, Vol. 1*. Copenhagen: Christian Ejlers.

Galtung, J. (1976). 'Three approaches to peace: peacekeeping, peacemaking, and peacebuilding', in Galtung, J., *Peace, War and Defence: Essays in Peace Research Vol. 3*. Copenhagen: Christian Ejlers.

Galtung, J. and I. Eide (1976). 'Some factors affecting local acceptance of a UN force: a pilot project report from Gaza', in Galtung, J., *Peace, War and Defence: Essays in Peace Research Vol. 3*. Copenhagen: Christian Ejlers.

Galtung, J. and H. Hveem (1976). 'Participants in peacekeeping forces', in Galtung, J. *Peace, War and Defence: Essays in Peace Research, Vol. 3*. Copenhagen: Christian Ejlers.

Galtung, J. (1985). 'Twenty-five years of peace research: ten challenges and some responses', *Journal of Peace Research*. 22(2):141–58.

Geva, N. and A. Mintz (1993). 'Experimental analysis of conflict processes project: preliminary findings', *International Studies Notes*. 18(2):15–20.

Glasl, F. (1982). 'The process of conflict escalation and roles of third parties', in Bomers, G.B.J. and R.B. Peterson (eds), *Conflict Management and Industrial Relations*. Boston, MA: Kluwer Nijhoff.

Glenny, M. (1990). *The Rebirth of History: Eastern Europe in the Age of Democracy*. London: Penguin.

Glenny, M. (1992). *The Fall of Yugoslavia: The Third Balkan War*. London: Penguin.

Goertz, G. and P.F. Diehl (1993). 'Enduring rivalries: theoretical constructs and empirical patterns', *International Studies Quarterly*. 37:147–71.

Gordenker, L. and Weiss, T.G. (eds)(1991). *Soldiers, Peacekeepers and Disasters*. London: Macmillan/IPA.

Goulding, M. (1993). 'The evolution of United Nations peacekeeping', *International Affairs*. 69(3):451–64.

Gow, J. (1991). 'Deconstructing Yugoslavia', *Survival*. 33(4):291–311.

Gow, J. and J.D.D. Smith (1992). 'Peacemaking, peacekeeping, European security and the Yugoslav war', *London Defence Studies, No. 11*: London: Brassey's/Centre for Defence Studies.

Grant, R. and K. Newland (eds)(1991). *Gender and International Relations*. Buckingham: Open University Press.

Greffenius, S. and J. Gill (1992). 'Pure coercion vs. carrot- and-stick offers in crisis bargaining', *Journal of Peace Research.* 29(1):39–52.

Grove, C.L. and I. Torbiorn (1985). 'A new conceptualization of intercultural adjustment and the goals of training', *International Journal of Intercultural Relations.* 9:205–33.

Grove, E. (1993). 'UN armed forces and the military staff committee', *International Security.* 17(4):172–82.

Gupta, A. and J. Ferguson (1992). 'Beyond "culture" space, identity, and the politics of difference', *Cultural Anthropology.* 7(1):6–23.

Gurr, T.R. (1993). *Minorities at Risk: A Global View of Ethnopolitical Conflict.* Washington, DC: United States Institute of Peace.

Gurr, T.R., with B. Harff (1993). 'The feasibility of an early warning system for ethnic conflicts in Europe', paper prepared for the PIOOM Symposium on Ethnic Conflicts and Human Rights Violations in Europe, 25 June, Leiden.

Haas, E.B. (1980). 'Why collaborate? Issue-linkage and international regimes', *World Politics.* 32(3):357–405.

Haas, E.B. (1986). *Why We Still Need the United Nations: Collective Management of International Conflict, 1945–1984.* Berkeley, CA: Institute of International Studies.

Haas, E.B. (1990). *When Knowledge is Power: Three Models of Change in International Organization.* Berkeley, CA: University of California Press.

Hagglund, G. (1990). 'Peacekeeping in a modern war zone', *Survival.* 32(3):233–40.

Hannigan, T.P. (1990). 'Traits, attitudes, and skills that are related to intercultural effectiveness and their implications for cross-cultural training: a review of literature', *International Journal of Intercultural Relations.* 14:89–111.

Harbottle, M. (1970). *The Impartial Soldier.* London: Oxford University Press.

Harbottle, M. (1971). *The Blue Berets: The Story of the United Nations Peacekeeping Forces.* London: Leo Cooper.

Harbottle, M. (1979). 'Cyprus: an analysis of the UN's third party role in a "small war"', in Worsley, P. and P. Kitromilides (eds), *Small States in a Modern World: The Conditions of Survival.* Cyprus: New Cyprus Assoc.

Harbottle, M. (1980). 'The strategy of third party interventions in conflict resolution', *International Journal.* 35(1):118–31.

Harbottle, M. (1984). 'The United Nations and its capacity for keeping the peace', *Fellowship Briefing No.4*, The Fellowship of Reconciliation, UK.

Harbottle, M. (1991). *What is Proper Soldiering?: A Study on New Perspectives for the Future Uses of the Armed Forces in the 1990's.* Oxon, UK: The Centre for International Peacebuilding.

Harleman, C. (1990). 'Considerations for peacekeeping training', unpublished paper prepared for the International Peace Academy.

Harleman, C. (1991a). 'Peacekeepers for a changing world', paper presented to the United Nations Special Committee on Peacekeeping Operations.

Harleman, C. (1991b). 'Education and training of Swedish UN-Troops at the United Nations Training Center (UNTC), Almnaes, Sweden', unpublished paper.

Harleman, C. (1992a). 'Requirements for peacekeeping training within the United Nations', *UNITAR Newsletter*. 4(1):4–6.

Harleman, C. (1992b). 'Regional conflicts: peacekeeping and disarmament', *United Nations Disarmament Quarterly Review* 3:171–90.

Harrison, S.S. (1989). 'Paths to Peace in Afghanistan: the Geneva Accords and after', *Occasional Paper on Peacekeeping, No. 1.* New York: International Peace Academy.

Harrod, J. and N. Schrijver (1988). *The UN Under Attack.* Aldershot: Gower.

Hashmi, S.H. (1993). 'Is there an Islamic ethic of humanitarian intervention?' *Ethics and International Affairs.* 7:55–73.

Hay, R. (1990). 'Humanitarian ceasefires: an examination of their potential contribution to the resolution of conflict', *Working Paper, No. 28.* Ottawa, Canada: Canadian Institute for International Peace and Security (CIIPS).

Hendrickson, D.C. (1993). 'The ethics of collective security', *Ethics and International Affairs.* 7:1–15.

Higgins, R. (1970). *United Nations Peacekeeping, 1946–1967, Documents and Commentary: Vol. 2, Asia.* London: Oxford University Press.

Higgins, R. (1981). *United Nations Peacekeeping: Documents and Commentary, Vol. 4, Europe 1946–1979.* Oxford: Oxford University Press.

Higgins, R. (1993). 'The new United Nations and former Yugoslavia', *International Affairs.* 69(3):465–83.

Hill, B.J. (1982). 'An analysis of conflict resolution techniques: from problem-solving workshops to theory', *Journal of Conflict Resolution.* 26(1):109–38.

Hill, W.F. (1977). *Learning: A Survey of Psychological Interpretations.* London: Methuen.

Hind, D. (1989). *Transferable Personal Skills: A Student Guide.* Sunderland: Business Education Publishers.

Hoffman, M. (1992). 'Third party mediation and conflict resolution in the Post-Cold War world', in Baylis, J. and N.J. Rengger (eds), *Dilemmas in World Politics.* Oxford: Clarendon Press, pp. 261–86.

Holiday, D. and W. Stanley (1993). 'Building the peace: preliminary lessons from El Salvador', *Journal of International Affairs.* 46(2): 415–38.

Holst, J.J. (1990). 'Enhancing peacekeeping operations', *Survival.* 32(3): 264–75.

Honeyman, C. (1988). 'In practice: five elements of mediation', *Negotiation Journal.* 4(2)(April): 149–60.

Horowitz, D.L. (1985). *Ethnic Groups in Conflict.* Berkeley, CA: University of California Press.

Hoskyns, C. (1965). *The Congo Since Independence: January 1960–December 1961.* London: Oxford University Press.

Human Rights Watch (1993). *The Lost Agenda: Human Rights and UN Field Operations.* New York: Human Rights Watch.

Hume, C.R. (1991). 'Negotiations before peacekeeping', *Occasional Papers on Peacekeeping, No. 5.* New York: International Peace Academy.

Huntington, S.P. (1993). 'The clash of civilizations', *Foreign Affairs.* 72(3): 22–49.

Inbar, I. (1991). 'Great power mediation: the USA and the 1983 Israeli-Lebanese agreement', *Journal of Peace Research*. 28(1):71–84.

Ingram, J.C. (1993). 'The future architecture for international humanitarian assistance', *Working Paper, No. 138*. Canberra: Peace Research Centre, The Australian National University.

International Peace Academy (1984). *Peacekeeper's Handbook*. New York: Pergamon Press.

Isard, W. (1992). *Understanding Conflict and the Science of Peace*. Oxford: Blackwell.

Jacovides, A.J. (1977). 'The Cyprus problem and the United Nations', in Attalides, M.A. (ed.), *Cyprus Reviewed*. Nicosia: The Jus Cypri Association.

James, A. (1984). 'Options for peacekeeping', in Howe, J.O. (ed.), *Armed Peace: The Search for World Security*. London: Macmillan.

James, A. (1989). 'The UN force in Cyprus', *International Affairs*. 65(3):481–500.

James, A. (1990a). *Peacekeeping in International Politics*. London: Macmillan.

James, A. (1990b). 'International peacekeeping: the disputants' view', *Political Studies*. 18(2):215–30.

Jaster, R.S. (1990). 'The 1988 Peace Accords and the future of South-Western Africa', *Adelphi Papers No. 253*. London: International Institute for Strategic Studies.

Job, C. (1993). 'Yugoslavia's ethnic furies', *Foreign Policy*. No. 92:52–74.

Johansen, R.C. (1990). 'UN peacekeeping: the changing utility of military force', *Third World Quarterly*. 12(2):53–70.

Jonah, J.O.C. (1990). 'The military talks at Kilometer 101: the UN's effectiveness as a third party', *Negotiation Journal*. 6(1):53–70.

Kant, E. (1939). *Perpetual Peace: A Philosophical Proposal*. London: Peace Book Company.

Katz, N.H. and J.W. Lawyer (1985). *Communication and Conflict Resolution Skills*. Dubuque, Iowa: Kendall/Hunt.

Kaufman, S. and G.T. Duncan (1988). 'The role of mandates in third party intervention', *Negotiation Journal*. 4(4):403–12.

Kaufman, S. and G.T. Duncan (1992). 'A formal framework for mediator mechanisms and motivations', *Journal of Conflict Resolution*. 36(4):688–708.

Kealey, D.J. (1990). *Cross-cultural Effectiveness: A study of Canadian Technical Advisors Overseas*. Quebec, Canada: Canadian International Development Agency (CIDA).

Kelman, H.C. (1972). 'The problem-solving workshop in conflict resolution', in Merritt, R.L. (ed.), *Communication in International Politics*. Urbana: University of Illinois Press.

Kelman, H.C. (1977). 'The conditions, criteria, and dialectics of human dignity', *International Studies Quarterly*. 21(3):529–52.

Kelman, H.C. (1978). 'Israelis and Palestinians: psychological pre-requisites for mutual acceptance', *International Security*. 3(1):162–86.

Kelman, H.C. (1982). 'Creating the conditions for Israeli-Palestinian negotiations', *Journal of Conflict Resolution*. 26(1)(March):29–41.

Kelman, H.C. (1985). 'Overcoming the psychological barrier: an analysis of the Egptian–Israeli peace process', *Negotiation Journal*. 1(3):213–34.

Kelman, H.C. and S.P. Cohen (1979). 'Reduction of international conflict: an interactional approach', in Austin, W.G. and S. Worchel (eds), *The Social Psychology of Intergroup Relations*. Monterey, CA: Brooks/Cole.

Kelman, H.C. and S.P. Cohen (1976). 'The problem-solving workshop: a social-psychological contribution to the resolution of international conflict', *Journal of Peace Research*. 13(2):79–90.

Keohane, R. (ed.)(1986). *Neorealism and Its Critics*. New York: Colombia.

Kirgis, F.L. (1993). *International Organizations in Their Legal Setting*. St. Paul, MN: West Publishing, 2nd edn.

Klare, M.T. and D.C. Thomas (eds)(1991). *World Society: Trends and Challenges at Century's End*. New York: St. Martin's Press.

Kolb, David A. (1984). *Experiential Learning*. New Jersey: Prentice-Hall.

Krepon, M. and J.P. Tracey (1990). '"Open Skies" and UN peace-keeping', *Survival*. 32(3):251–63.

Kriesberg, L. (1987). 'Timing and the initiation of de-escalation moves', *Negotiation Journal*. 3(4):375–84.

Kriesberg, L. (1988). 'Strategies of negotiating agreements: Arab–Israeli and American–Soviet cases', *Negotiation Journal*. 4(1):19–29.

Kriesberg, L. (1991). 'Formal and quasi-mediators in international disputes: an exploratory analysis', *Journal of Peace Research*. 28(1):19–28.

Kriesberg, L. and S.L. Thorson (eds)(1991). *Timing the De-escalation of International Conflicts*. Syracuse, NY: Syracuse University Press.

Kriesberg, L., T.A. Northrup and S.J. Thorson (eds)(1989). *Intractable Conflicts and Their Transformation*. Syracuse, NY: Syracuse University Press.

Kuhn, T.S. (1962). *The Structure of Scientific Revolutions*. Chicago: University of Chicago Press.

Kuzmanic, T. and A. Truger (eds)(1993). *Yugoslavia War*. Ljubljana, Slovenia/ Schlaining, Austria: Peace Institute Ljubljana/Study Centre for Peace and Conflict Resolution, 2nd Ed.

Kyle, K. (1984). 'Cyprus', *Report No. 30*. Minority Rights Group.

Laue, J.H. (1982). 'Ethical considerations in choosing intervention roles', *Peace and Change*. 8(2/3)(summer):29–41.

Lawson, S. (1992). 'Politics of authenticity: ethnonationalist conflict and the state', *Working Paper, No. 125*. Canberra: Peace Research Centre, The Australia National University.

Lawson, S. (1993). 'Institutionalizing peaceful conflict: political opposition and the challenge of democratization in Asia', *Australian Journal of International Affairs*. 47(1):15–30.

Lederach, J.P. (1990). 'Training on culture: four approaches', *Conciliation Quarterly*. 9(1): 6, 11–13.

Legum, C. (1988). *The Battlefronts of Southern Africa*. New York: Africana.

Leitch, M.L. (1986/7). 'The politics of compromise: a feminist perspective on mediation', *Mediation Quarterly*. 14/15: 163–75.

Lennung, S-A. (1974/5). 'Implicit theories in experiential group practices – a pedagogical approach', *Interpersonal Development*. 5:37–49.

Levi, A.M. and A. Benjamin (1976). 'Jews and Arabs rehearse Geneva: a model of conflict resolution', *Human Relations*. 29(11):1035–44.

Levi, A.M. and A. Benjamin (1977). 'Focus and flexibility in a model of conflict resolution', *Journal of Conflict Resolution*. 21(3)(September): 405–25.

Lewer, N. and O. Ramsbotham (1993). 'Something must be done: towards an ethical framework for humanitarian intervention in international-social

conflict', *Peace Research Report, No. 33.* Bradford: Department of Peace Studies, University of Bradford.

Lewicki, R.J. (1982). 'Ethical concerns in conflict management', in Bomers,
G.B.J. and R.B. Peterson (eds), *Conflict Management and Industrial Relations.*
Boston, MA: Kluwer Nijhoff.

Light, M. (1984). 'Problem-solving workshops: the role of scholarship on conflict resolution', in Banks, M. (ed.), *Conflict in World Society: A New Perspective
on International Relations.* Brighton: Wheatsheaf.

Light, M. and A.J.R. Groom (eds) (1985). *International Relations: A Handbook of
Current Theory.* London: Pinter.

Liu, F.T. (1990). 'United Nations Peacekeeping: Management and Operations',
*Occasional Papers on Peacekeeping, No. 4.* New York: International Peace Academy.

Liu, F.T. (1992). 'United Nations peacekeeping and the non-use of force',
*IPA Occasional Paper Series.* Boulder, CO: Lynne Rienner.

Luard, E. (1966). *The Evolution of International Organizations.* London: Thames
& Hudson.

Luard, E. (1975). *The United Nations: How It Works and What It Does.* London:
Macmillan.

MacInnis, J.A. (1989). 'Cyprus: Canada's perpetual vigil', *Canadian Defence
Quarterly.* 19(1):21–6.

Mackenzie, L. (1993). 'Military realities of UN peacekeeping operations',
*RUSI Journal.* 138(1):21–4.

Mackinlay, J. (1989). *The Peacemakers: An Assessment of Peacekeeping Operations at
the Arab-Israel Interface.* London: Unwin Hyman.

Mackinlay, J. (1990). 'Powerful peace-keepers', *Survival.* 32(3):241–50.

Mackinlay, J. and J. Chopra (1992). 'Second generation multinational operations', *The Washington Quarterly.* 15(3):113–31.

MacQueen, N. (1983). 'Ireland and the United Nations Peacekeeping Force
in Cyprus', *Review of International Studies.* 9:95–108.

McCaffery, J.A. (1986). 'Independent effectiveness: a reconsideration of
cross-cultural orientation and training', *International Journal of Intercultural
Relations.* 10(2):159–78.

McDonald, R. (1988/9). 'The problem of Cyprus', *Adelphi Papers No. 234.*
London: International Institute for Strategic Studies.

Mandell, B.S. and B.W. Tomlin (1991). 'Mediation in the development of
norms to manage conflict: Kissinger in the Middle East', *Journal of Peace
Research.* 28(1):43–56.

Mandell, B. and R.J. Fisher (1992). 'Training third-party consultants in international conflict resolution', *Negotiation Journal.* 8(3):259–71.

Martin, J.N. (1986). 'Training issues in cross-cultural orientation', *International Journal of Intercultural Relations.* 10(2):103–16.

Maxwell, M. (1990). *Morality Among Nations: An Evolutionary View.* Albany, NY:
State University of New York Press.

Miall, H. (1992). *The Peacemakers: Peaceful Settlement of Disputes Since 1945.*
London: Macmillan.

Midlarsky, M. (ed) (1992). *The Internationalization of Communal Strife.* London:
Routledge.

Miller, L.H. (1990). *Global Order: Values and Power in International Politics.*
Boulder, CO: Westview, 2nd edn.

Mills, S.R. (1989). 'The financing of United Nations peacekeeping operations: the need for a sound financial basis', *Occasional Papers on Peacekeeping, No. 3*. New York: International Peace Academy.

Mintz, A. and N. Geva (1993). 'Why don't democracies fight each other?', *Journal of Conflict Resolution*. 37(3):484–503.

Mitchell, C.R. (1973). 'Conflict resolution and controlled communication: some further comments', *Journal of Peace Research*. 10:123–32.

Mitchell, C.R. (1981a). *Peacemaking and the Consultant's Role*. Westmead: Gower.

Mitchell, C.R. (1981b). *The Structure of International Conflict*. London: Macmillan.

Mitchell, C.R. (1989). 'Conflict resolution and civil war: reflections on the Sudanese settlement of 1972', *Working Paper No. 3*. Fairfax, VA: Center for Conflict Analysis and Resolution, George Mason University.

Mitchell, C.R. (1991). 'A willingness to talk: conciliatory gestures and de-escalation', *Negotiation Journal*. 7(4):405–29.

Mitchell, C.R. and K. Webb (eds) (1988). *New Approaches to International Mediation*. Westport: Greenwood.

Mitchell, R. (1988). 'Peacekeeping and peacemaking in Cyprus', *Background Paper, No. 23*. Ottawa, Canada: CIIPS.

Morgenthau, H.J. (1960). *Politics Among Nations*. New York: Knopf (3rd edn., 1st edn. pub. 1948).

Moser, Y. (1993). 'United Nations warriors or peacekeepers: examining the logic of combating war with soldiers', *Nonviolence International Papers*. Bangkok: Nonviolence International.

Moskos, C.C. (1976). *Peace Soldiers: The Sociology of a United Nations Military Force*. Chicago: Chicago University Press.

Nader, L. (1972). 'Some notes on John Burton's paper on "resolution of conflict"', *International Studies Quarterly*. 16(1):53–8.

Nelson, C. (1989). 'The initiation of United Nations peacekeeping forces: problems and reform proposals', *International Affairs Bulletin*. 3(1):30–44.

Nelson, R.W. (1985). 'Multinational peacekeeping in the Middle East and the United Nations model', *International Affairs*. 61(1):67–89.

Nordstrom, C. and J. Martin (eds) (1992). *The Paths to Domination, Resistance, and Terror*. Berkeley, CA: University of California Press.

Northrup, T.A. (1992). 'The dynamics of identity in personal and social conflict', in Kriesberg, L., T.A. Northrup and S.J. Thorson (eds), *Intractable Conflicts and Their Transformation*. Syracuse: Syracuse University Press.

Norton, A.R. and T.G. Weiss (1990a). 'Superpowers and peacekeepers', *Survival*. 32(3):212–20.

Norton, A.R. and T.G. Weiss (1990b). 'UN peacekeepers: soldiers with a difference', *Headline Series, No. 292*. New York: Foreign Policy Association.

O'Brien, C. C. (1962). *To Katanga and Back: A UN Case History*. New York: Simon and Schuster.

Ogata, S. (1993). 'The UN response to the growing refugee crisis', *Japan Review of International Affairs*. 7(3):202–15.

Ogunbanwo, S. (1991). 'The United Nations disarmament training for diplomats: hopes for the future', *Bulletin of Peace Proposals*. 22(1):49–53.

Osgood, C.E. (1962). *An Alternative to War and Surrender*. Urbana: University of Illinois Press.

Ottaway, M. (1991). 'Mediation in transnational conflict: Eritrea', *The Annals, AAPSS.* 518:69–81.

Paige, R.M. (1986). 'Trainer competencies: the missing conceptual link or orientation', *International Journal of Intercultural Relations.* 10(2):135–58.

Parsons, A. (1983). 'The United Nations and international security', *Millennium.* 12(2):101–9.

Pearson, F.S. and J.M. Rochester (1992). *International Relations: The Global Condition in the Late Twentieth Century.* New York: McGraw-Hill, 3rd. edn .

Pederson, P. (1983). 'The transfer of intercultural training skills', *International Journal of Psychology.* 18:333–45.

Popper, K.R. (1957). *The Poverty of Historicism.* London: Routledge & Kegan Paul.

Popper, K.R. (1959). *The Logic of Scientific Discovery.* London: Hutchinson.

Posen, B.R. (1993). 'The security dilemma and ethnic conflict', *Survival.* 35(1):27–47.

Potapchuk, W. and C. Carlson (1987). 'Using conflict analysis to determine intervention techniques', *Mediation Quarterly.* 16:31–43.

Prein, H. (1984). 'A contingency approach for conflict intervention', *Group and Organization Studies.* 9(1): 81–102.

Premdas, R.R. (1991). 'The internationalization of ethnic conflict: some theoretical explanations', in de Silva, K.M. and R.J. May (eds), *Internationalization of Ethnic Conflict.* London: Pinter.

Princen, T. (1991). 'Camp David: problem-solving or power politics as usual?', *Journal of Peace Research.* 28(1): 57–69.

Prins, G. (1991). 'The United Nations and peacekeeping in the Post-Cold War world: the case for naval power', *Bulletin of Peace Proposals.* 22(2): 135–55.

Pruitt, D.G. and P.J. Carnevale (1993). *Negotiation in Social Conflict.* Buckingham: Open University Press.

Pugh, M.C. (1992). 'Multinational maritime forces: a breakout from traditional peacekeeping?', *Southampton Papers in International Policy, No. 1.* Southampton, UK: Mountbatten Centre for International Studies.

Ramphal, S. (1992). 'Globalism and meaningful peace: a new world order rooted in international community', *Security Dialogue.* 23(3): 81–7.

Renner, M. (1993). 'Critical juncture: the future of peacekeeping', *Worldwatch Paper No. 114.* Washington, DC: Worldwatch Institute.

Renninger, J.P. *et al.* (1982). 'Assessing the United Nations scale of assessments: is it fair? is it equitable?', *Policy and Efficacy Studies, No. 9.* New York: UNITAR.

Rifkin, J. (1984). 'Mediation from a feminist perspective', *Law and Inequality.* 21(1):21–31.

Rikhye, I.J. (1964). 'Preparation and training of United Nations peacekeeping forces', *Adelphi Paper, No. 9.* London: IISS.

Rikhye, I.J. (1970). 'Training for Peacekeeping', paper presented to the Institute of Vredesvraagstikken, Netherlands, December, 1970.

Rikhye, I.J. (1984). *The Theory and Practice of Peacekeeping.* London: Hurst.

Rikhye, I.J. (1989). 'The future of peacekeeping', *Occasional Papers, No. 2* New York: International Peace Academy.

Rikhye, I.J., M. Harbottle and B. Egge (1974). *The Thin Blue Line: International Peacekeeping and Its Future.* New Haven: Yale University Press.

Rikhye, I.J. and K. Skjelsbaek (eds) (1990). *The United Nations and Peacekeeping: Results, Limitations and Prospects.* London: Macmillan.

Rittberger, V. (1988). 'International regimes and peaceful conflict resolution', in Wallensteen, P. (ed.), *Peace Research: Achievements and Challenges.* London: Westview Press, pp. 144–65.

Roberts, A. and B. Kingsbury (eds) (1988). *United Nations, Divided World: The UN's Role in International Relations.* Oxford: Clarendon Press.

Roberts, A. (1993). 'Humanitarian war: military intervention and human rights', *International Affairs.* 69(3):429–49.

Rochester, J.M. (1990). 'Global policy and the future of the United Nations', *Journal of Peace Research.* 27(2):141–54.

Rosenau, J. (1992a). 'The United Nations in a turbulent world', *IPA Occasional Paper Series.* Boulder, CO: Lynne Rienner.

Rosenau, J. (1992b). 'Normative challenges in a turbulent world', *Ethics and International Affairs.* 6:1–19.

Ross, L. and C. Stillinger (1991). 'Barriers to conflict resolution', *Negotiation Journal.* 7(4):389–404.

Ross, M.H. (1992). 'The language of success and failure in ethnic conflict management', paper presented for the First International Conference of the Ethnic Studies Network, 8–10 June, Northern Ireland.

Rothchild, D. and C. Hartzell (1991). 'Great- and medium-power mediation: Angola', *The Annals, AAPSS.* 518:39–57.

Rothman, J. (1989). 'Supplementing tradition: a theoretical and practical typology for international conflict management', *Negotiation Journal.* 5(3): 265–77.

Rothman, J. (1991). 'Conflict research and resolution: Cyprus', *The Annals, AAPSS.* 518:95–108.

Rothman, J. (1992). *From Confrontation to Cooperation.* London: Sage.

Rubin, J.Z. (1989). 'Some wise and mistaken assumptions about conflict and negotiation', *Journal of Social Issues.* 45(2):195–209.

Rubinstein, R.A. (1989). 'Culture, international affairs, and multilateral peacekeeping: confusing process and pattern', *Cultural Dynamics.* 2(1):41–61.

Russett, B. and J.S. Sutterlin (1991). 'The UN in a new world order', *Foreign Affairs.* 70(2):69–83.

Saito, S. (1993). 'The United Nations and the issue of a fluid global security', *Japan Review of International Affairs.* 9(3):234–53.

Salla, M.E. (1993). 'The efficacy of nonviolence in international relations: a critique', *Australian Journal of Political Science.* 28(3):458–80.

Samatar, S.S. (1991). *Somalia: A Nation in Turmoil.* London: Minority Rights Group.

Sandole, D.J.D. (1986). 'Traditional approaches to conflict management: short-term gains vs. long-term costs', *Current Research on Peace and Violence.* 9(3):119–24.

Sandole, D.J.D. and I. Sandole-Staroste (eds) (1987). *Conflict Management and Problem Solving: Interpersonal to International Applications.* London: Francis Pinter.

Saunders, H.H. (1985). 'We need a larger theory of negotiation: the importance of prenegotiating phases', *Negotiation Journal.* 1(3):249–62.

Schmidt, H. (1992). 'The search for global order: problems of survival', *Security Dialogue.* 23(3):41–56.

Shapiro, D., R. Drieghe, and J. Brett (1985). 'Mediator behavior and the outcome of mediation', *Journal of Social Issues.* 41(2):101–14.

Sheppard, B.H. (1984). 'Third party conflict intervention: a procedural framework', *Research in Organizational Behavior.* 6:141–90.

Sherry, G.L. (1986) 'The United Nations, international conflict, and American security', *Political Science Quarterly.* 101(5):753–71.

Sherry, G.L. (1990). 'The United Nations reborn: conflict control in the post-cold war world', *Critical Issues.* 2:1–32.

Simon, D. (1991). 'Independent Namibia one year on', *Conflict Studies, No. 239.* London: Research Institute for the Study of Conflict and Terrorism.

Sites, P. (1973). *Control: The Basis of Social Order.* New York: Dunellen.

Sivard, R.L. (Annual 1974– ). *World Military and Social Expenditures.* Leesburg, VA: World Priorities.

Skjelsbaek, K. (1986). 'Peaceful settlement of disputes by the United Nations and other intergovernmental bodies', *Cooperation and Conflict.* 21(3):139–54.

Skjelsbaek, K. (1989). 'United Nations peacekeeping and the facilitation of withdrawals', *Bulletin of Peace Proposals.* 20(3):253–64.

Skjelsbaek, K. (1991). 'The UN Secretary-General and the mediation of international disputes', *Journal of Peace Research.* 28(1):99–115.

Skogmo, B. (1989). *UNIFIL: International Peacekeeping in Lebanon, 1978–1988.* London: Lynne Rienner.

Small, M. and J.D. Singer (1979). *Explaining War: Selected Papers from the Correlates of War Project.* Beverley Hills, CA: Sage.

Smith, M., R. Little, and M. Shackleton (eds)(1981). *Perspectives on World Politics.* London: Croom Helm.

Smith, William, P. (1985). 'Effectiveness of a biased mediator', *Negotiation Journal.* 1(4):363–72.

Smoker, P., R. Davies and B. Munske (eds)(1990). *A Reader in Peace Studies.* New York: Pergamon Press.

Sohn, L.B. (1987). 'Peaceful settlement of disputes and international security', *Negotiation Journal.* 3(2):155–65.

Solarz, S.J. (1990). 'Cambodia and the International Community', *Foreign Affairs.* 69(2):99–115.

Somerville, K. (1993). 'The failure of democratic reform in Angola and Zaire', *Survival.* 35(3):51–77.

Sorensen, G. (1992). 'Utopianism in peace research: the Gandhian heritage', *Journal of Peace Research.* 29(2):135–44.

Soroos, M.S. (1986). *Beyond Sovereignty: The Challenge of Global Policy.* Colombia: University of South Carolina Press.

Soroos, M.S. (1990a). 'Global policy studies and peace research', *Journal of Peace Research.* 27(2):117–25.

Soroos, M.S. (1990b). 'The challenge of global policy', *Journal of Peace Research.* 27(2):113–15.

Spencer, D.E. and W.I Spencer (1992). 'The International Negotiation Network: A New Method of Approaching Some Very Old Problems', *INN Occasional Paper Series.* 2(2).

Spencer, D.E., W.J. Spencer, and H. Yang (1992). 'Closing the mediation gap: the Ethiopia/Eritrea experience', *Security Dialogue.* 23(3):89–99.

Stein, J.G. (1985). 'Structures, strategies and tactics of mediation: Kissinger and Carter in the Middle East', *Negotiation Journal.* 1(4):331–47.

Stein, J.G. (1989a). 'Getting to the table: processes of international prenegotiation', *International Journal.* 44:231–6.

Stein, J.G. (1989b). 'Prenegotiation in the Arab-Israeli conflict: the paradoxes of success and failure', *International Journal.* 44:410–41.

Stein, J.G. (1989c). 'Getting to the table: the triggers, stages, functions, and consequences of prenegotiations', *International Journal.* 44:475–504.

Stiles K.W. and M. MacDonald (1992). 'After consensus what?: performance criteria for the UN in the post-Cold War era', *Journal of Peace Research.* 29(3):299–312.

Stockholm International Peace Research Institute (SIPRI) (Annual 1973– ). *SIPRI Yearbook: World Armaments and Disarmament.* Oxford: Oxford University Press.

Sussman, N.M. (1986). 'Re-entry research and training: methods and implications', *International Journal of Intercultural Relations.* 10(2):235–54.

Swift, R.N. (1974). 'United Nations military training for peace', *International Organization.* 28(2):267–80.

Taylor, P. and A.J.R. Groom (eds)(1988). *International Institutions at Work.* London: Pinter.

Thakur, R. (1993). 'The United Nations in a changing world', *Security Dialogue.* 24(1):7–20.

Thomas, A.J. (1979). 'International law and the Turkish invasion of Cyprus', in Worsley, P. and P. Kitromilides (eds), *Small States in the Modern World: The Conditions of Survival.* Cyprus: New Cyprus Assoc.

Thompson, W.S. *et al.* (eds)(1991). *Approaches to Peace: An Intellectual Map.* Washington, DC: United States Institute of Peace.

Thornton, T.P. (1991). 'Regional organizations in conflict management', *The Annals, AAPSS.* 518:132–42.

Tickner, J.A. (1992). *Gender in International Relations.* New York: Colombia University Press.

Tillett, G. (1991). *Resolving Conflict: A Practical Approach.* Sydney: Sydney University Press.

Tomlin, B.W. (1989). 'The stages of prenegotiation: the decision to negotiate North American free trade', *International Journal.* 44:254–79.

Touval, S. (1985). 'The context of mediation', *Negotiation Journal.* 1(4):373–8

Touval, S. (1989). 'Multilateral negotiation: an analytic approach', *Negotiation Journal.* 5(2):159–74.

Tromp, H. (1993). 'Conflict and crisis management: the Yugoslav case', *Peace and the Sciences.* Vienna: International Institute for Peace, pp. 33–9.

Umbricht, V. (1988). *Multilateral Mediation: Practical Experiences and Lessons.* Boston: Martinus Nijhoff.

United Nations (1990). *The Blue Helmets: A Review of United Nations Peacekeeping, 2nd. Ed.* New York: UN Department of Public Information.

UNITAR (1987). *The United Nations and the Maintenance of International Peace and Security.* Lancaster: Martinus Nijhoff.

United Nations Office of Legal Affairs (1992). *Handbook on the Peaceful Settlement of Disputes Between States.* New York: United Nations.

Urquhart, B. (1972). *Hammarskjold.* New York: Knopf.

Urquhart, B. (1981). 'International peace and security: thoughts on the twentieth anniversary of Dag Hammarskjold's death', *Foreign Affairs.* 60(1):1–16.

Urquhart, B. (1987). *A Life in Peace and War.* London: Weidenfeld & Nicolson.
Urquhart, B. (1989). 'The future of peacekeeping', *Negotiation Journal.* 5(1): 25–32.
Urquhart, B. (1989). 'The United Nations system and the future', *International Affairs.* 65(2):225–31.
Urquhart, B. (1990). 'Beyond the "sheriff's posse"', *Survival.* 32(3):196–205.
Urquhart, B. (1991/92). 'The United Nations: from peacekeeping to a collective system?', *Adelphi Papers, No. 265.* London: International Institute for Strategic Studies :18–29.
Urquhart, B. and E. Childers (1990). 'A world in need of leadership: tomorrow's United Nations', *Development Dialogue.* 1–2.
Ury, W.L. (1987). 'Strengthening international mediation', *Negotiation Journal.* 3(3):225–9.
Ury, W.L. *et al.* (1988). 'Designing an effective dispute resolution system', *Negotiation Journal.* 4(4):413–31.
van de Vliert, E. (1992). 'Questions about the strategic choice model of mediation', *Negotiation Journal.* 8(4):379–86.
van Wynen-Thomas, A. (1979). 'The Turkish invasion of Cyprus: legal aspects of the regional and United Nations actions', in Worsley, P. and P. Kitromilides (eds), *Small States in a Modern World: The Conditions of Survival.* Cyprus: New Cyprus Assoc.
Vayrynen, R. (1985). 'Is there a role for the United Nations in conflict resolution', *Journal of Peace Research.* 22(3):189–96.
Vayrynen, R. (1985). 'The United Nations and the resolution of international conflicts', *Cooperation and Conflict.* 20(3):141–71.
Vayrynen, R. (ed.)(1989). *The Quest for Peace.* London: Sage.
Vayrynen, R. (ed.)(1991). *New Directions in Conflict Theory: Conflict Resolution and Conflict Transformation.* London: Sage.
Walker, J. (1993). 'International mediation of ethnic conflicts', *Survival.* 35(1):102–17.
Walker, R.B.J. (1988). *One World, Many Worlds: Struggles for a Just World Peace* Boulder, CO: Lynne Rienner.
Wall, J.A. (1981). 'Mediation: an analysis, review, and proposed research', *Journal of Conflict Resolution.* 25(1):157–80.
Wall, J.A. and A. Lynn (1993). 'Mediation: a current review', *Journal of Conflict Resolution.* 37(1):160–94.
Wallensteen, P. (ed.)(1988). *Peace Research: Achievements and Challenges.* London: Westview Press.
Wallensteen, P. and K. Axell (1993). 'Armed conflict at the end of the Cold War, 1989–92', *Journal of Peace Research.* 30(3):331–46.
Waltz, K. (1959). *Man, the State, and War.* New York: Colombia.
Waltz, K. (1979). *Theory of International Politics.* New York: Random House.
Weathersby, R. (1992). 'Developing a global perspective: a crucial "changing of the minds"', *Journal of Management Education.* 16:10–27.
Weber, T. (1989). 'The problems of peacekeeping', *Interdisciplinary Peace Research.* 1(2):3–26.
Weber, T. (1993). 'From Maude Royden's peace army to the gulf peace team: an assessment of unarmed interpositionary peace forces', *Journal of Peace Research.* 30(1):45–64.

Wehr, P. (1979). *Conflict Regulation.* Boulder: Westview Press.

Wehr, P. and J.P. Lederach (1991). 'Mediating conflict in Central America', *Journal of Peace Research.* 28(1):85–98.

Weingarten, H.R. and E. Douvan (1985). 'Male and female visions of mediation', *Negotiation Journal.* 1(4):349–57.

Weiss, T.G. (ed.)(1990). *The United Nations in Conflict Management: American, Soviet and Third World Views.* New York: International Peace Academy.

Weiss, T.G. (1993). 'New challenges for UN military operations: implementing and agenda for peace', *The Washington Quarterly.* 16(1):51–66.

Weiss, T.G. and K.M. Campbell (1991). 'Military Humanitarianism', *Survival.* 33(5):451–65.

Weiss, T.G. and L. Minear (1991). 'So international ethics matter?: humanitarian politics in the Sudan', *Ethics and International Affairs.* 5:197–214.

Weston, B.H. (1992). 'Toward a Post-Cold War global security: a legal perspective', *Waging Peace Series, No. 32.* Santa Barbara, CA: Nuclear Age Peace Foundation.

Williams, D. (1987). *The Specialized Agencies and the United Nations: The System in Crisis.* London:C. Hurst and Company.

Winham, G.R. (1989). 'The prenegotiation phase of the Uruguay round', *International Journal.* 44:280–303.

Wiseman, H. (ed.)(1983). *Peacekeeping: Appraisals and Proposals.* Oxford: Pergamon Press.

Wiseman, H. (1991). 'Civilian participation in UN peacekeeping operations', paper presented to the International Peace Academy's, *Vienna Seminar,* 7–18 July 1991.

Woodhouse, T. (ed.)(1991). *Peacemaking in a Troubled World.* Oxford: Berg.

Woodhouse, T. (1992). 'Improving the good instrument:active mediation and conflict resolution in the New World Order', *Occasional Paper, No. 24.* Perth, Australia: Indian Ocean Centre for Peace Studies (IOCPS).

World Commission on Environment and Development (1987). *Our Common Future.* Oxford: Oxford University Press.

Wright, Q. (1965). 'The escalation of international conflicts', *Journal of Conflict Resolution.* 4(4):434–49.

Yalem, R.J. (1971). 'Controlled communication and conflict resolution', *Journal of Peace Research.* 8:263–72.

Young, N. (1987). 'The peace movement, peace research, peace education and peacebuilding', *Bulletin of Peace Proposals.* 18(3):331–49.

Young, O.R. (1986). 'International regimes: toward a new theory of institutions', *World Politics.* 39(1):104–22.

Zartman, I.W. (1985). 'Negotiating from asymmetry: the North-South stalemate', *Negotiation Journal.* 1(2):121–38.

Zartman, I.W. (1989). 'Prenegotiation: phases and functions', *International Journal.* 44:237–53.

Zartman, I.W. (1991). 'Conflict and resolution: contest, cost and change', *Annals, AAPSS.* 518(Nov):11–22.

# Index

abilities  *see* skills
adjudication  107
adjustment cycle  171–2
  for military peacekeepers  175–7
advocacy, by third parties  106
Agency for Personnel Service Overseas
  (APSO)  199–200
Ahtisaari, Marti  61–2, 69, 70
  *see also* UNTAG
Alliance, Treaty of  46
Amnesty International  21
  *An Agenda for Peace*  22, 24, 141, 195–6,
    216–18
Angola  26, 59, 61, 62, 65
  *see also* UNAVEM; UNTAG
Angolan peace accords  27
apartheid  61
arbitration  107
Atlantic Charter  1
attribution training  170
attitudes
  in cross-cultural interaction  168
  in peacekeeping  205–6, 212–13
  *see also* cross-cultural interaction
    training
Austrian Study Centre for Peace and
  Conflict Resolution (ASPR)  181
  training for peacekeeping  203
Azar, Edward E.  97–8
  *see also* protracted social conflict

Bercovitch, Jacob  104, 107–8, 121, 147,
  151, 154
Bosnia-Herzegovina
  recognition of  73–4
  referendum  73
  *see also* UNPROFOR
Boulding, Kenneth  94–5
Boutros-Ghali, Boutros  22, 36, 78, 79,
  80–1, 82, 129, 131–2, 134, 141, 153,
  216–18
  *see also An Agenda for Peace*
Burton, John  90, 94–5, 97, 104, 109, 114

Canadian Forces  181, 183–8, 191
  Directorate of Peacekeeping
    Operations (CF–DPKO)  183
  Douglas Report  183, 185–6, 204

International Peacekeeping Training
  Centre  186–7
  negotiation training  187–8
  training  183–5:  pre-rotation
    training  184; critique of  185–6
  *see also* training for peacekeeping
cantonment  33
Carrington, Lord Peter  74–5, 80–1
case-by-case approach to conflict
  management  143–4
  and peacekeeping training  182, 183
Churchill, Winston  1
civilian participation in
  peacekeeping  23, 195–6, 217
  types of  196
  United Nations staff  196:  training
    for UNTAG  197–9
civilian police  *see* United Nations
  civilian police
civilian training  *see* training for
  peacekeeping
CNN-effect  22
code of conduct  *see* UNTAG
cognitive-behaviour modification  170
Cold War  10, 11–12, 22–3, 129–30
collective security  *see* Security Council
communication skills  167, 169–70
  and success  174
  *see also* abilities; cross-cultural
    interaction training; skills
compromise  105
conceptual framework for
  peacekeeping  155
  strategic versus conceptual
    thinking  207
concert of powers  3, 8, 9, 10
conciliation  105, 107
  definition  110–11
confidence-building measures  57, 59,
  125, 126, 128
  related to peacebuilding  132
conflict
  causes of  99–103;  contingency
    theory  99–100; inherency
    theory  100; objective
    conflict  101–2; subjective
    conflict  102–3
  ideographic approach to  116–18

issues 11–12, 148
multi-level 96
non-linearity of 119
normative approach to 116–18
structure and process 98–9
theory 96–104
trends 20–2
*see also* human needs theory;
    protracted social conflict;
    structural violence; conflict
    management
conflict analysis 105
*see also* problem-solving
conflict attitudes 98
conflict behaviour 98, 105
conflict escalation/de-escalation 98–9,
    118–19
stage 4 escalation 150
conflict management 104–23
conflict resolution 104–5;
    definition 105; roles of 109–11
conflict settlement 101, 104–5;
    definition 105; roles of 107–8,
    110–11
issues in 148
*see also* contingency theory; third
    parties; third party intervention;
    evaluation of conflict
    management
conflict situation 98, 125
conflict widening 98
Congo *see* ONUC
constabulary ethic 175–6
constructionism 92
consultation 107
and contingency theory 116
as peacebuilding 150
definition 109
Contadora Group 26
contingency theory 100, 104, 115–23
complementarity 116, 159–60
critique of 121–3
empirical evidence from 119–20
and ethical issues 118
escalation and typology 118–19
normative nature of 116–17
and peacekeeping *see* peacekeeping
and protracted social conflict 119,
    120–1
controlled impasse 125
Cornwallis proposal 186–7
*see also* Canadian Forces
crisis management 8
Croatia, recognition of 73

*see also* UNPROFOR
Croatian Army (CA), offensives into pink
    zones 78
Croatian Democratic Union (HDZ) 72
cross-cultural adjustment theory 171–2
and peacekeeping 175–7
cross-cultural interaction training 165
definition 166
developing training
    programmes 172–3
factors necessary for success 167
skills of 167–70
techniques of 170–1
*see also* training for peacekeeping;
    skills; attitudes; selection process;
    fact-oriented training;
    interactional learning;
    experiential learning
crude law of social relations 98
de Cuellar, Javier Perez 7, 30, 36, 130,
    141–2
cultural awareness training 170
culture shock 171, 176
Curle, Adam 93–5
cycle of development, conceptualization
    process 164–5
Cyprus *see* UNFICYP

Danish Defence Force *see* Nordic
    militaries
data-set 154, 156
Declaration of United Nations 1, 2
deep-rooted conflict 20, 24, 126
*see also* conflict; human needs theory;
    protracted social conflict
de-escalation of conflict *see* conflict
    escalation/de-escalation
Democratic Turnhalle Alliance
    (DTA) 69, 70
Denmark *see* Nordic militaries
Department of Humanitarian Affairs
    (DHA) 34, 133, 143
Department of Peacekeeping
    Operations (DPKO) 7, 34, 130
'focal point' for training 180
and training 179–80, 195
Department of Peace Operations 130,
    133
Department of Political Affairs
    (DPA) 130
preventive capability 130
dependent variables 154–5
destructive conflict 96–7
Diehl, Paul F. 41–2, 148–9, 156

Directorate of Peacekeeping
　　Operations　*see* Canadian Forces
dissemination　164
disputes, definition　97
DOMREP　17, 26
Dumbarton Oaks Conversations　1–2

ECOMOG　29
Economic and Social Council
　　(ECOSOC)　2, 3
enforcement　5, 10–11, 24, 212–13, 224–5
　versus peaceful third party
　　activity　211–12
　*see also* United Nations Charter
Enlightenment, the　91
escalation of conflict　*see* conflict
　escalation/de-escalation
*Esquipulas II* Agreement　26, 159
Establishment, Treaty of　46
ethics　*see* third party intervention
European Community, in former
　　Yugoslavia　72
　European Community's Conference on
　　Yugoslavia (ECCY)　74–5, 80–1
　recognition of Croatia and
　　Slovenia　73
　*see also* UNPROFOR
European Community's Conference on
　　Yugoslavia (ECCY)　*see* European
　　Community
experience/expertise fallacy　168, 228–9
experiential learning　170, 172, 177
　and simulations exercises　180–1
　versus 'situation exercises'　180–1
evaluation of conflict
　　management　112–13
　*see also* conflict management

facilitation　107, 126
　definition　109
facilitator, definition　109
fact-finding　107
fact-oriented training　170, 171, 177,
　　180, 205, 209, 215
Federal Republic of Yugoslavia
　　(FRY)　71, 76
　*see also* UNPROFOR
Field Operations Division (FOD)　34
Fifth Committee, General Assembly　6–7
Finnish Defence Force　*see* Nordic
　　militaries
First Committee, General Assembly　6
Fisher, Ronald and Loraleigh
　　Keashly　108, 119, 121–2

FMLN (Frente Farabundo Martí para la
　　Liberación Nacional)　27
Force Commander　34, 35, 39–40
　training for　195
　*see also* peacekeeping
Fourth Committee, General Assembly　6

Galtung, Johan　41, 92, 93–5, 133, 149
General Assembly　2, 3
　functions　6
　organization　6
　Committees　6–7
Geneva Declaration　57
　*see also* UNFICYP
good offices　105, 107
Goulding, Marrack　127, 142
Green Line　49–50
Groom, A.J.R.　90, 95–6
Grove, Cornelius, L. and Ingemar
　　Torbiorn　171–2, 175–7
Guarantee, Treaty of　46–7
Gulf War　5, 11, 24, 30–1

Haas, Ernst　11, 41–2
Hammarskjold, Dag　7, 13, 14, 15
Harbottle, Michael　53–4, 142–3,
　　214–15
　*see also* UNFICYP
Heiberg, Marianne　41, 204–5
horizontal conflict　149
human development　93–4
humanitarian intervention　10, 28–9,
　　33, 138
　in Bosnia　79–86
　ethics in　114
　*see also* UNOSOM; UNPROFOR
human needs theory　90, 94–5
　critique of　95
　generic theory of conflict　90
　needs, values, interests　94
　universal, cultural and transitory
　　needs　94
　*see also* peace
human rights　10, 21, 138–9
Human Rights Watch　75

idealism　89
impartial, third party　106–7, 126
　loss of impartiality　136
in-country peacebuilding　132
　*see also* peacebuilding
independent variables　154–5
inherency theory　*see* conflict
interactional learning　170, 180

intercultural adjustment *see*
cross-cultural adjustment theory
interdependence *see* pluralism
inter- and intra-state conflict 20, 24,
128, 148
*see also* conflict
Interim Offices 24–5, 143
intermediary 106
international civil servants 7
International Committee of the Red
Cross (ICRC) 136
International Conference on Former
Yugoslavia (ICFY) 75, 79
International Court of Justice (ICJ) 2,
3, 60–70
International Peace Academy 127,
181
training for peacekeeping 201–2
Vienna Seminar 202; *see also*
simulation exercises
*see also Peacekeeper's Handbook*
International Peacekeeping Training
Centre *see* Canadian Forces
international regimes 132
international relations 88–91
intervenors *see* third parties
Irish Defence Forces 181, 188–91
training for service with UNIFIL 188–9
United Nations school 190
*see also* training for peacekeeping
Irish Garda, training for
UNTAG 199–200
issues, process and context 154–6
*see also* conflict; conflict management;
contingency theory

joint-costing 105, 111

Katanga secession 14
*see also* ONUC
Kealey, Daniel 173–5
Keashly, Loraleigh *see* Fisher, Ronald
and Loraleigh Keashly
Knin 77
Korean War 10–11
Kosovo 84

Laue, James 105, 106
Lausanne, Treaty of 46
League of Nations 60
London Agreement 46

Macedonia *see* UNPROFOR
Machiavelli, Niccolo 89, 91

macro-level conflict
management 133–4
*see also* peacekeeping
mandates 37–8
ambiguity 38
Marxism, influence on peace
research 92
mediation 105, 154
and contingency theory 115–16
definition 107–8
insider-partial/outsider-neutral
mediators 122, 159
as peacemaking 150
success, predictors of 154
*Médecins Sans Frontières* 135–6
Miall, Hugh 11, 148–9
micro-level conflict management 133–4
*see also* peacekeeping
military culture 175
Military Observers *see* United Nations
Military Observers
Military Staff Committee (MSC) 9
Milosevic, Slobodan 72, 73
*see also* UNPROFOR
MINURSO 27–8
Mitchell, Christopher 98, 104, 106
Mogadishu 28–9
Moscow Declaration 1
Moskos, Charles C. 42, 175–7, 191
multilateral diplomacy 37

Namibia *see* UNTAG
national service armies 181, 225–6
negative peace *see* peace
negotiation 105, 107
definition 110
power in 110
negotiation training *see* Canadian Forces
neutrality *see* impartial
Nicosia 48, 49
Non-Governmental Organizations
(NGOs) 9, 88, 132
non-interference 4
Nordic militaries 181, 183, 191–4
conflict resolution skills
training 194, 208
training 191–4
*see also* training for peacekeeping
Nordic Stand-By Forces 192
training for 192–3, 209
Norwegian Defence Force *see* Nordic
militaries

objective conflict *see* conflict

Office of General Services (OSG) 34
Office of Human Resources Management
    (OHRM) 180, 196–200
ONUC 13–15, 17
    funding crisis 15–16
ONUCA 26
ONUMOZ 29
ONUSAL 10, 27, 33
ONUVEH 27
ONUVEN 26–7, 33
Organization of Africa Unity (OAU) 18
OSGAP 30
outcomes *see* success
Ovamboland 59, 60, 64, 65, 67
    *see also* UNTAG
Overseas Technical Advisors, training
    of 173–5
Owen, Lord David 75

Paphos, UN activity in 53–4
peace, negative and positive 92, 93–5,
    113, 126
    positive peace and success 113
peacebuilding 124, 216–17
    definitions 132
    institutions engaged in
        peacebuilding 132–3
    need for coordination of 132–3, 134–5
    post-conflict peacebuilding 130–1
    pre-conflict peacebuilding 132
peacekeeping
    abuses by peacekeepers 43, 85
    *ad hoc* nature 16, 22–3, 218
    basic principles 13, 25
    birth of 8–16
    conceptual framework 42–3,
        141–61; contingency theory and
        peacekeeping 150–61; summary
        of arguments for 162–3
    cultural variables in 165, 175–7,
        204–5, 229–30
    definitions 124–9, 207–8; inadequacy
        of 139–40
    ethics of intervention 148–9, 228
    evolution of 142
    Fifth Committee 6–7
    finances 36–7
    as a form of third party
        intervention 126, 143, 145–9,
        211–20
    functions 31–3, 107, 218, 152–3
    macro-level 133–4, 142–3, 150; links
        with peacemaking and
        peacebuilding 134–7; problems

with linking peacemaking and
        peacekeeping 147–8
    micro-level 110, 133–4, 142–3,
        151–3; links with peacemaking
        and peacebuilding 137–9, 218;
        as pre-peacebuilding 152; roles
        at 137
    management 34–6
    multidimensional
        peacekeeping 23–5; difference
        between classical and
        multidimensional 145–6;
        innovations 33–4
    overview of 16–19, 25–30
    problems caused by expansion
        of 146–9
    statistics on 23
    success 40–2, 43–4, 131, 154–5, 174,
        176
    training of 147, 158–9
    *see also* cross-cultural interaction
        training; training for
        peacekeeping; troop-contributing
        countries; skills
peacekeeping, broad functional
    definitions 126–7
*Peacekeeper's Handbook* (International
    Peace Academy) 130
peacekeeping, narrow functional
    definitions 125–6
peacemaking 34, 124, 216–17
    definition 129
    problems with 130
    related to peacekeeping 130–1, 147–8
peace operations 153
peace research 91–5, 103
    connection to peace education and
        peace movements 92
    as structuralism 95–6
Pearson, Lester 13
Pederson, Paul 172–3
Permanent Five (P–5) 2, 10
    veto 3–4, 5
    *see also* Security Council
personality traits
    in cross-cultural interaction 168–9
    in peacekeeping 186, 206
    *see also* cross-cultural interaction
        training
pink zones *see* UNPROFOR
pluralism 89–91, 103
POLISARIO (Popular Front for the
    Liberation of Saguia el-Hamra and
    Río de Oro) 28

positive peace   *see* peace
post-Cold War   22–3
post-conflict peacebuilding   *see*
    peacebuilding
post-traumatic stress syndrome
    (PTSS)   190–1
pre-conflict peacebuilding   *see*
    peacebuilding
pre-mediation   152
pre-negotiation   152, 153
pre-peacebuilding   152, 157
preventive diplomacy   130, 216
problem-solving   105
    problem-solving workshops   109
    *see also* conflict management;
        consultation
professional armies   181, 182, 188,
    225–6
professionalization of
    peacekeeping   221, 225–8
protracted social conflict (PSC)   42–3,
    97–8, 146
    and contingency theory   120–1
    as less amenable to conflict
        management   147–8
    *see also* conflict
provention   95
psychological aspects of conflict   98–9
    *see also* conflict

Reagan, Ronald   18–19
realism   89, 97, 101, 103, 115
reform   *see* United Nations
refugees   21
regional training centres   179, 201,
    230–1
regional training programmes   *see*
    Nordic militaries
RENAMO (Mozambique National
    Resistance Movement)   29
'Republic of Serbian Krajina'   72
    *see also* UNPROFOR
Roosevelt, Franklin D.   1

Sarajevo   *see* UNPROFOR
scarcity of resources   101–2
Second Committee, General
    Assembly   6
Secretariat   7
Secretary-General   2, 3, 7
    Article 99   7
    *see also* Secretariat
Security Council   2, 3, 9
    collective security   10, 12

crisis management   8
    functions   4–6
    informal consultations   6, 9
    stalemate in   11–12
    voting   5
selection process   167, 206–7
    *see also* cross-cultural interaction
        training
'Serbian Autonomous Region of
    Krajina'   *see* 'Republic of Serbian
    Krajina'
Sherry, George   125
simulation exercises   *see* training for
    peacekeeping
situation room   35
Sixth Committee, General Assembly   6
skills
    contact skills   209, 212, 216, 218–20,
        224–5
    non-contact skills   208–9, 213, 218–20
    for third parties   111–12, 169–170
    skills for cross-cultural
        interaction   167–170
    skills for peacekeeping   205
    *see also* third parties; cross-cultural
        interaction training
Slovenia, recognition of   73
    *see also* UNPROFOR
sovereignty   4, 10, 38
Special Committee on Peacekeeping
    Operations (C-34), General
    Assembly   6–7, 164
    creation of   15
Specialized Agencies   3
*status quo*   8, 43–4, 125–6, 149, 150
    limitations of, in relation to
        peacekeeping   128–9, 139
Staff Officers   *see* United Nations Staff
    Officers
Stoltenberg, Thorvald   75, 86
structural violence   21–2, 91–2, 113
    *see also* conflict
subjective conflict   *see* conflict
success   40–2, 43–4, 113, 131, 154–5,
    174–6
    *see also* mediation; peacekeeping; third
        party intervention
Suez crisis   *see* UNEF I
SWAPO (South West Africa People's
    Organization)   60, 61, 67, 70
    disruption of UNTAG   64–6
    *see also* UNTAG
SWAPOL (South West Africa Police)   *see*
    UNTAG

Swedish Defence Force   *see* Nordic
    militaries

Thant, U   48, 50, 53
theory–practice link   164–6, 177
Tito, Josep   71
Third Committee, General Assembly   6
third parties   106, 140
    roles of intervenors   107–11
    skills of intervenors   111–12, 169–70
    *see also* skills
third party intervention   105, 106–7
    ethics of   114, 210
    evaluation of   112–13
    decision to intervene,
        peacekeeping   148–9
    success in   113
    typology of   107–11
    *see also* conflict management;
        contingency theory; peacekeeping
Torbiorn, Ingemar   *see* Grove,
    Cornelius, L. and Ingemar Torbiorn
trainers, role of   172–3, 229
training for peacekeeping   43, 179–210
    civilian training   195–200;   critique
        of   205, 208–10
    critique of   203–10, 219–20
    current training provision,
        summary   179–81
    links between theory, training and
        practice   164–6, 175–7
    institutionalization, lack of   179
    international agency training   200–3
    military training   182–95; critique
        of   205, 208–10
    military versus peacekeeping
        training   191–2, 205–6, 211–12,
        213, 221–8
    national training centres   182, 193–4
    simulation exercises   180, 202
    types of: in-country   180, 183, 197,
        199–200; mission-site   180, 183,
        197; UN Headquarters   180, 195,
        197; international agency   180
    *see also* cross-cultural interaction
        training; Irish Defence Forces;
        Canadian Forces; Nordic
        militaries
training programmes, development
        of   172–3
    evaluation of   173
transformation of societies   93, 105, 133
    *see also* peace, Curle

troop-contributing countries   39–40,
    43, 179, 183
    traditional troop-contributors   182
    *see also* training for peacekeeping
Trusteeship Council   3
Tudjman, Franjo   72, 73
    *see also* UNPROFOR

values   94, 102–3
    in conflict management   148–9
    in the study of conflict   116–18
vertical conflict   149
*Vienna Seminar*   *see* International Peace
        Academy
violence   100–1
    control of, in peacekeeping   150,
        152–3
    prevention of, in post-Cold War
        world   137
    suppression of   149
    *see also* structural violence; conflict

UNAMIR   29
UNAVEM   26
UNAVEM II   27
UNDOF   18
UNEF I   12–13, 17
UNEF II   18
UNFICYP   17, 46–59, 134, 137–8, 145,
        146, 175–6
    *aide-mémoire*   49
    buffer zone   51
    creation of   47–50
    crisis (1974)   56–8
    Geneva Declaration   57
    mandate and functions   50–5
    peacebuilding activities   52–3
    recent developments   58–9
    training   187–8
    *see also* confidence-building measures;
        United Nations civilian police
UNGOMAP   30, 134
UNICEF   132
UNIFIL   18, 137
    training   188–90, 204–5
UNIKOM   25, 30
UNIIMOG   26
UNITA (National Union for the Total
        Independence of Angola)   27
UNITAF   28
UNMIH   27, 29–30
UNMOGIP   17
UNOGIL   17